Confessions
of a Weekend Warrior

Confessions
of a Weekend Warrior

*Thirty-Five Years
in the National Guard*

Brig. Gen. Paul "Greg" Smith,
US Army (retired)

McFarland & Company, Inc., Publishers
Jefferson, North Carolina

Library of Congress Cataloging-in-Publication Data

Names: Smith, Paul G. (Paul Gregory), 1957– author.
Title: Confessions of a weekend warrior : thirty-five years in the national guard
Description: Jefferson, North Carolina : McFarland & Company, Inc.,
Publishers, 2024 | Includes bibliographical references and index.
Identifiers: LCCN 2024015152 | ISBN 9781476694108 (paperback : acid free paper) ∞
ISBN 9781476652634 (ebook)
Subjects: LCSH: United States—National Guard—Biography. |
Smith, Paul G. (Paul Gregory), 1957- | United States—National Guard—
Military life. | Massachusetts. National Guard—History—20th century. |
United States. Army—Officers—Biography.
Classification: LCC UA250 .S65 2024 | DDC 355.3/709744092 [B]—dc23/eng/20240404
LC record available at https://lccn.loc.gov/2024015152

British Library cataloguing data are available

ISBN (print) 978-1-4766-9410-8
ISBN (ebook) 978-1-4766-5263-4

Front cover image: Brig. Gen. Paul G. Smith of Ashburnham, Massachusetts
stands in the doorway of a vehicle at the National Guard Armory
in Worcester, Massachusetts, May 16, 2014 photograph
(Worcester Telegram & Gazette, © Christine Peterson, USA Today Network).

Printed in the United States of America

*McFarland & Company, Inc., Publishers
Box 611, Jefferson, North Carolina 28640
www.mcfarlandpub.com*

To the men and women of America's National Guard
who carry on the Minuteman tradition.
"Always Ready, Always There!"

Table of Contents

Preface

When I first set foot in a National Guard armory I was confused by the chaos. Shouts mingled with the clang of equipment and the roar of truck motors echoed in the cavernous hall. I coughed when the mix of cigarette smoke, engine fumes, and cleaning fluid tickled my throat. Some soldiers bustled about carrying sheaves of paperwork while other groggy warriors lounged about in clusters. Faded photos of doughboys in the Great War and GI from World War II hung in dusty frames on the walls while curled, yellowed notices dangled from bulletin boards like autumn leaves. Bewildered new recruits in civilian clothes loitered against the walls, nervously wondering what they'd gotten themselves into. I shared their misgivings.

Suddenly a paunchy sergeant strutted into the center of the hall and bellowed "Fall In!" Those two words were like a magic spell as the engines were silenced, the cigarette butts were stubbed out, the sleepers sprung to life, and 150 people formed a tight, silent rectangle, in which every person had their place. From my spot in the back of the formation I observed that the professionalism of the group fanned out like a spectrum from front to rear—officers stood erect and polished in front, followed by squared away sergeants. Soldiers in the front ranks seemed more alert than those who arrived late and slunk into the rear ranks. Finally the teenagers in civilian clothes formed the last line as they shifted and fidgeted.

Soon a lone figure marched to the front of the rectangle. All eyes were on him and every ear listened attentively. In a booming voice he described his expectations for the day's activities, mixing his directives with criticism, praise, warnings, and witticisms. Although he was younger than half of the formation, it was clear to me that he was regarded with affection and deep respect. I remember feeling admiration for the way he motivated this disparate throng of people as well as a sense of awe at the responsibility he bore to lead this military organization. Could I ever become a confident, respected commander like this officer? I wasn't sure.

And so, in 1979 I began my journey in the National Guard. At that time the Guard was reviled by active-duty forces as an undisciplined swarm of "weekend warriors," who played at soldiering. The bitter aftertaste of the Kent State Massacre lingered, when frightened and confused National Guardsmen fired into a crowd of college students, killing four and wounding nine others.[1] Many Americans viewed the Guard as a gaggle of card-playing, beer-swilling amateurs who had joined up to avoid combat duty in Vietnam. But I began to see an entirely different picture.

In short order I came to realize that maybe these citizen-soldiers couldn't march very well or execute battle drills with precision, but when disaster struck, they saved people's lives with remarkable initiative and dedication. I soon valued the ingenuity, flexibility, and adaptability that their active-duty counterparts couldn't begin to match. Over time I treasured the enduring traditions, legacies, and community connections that made the National Guard a tight-knit family of Minutemen and Minutewomen.

A funny thing happened over the next 35 years—I grew from being a hesitant sort of military tourist to a committed commander who did my best to fulfill my responsibilities to the nation and the people I led. Simultaneously the National Guard gradually developed from a third-string amateur organization to a highly effective fighting force that today forms an integral element of the world's most powerful military.

One Sunday morning, when I actually became a commander, I had one of life's epiphanies. As I paced in front of the formation waiting for the sergeants to form their platoons. I inhaled the mingled scents of stale cigarette smoke, aftershave, last night's lingering alcohol, and perfume. I spotted the gap-toothed smile of an unshaven face as he laughed, the drooping eyelids of a young mother trying to wake up, and the alert clear-eyed gaze of a teenage soldier just returned from basic training. Suddenly I understood that these were much the same faces that stood firm on Concord's North Bridge, held the line at Gettysburg, and fought back the Nazis at Bastogne. They weren't all pretty, or intelligent, or even physically fit, but these citizen-soldiers were American patriots who would lay down their lives, if necessary, to protect this nation and safeguard its citizens. And I was proud to be one of them.

*   *   *

So I wrote this book for many reasons. First, I wanted to paint a realistic portrait of the National Guard. I think some Americans believe that Guardsmen are permanently gathered in their armories, awaiting the next deployment or mission. I'm not sure many people realize that their local mechanic, attorney, electrician, or child's teacher is actually a member of the National Guard who will drop their civilian lives to respond to duty within a few hours' notice. I'm also not sure that many understand that Guardsmen can be called to duty for missions that vary from combat action and peacekeeping overseas to giving Covid shots and driving school buses here at home. Although I may poke fun at the old ways, I hope I conveyed the admiration and respect I hold for the soldiers and airmen with whom I served and those who continue to serve.

Second, I wanted to offer a few lessons for those who aspire to lead others. There are many, many instructive books about leadership theories and practices. This isn't one of them. I certainly wouldn't call myself an expert on the subject, but I learned some important truths about leadership along the way—mainly through trial and lots of error. While I gained insights from my superiors who served as role models, some of the most important lessons were taught by sergeants and soldiers whom I led. But perhaps I gained the greatest wisdom from my own failures and I'm grateful to those who picked me up afterwards, dusted me off, and continued to trust me. I certainly wouldn't recommend that aspiring leaders seek out failure, but when it happens, it can be a damn good teacher.

Finally, I wanted to tell the story of my own awkward, bumpy military career. I survived an odyssey during which I transformed from a gawky, hesitant cadet to a committed commander. When people ask me why I served for so many years, I often respond, "I just forgot to get out." But there's much more to the story than that. I gradually became part of a military family that educated me, scolded me, consoled me, and embraced me. My transformation and growth were facilitated by a host of officers, sergeants, buddies, and ordinary soldiers who were willing to tolerate my awkward missteps, headstrong bombast, and foolish escapades and not lose faith in me. Somehow they saw a spark of something that made them believe in me and they convinced me to believe in myself. I hope I've painted a loving and respectful portrait of our military family, America's National Guard.

Son of the Greatest Generation

There aren't many photos of me that have survived from my childhood. One is my first school photo from kindergarten. Another shows me at about seven years of age dressed in a blue Civil War uniform as I stiffly saluted the photographer.

When people ask me why I joined the Army, I often respond, "There was no way I could not have become a soldier." Pardon the double negative, but serving in the military wasn't so much a choice in my case, it was kind of an inevitable fate. Let me explain:

Like it or not, the United States of America is a warrior nation. During our nearly 250 year existence, when we haven't been locked in battle with the Brits, Germans, Japanese, Al Qaeda, or ISIS, we've been busy forcibly relocating our reluctant Native American brothers and sisters or killing our regional neighbors during the Civil War. Oh yes, and then there have been those minor armed forays into Latin America, Southeast Asia, or Africa to spread democracy and stability.

We love football (which is really just stylized warfare with scantily clad cheerleaders looking on), mixed martial arts—the bloodier, the better—boxing, worldwide wrestling, hunting, and of course, the National Rifle Association. As nations go, we're a lot more violent than most.

I think my DNA had "U.S." imprinted on it when I was issued to my parents upon my entry into America. My earliest playthings were plastic soldiers, little tanks, and cap pistols. I had the finest dressed, best equipped, most fearsome G.I. Joe dolls (complete with cheek scars) in the neighborhood.

When my little band of fellow commandos and I weren't stalking each other in the pine forests wielding sticks as Thompson submachineguns, we were constructing snow fortifications and sallying forth to assault each other with hard packed snowball grenades. If we got our homework done at night, we watched "Combat," or "Rat Patrol," or "Hogan's Heroes" on television.

As a little boy I was particularly fascinated by the Civil War. One day I asked my aunt, "Did anyone from our family fight in the Civil War?"

She looked up from her knitting and said, "My great grandfather went away to fight and never came back, the bum."

Until I was well into my adult years I pictured my ancestor as a deserter or carpetbagger who abandoned his family, but that was far from the truth. Together with my son, we discovered that, after arriving from Ireland, Private George Lavis, 41 years of age, enlisted in the 28th Massachusetts Regiment. In 1864 he was shot through the lungs during the Battle of the Wilderness and treated at the Armory Square Hospital in Washington, D.C. Abraham Lincoln and Walt Whitman frequently visited wounded soldiers at this hospital, so it's likely that George Lavis met them. Unfortunately George succumbed to his wounds and was one of the first thousand Union casualties to be buried on the front lawn of Robert E. Lee's Virginia plantation. Today we call this place Arlington National Cemetery.

The family may never have known that George was buried at Arlington because the name on his headstone was incorrect, until we requested that it be changed. We later learned that George was illiterate and probably couldn't spell his own name.

The more we learned about the Lavis family, the less my aunt's response surprised me. Because of his age, George wasn't subject to conscription. Instead he volunteered to serve, which may seem patriotic to us, but it may have also seemed irresponsible to his wife and children. When George died he left behind a widow with six growing children to feed. Margaret Lavis was faced with starvation for her children because there was no source of income to support them. Her husband's noble sacrifice for the nation may have been irrelevant to her as she scraped and struggled to provide for her impoverished family. Eventually she remarried and secured a pension for her children, but that was many years after the war.

As a member of a vast Irish-American extended family, I was surrounded by World War II veterans in the 1960s. Some of them discussed their wartime experiences freely, some offered fictional stories to hide the truth, and some preferred to keep that part of their experience locked away. My father served as a naval intelligence officer in the Pacific. He was more than willing to talk about the reports he processed and the annexes he wrote, but that did little to fire a youthful imagination. Uncle Arthur related funny stories about training as a cavalryman at Camp Drum, New York (a place with which I would later become intimately familiar). I remember how he chuckled when he told us about his later Army career firing anti-aircraft guns in the Aleutian Islands, carefully avoiding any hits on unidentified aircraft. He explained that the gun crew only wanted to qualify for combat pay.

Uncle Bill, the older of my mother's brothers, had a very funny comedy routine about how the Navy came to recruit him while he was hiding under the bed. After he died, I learned that Bill operated a clandestine observation post in the jungle at Guadalcanal from which he reported on Japanese naval movements. If he were captured, he would have been beheaded like other coastal observers, and he probably knew this. When he was eventually relieved from his post, he weighed less than 100 pounds.

My mother's younger brother, Bob, was a quiet, gentle man who worked for the Catholic Church and rarely spoke about his time in the Army. Uncle Bob was graduated early from high school in February 1944 so he and his classmates could enlist in the war effort. He served in the famed 10th Mountain Division. I found out that Bob was awarded a Purple Heart and a Bronze Star for valor in the Po Valley campaign in Italy at 19 years of age. There always seemed to be a silent sadness that surrounded Bob. He died before he turned 55.

I was also fortunate to have two granduncles who shared their stories from the War to End All Wars—World War I. Uncle Frank was a prim and proper widower who was a frequent dinner guest at our house after his wife died. Despite his reserved, strait-laced manner, a special bond grew between us when he noticed my fascination with all things military. I remember the sparkle in Uncle Frank's eyes when he described life in the trenches and how wonderful it was to have leave in Paris. He brought me French coins, bullet shells, and his engineer compass. Once he gave me his brown wool sergeant's stripes.

"You were a sergeant, Uncle Frank?" I asked with admiration.

"Oh, yes, I was a sergeant several times," he replied.

"Why were you a sergeant so many times?" I asked, a bit puzzled.

"Well, you see, my mother lived about a half mile from the Army post where I was stationed before we went overseas," he explained. "Instead of Army food, which was pretty bad, I preferred my mother's cooking."

"That makes sense," I said.

"I guess it didn't make sense to my company commander," he smiled. "Every now and then they'd catch me coming or going to my mother's house through a hole in the fence and I'd lose my sergeant stripes. But that was okay, because I'd get them back in a day or two."

The other World War I veteran in the family, Uncle Owen, was a first class storyteller and entertainer, although he had a casual relationship with the truth. He regaled us with vivid tales about driving his rickety truck through muddy roads under fire, the horror of gas attacks, and the fear of artillery barrages in the trenches of France. There was just one problem ... he was never there.

Many years after Owen died, I was visiting the state's military archive.

The curator asked if I had any relatives whose military records I would like to see. Remembering Uncle Owen's wonderful tales of the Great War, I asked to see his records. The curator returned after a few minutes with a file folder. Opening the file, he said, "Ah, yes, Corporal Owen Smith, 101st Field Trains…, Well, it appears he never left Fort Dix, New Jersey."

The year 1967 was an important one in my military education and I owe it all to the Boston Red Sox. The previously pathetic Red Sox had a phenomenal season that year during which they won so many close games in the 9th inning that they were nicknamed, "The Cardiac Kids." In typical Boston sports hyperbole, "The Impossible Dream" season, as it was dubbed, resulted in the American League championship pennant followed by a heartbreaking loss in Game 7 of the World Series. Oh, what could have been!

Throughout the spring and summer of 1967, every Red Sox fan was glued to the TV or radio as they followed this incredible baseball season, and I was no exception. In addition, it was oh so satisfying to read about the Sox's latest triumph in the following day's newspaper. Before long I found myself eagerly immersed in the adult news cycle. I hungrily devoured newspapers, magazines, and radio and television news in search of information about the latest Red Sox triumph. However, while I scoured news sources for sports information, I began to absorb domestic and international news almost by osmosis.

In the summer of 1967 I quickly became captivated by the David and Goliath narrative of brave little Israel's victory over its greedy Arab neighbors in the Six Day War. I can still see the photos of Moshe Dayan with his black eye patch as he perched gallantly atop a tank turret. Here was a story that was almost as thrilling as the Red Sox, but it involved real life and death consequences.

Soon the stark photos of wounded U.S. military personnel as they were loaded onto helicopters and the haunted stares of teenaged infantrymen in Vietnam leapt off the pages of *Life* magazine and lodged in my consciousness. I found myself monitoring the news from Vietnam as eagerly as I had followed developments in the Sinai or the box scores at Fenway. As news coverage of the Vietnam War became more grim, I hoped and prayed that the war would soon be over—at least before my older brothers were eligible for the draft.

One Sunday in 1968 my father invited me to accompany him to the men's group breakfast at church. There was a special guest this Sunday—a young man from our parish was home on leave and he was going to tell us what was really going on in Vietnam. Scott, whom I vaguely remembered as a friend of my older sister, stepped up to the podium in his dress uniform with all the colorful ribbons on his chest and began to talk about life as a helicopter pilot in combat. Some of his stories were funny, some were exciting, and some were sad. I was so eager to hear what he had to say that I hardly touched my pancakes.

When Scott finished his presentation, the club president invited audience members to ask any questions they might have. I remember the first question: "First of all, thank you for what you and our boys are doing over there, son," the pot-bellied middle-aged speaker began. "But what a lot of us really want to know is whether we can believe what we're hearing on TV. Are we winning this war or not?"

Scott took his time before he answered. "In all honesty, Sir, I don't believe that we are winning this war. In fact, I'm not really sure that Vietnam is worth the cost in dollars and bloodshed. I don't know if we belong in Vietnam anymore." An awkward silence followed his answer.

Someone else tried to lighten the atmosphere by asking about the food, and Scott seemed happy to joke about "C" rations and powdered eggs. Somebody else asked a technical question about flying a helicopter, but uncomfortable doubt about the war in Vietnam had been unleashed, and, like squeezed toothpaste, there was no getting it back into the tube.

On the way home I asked my father about what we had heard. "Do you think it's true that we're losing the war in Vietnam, Dad?"

My father looked at me with a sad smile. "I think Scott is just tired and discouraged. He needs to come home, eat his mother's cooking, see his old friends, and get some rest. When it's time for him to go back to Vietnam, he'll have a better attitude and he'll see things differently." I nodded, but I wasn't entirely sure that my father was right.

As my older brothers approached graduation from college, they faced being drafted into the military and possible service in Vietnam. There was never much concern about my oldest brother, because he was missing two fingers from a snowblower accident in his teenage years—obviously he would be declared "4F," or medically excused from service.

For my other brother, it was a different matter. At first my father cheerfully brought home brochures about Navy Officer Candidate School to encourage my brother to follow his father's footsteps before the draft caught up with him. I don't think he was all that excited about the prospect of serving in the Navy. However, I was captivated.

I remember one glossy tri-fold brochure depicting a buff, tanned Navy ensign in a gleaming white uniform. This young god of naval warfare peered through binoculars over a sparkling blue sea from his princely perch on the bridge of a destroyer. When my brother wasn't looking, I'd pore admiringly over the brochure, emblazoned with the motto, "Campus to Quarterdeck." If the Navy accepted pre-teens, I would have signed up then and there, no questions asked.

Eventually the draft board classified my brother as 4F because of a medical condition that I don't think he was even aware of. He probably wasn't all that sorry to pass up the quarterdeck for a corporate office and law school.

As the 1960s passed, however, I grew further and further left of center in my political views. My oldest sister, Mary Ellen, emerged as a grassroots leader in Boston politics and a strident activist for school desegregation and gay rights. Her thinking certainly influenced my opinions at the time. I also looked up to my 8th grade Social Studies teacher, who encouraged us to read a wide spectrum of political science writing. I remember being surprised to find that Karl Marx's *Das Kapital* actually made as much sense to me as the Declaration of Independence. Throughout this time, tempers flared at home as my conservative father became angrier at my sister's political activities.

In April 1970 I found myself on Boston Common, standing beside my sister and 60,000 like-minded folks who were there to protest the war in Vietnam. I wore a little blue pin with a white dove on it. The bird had an olive branch in its beak and it fluttered above the words, "Peace Now!" Like everyone else, I cheered myself hoarse as Abbie Hoffman and Black Panther leaders harangued the crowd, not realizing that we were not much different from other mobs that were whipped into a frenzy by fanatics.[2]

But, when it was over, there was an unsettling dialog within me that was at odds against what I had heard:

"If war was always immoral, then who would have stopped Hitler?"

"Maybe it was wrong to intervene in a Vietnamese civil war, but did that really make our soldiers war criminals?"

"Ho Chi Minh and his forces were known to be brutal—was he really the equivalent of George Washington?"

The war in Vietnam eventually drew to a close. Nixon resigned and nothing much happened during the Ford years. I entered high school and became far more interested in girls, football, baseball, track, and sex, than I was concerned about politics. Don't get me wrong, I was a member of the varsity baseball, track, and football teams, but I was certainly not a starter. In retrospect, I was an angry little kid in a complicated family who just liked to butt heads with other kids—oh, and I knew that high school girls thought athletes were cool.

I grew my hair long, wore wide bell-bottom pants and tight shirts with long, pointy collars. For some reason, probably to get close to some girl I liked, I started volunteering at a day camp for children with special needs. Gradually, working with those wonderful kids became more than a nice thing to do—it gave me purpose and satisfaction and fulfillment— and it became a vocation (and, since most of my co-workers were female, it did wonders for my dating prospects). My focus for the future was to get into a good teachers' college that would prepare me for a career in special education. I didn't give the military a second thought.

High school graduation came and launched me into Fitchburg State College. My parents, after raising five other kids, were relieved that their last little bird was out of the nest. They moved away to Florida the day before I left for college. They made sure that my tuition was paid and even sent me a few bucks every month. College life was great. I had never been so free in all my life.

I quickly found out that I could maintain decent grades in college while drinking a lot of beer and partying almost every night. Sometimes I'd wake up in places and have no recollection of how I got there. Sometimes I'd disappear for a whole weekend and not clearly remember where I had been. One morning I woke up to a good friend shaking his fist in my face as he growled,

"If you ever talk to me like that again, I'll kick the shit out of you. I don't care if you're my buddy or not." I had no idea what he was talking about.

An incident on my first New Year's Eve in college may have served as a dangerous, but much needed, wakeup call. Because the college dorms were closed, I spent the Christmas holidays at my sister's apartment. I recall that my parents returned from Florida for a few days, but without a family home, it was an odd, disjointed Christmas. At the time I would have said it didn't matter to me, but in retrospect, it probably mattered a great deal.

The week after Christmas I broke up with my high school girlfriend because I thought I needed to be free to see other young women. It was ugly and it finally ended when I just stopped returning her calls. Looking back, I have few regrets in life, but I will always feel sorry for the pain that I caused that beautiful, kind young woman who was trying to save me from myself.

And so, on New Year's Eve I connected with a high school buddy who had just returned from Marine Corps boot camp. He was every inch a cocky, tough guy in his new biker leather jacket with all the buckles, a lean, hard look, and his shaved head. I had a thousand admiring questions for him as the two of us set out in my car to cruise the parties—two bad asses who answered to no one.

I never knew the reason, but a carful of angry young men began to follow us through the streets. At times we lost them, but suddenly they'd emerge from a side road, hollering threats at my friend. Finally we stopped at one of the parties we planned to visit and the threatening car pulled up a hundred yards away. "Let's just get this over with," my friend said. "We may get our asses beat, but we can't drive around with them chasing us all night."

I reached under the car's front seat and pulled out a machete I kept there because I thought it might be useful in a situation like this. "This might come in handy," I said, brandishing the weapon with bravado. "Give me that fucking thing," my friend grabbed the machete and threw it into the bushes. "You'll get us killed."

Moments later four guys walked over to us and hurled a few insults at my friend. They told me to get lost because I had nothing to do with their argument. In perhaps the only good decision I made that night, I stood my ground and said I wasn't going to just watch while four of them beat up my friend. And so it began with pushing, shoving, a few punches and a whole lot of bad language.

"Police!" somebody yelled, and the attackers started to flee into the darkness. But not before one of them hit me with a sucker punch to my jaw. I remember flying after the guy who punched me, screaming in rage. Just then two dark arms grabbed me and wrestled me to a halt. Then I saw the badge. Thankfully the police just let my friend and I go after we calmed down and promised not to go after the other guys. We then went to the house party where we drank too much and boasted about what we would have done to those four weaklings.

When I look back, I realize with a shudder, that if my friend hadn't thrown away that machete and, perhaps to a lesser degree, if that cop hadn't stopped me from retaliating on the sucker puncher, that night could have ended with serious charges or worse—and those charges would have prevented many of the good things that happened later in my life.

But I learned a few important lessons that night that would later influence my decision-making. Perhaps most importantly I learned never to bring weapons into a tense situation unless you're prepared to use them and accept the consequences. I also learned to take a longer view of those who make mistakes in a fit of anger or because of a lapse in judgment. As a wise person said, "There but for the grace of God go I."

I woke up on New Year's Day with a vicious headache, a mouth full of dust, a sore jaw, a pair of broken glasses, and a tearful phone message from a young woman who deserved a much better man than me.

I was out of control. Something needed to change.

"ROTC, It Sounds Like Some Bullshit to Me, to Me...."

> ROTC, ROTC, it sounds like some bullshit to me, to me,
> ROTC, it sounds like some bullshit to me.
> They made me a 2nd lieutenant,
> They gave me two bars of gold
> They called me a forward observer,
> I lived to be 6 seconds old.[3]
> Some mothers have sons in the Air Force
> Some mothers have sons on the sea
> Some mothers have sons who are assholes
> And they all join ROTC
> Oh, ROTC, ROTC, it sounds like some bullshit to me, to me,
> ROTC, it sounds like some bullshit to me.
> —Unofficial ROTC Cadet Song (Never sung
> within earshot of the cadre)

Through the crystal clear hindsight of time, I realize that I probably joined Army ROTC because I needed some structure in my unhinged 1970s' college life. At the time, it just seemed like a cool thing to do.

I must have thought about ROTC somewhat early in my freshman year of college because I recall a conversation with the ROTC office at the College of the Holy Cross. The arrogant voice on the other end of the phone line made it quite clear that the Navy ROTC program at the College of the Holy Cross was definitely not interested in a student from Fitchburg State College.

Then one day a fellow student in my music class showed up in an Army dress green uniform. When I asked him about it he sheepishly explained that ROTC cadets were required to wear their uniforms on campus one day each month. As weeks went by I asked him more and more questions about Army ROTC. The unit was located at Worcester Polytechnic Institute and they obviously accepted Fitchburg State College students. Students could sign up, get issued a full set of uniforms, which sounded really wonderful to me, and there was no service obligation until your junior year. The only requirements were to attend a free class at WPI one afternoon each week and participate in a weekend training exercise at Fort Devens every semester.

In January 1976 I filled out the registration paperwork to become a non-contract Army ROTC cadet. Just months before I signed the papers, the last Huey helicopters had lifted off from the rooftop of the U.S. embassy in Saigon with abandoned Vietnamese allies grasping in vain for the skids. I was joining the fighting force that won two world wars but had recently conceded defeat in a failed venture that had cost over 58,000 young American lives. What was I thinking?

A civilian clerk took me to the supply room, asked me my sizes, and tossed a wrinkled olive drab uniform at me. It was the first time I ever smelled the oily odor of Army equipment, like a combination of turpentine and moth balls. To some it might have been revolting, but it smelled like perfume to me—and it still does. In short order I screwed a misshapen ball cap on my head—the odd-looking one from the 1960s with the flat front and peak in the center, sort of like home plate on your forehead—and caught a used field jacket that was thrown my way. The olive drab pants and shirt had no possibility of fitting.

Finally the supply clerk beckoned me over to a locked cabinet from which he plucked a brand new pair of black combat boots with the tag still on them.

"Try these on to make sure they fit right," he directed. "A soldier's boots are the most important item of equipment he owns. If they don't fit right you'll tear up your feet on a ruck march."

I laced them up with quiet delight and commented, "They feel kind of stiff."

"Well, you got to break them in, Son," he said, looking at me like I was a simpleton. "Wear them around campus after you give them a good polishing. Don't get them dinged up, but wear them every chance you get. Just don't show up for the weekend exercise with boots that you haven't broken in real well."

I stuffed my first Army uniform into a well-worn cloth bag and returned to my dorm where I couldn't wait to try on every last item. I admired myself in front of the mirror. I was a member of the United States Army—sort of.

The first ROTC class I attended was basic leadership. To say that the study of leadership is the fundamental subject of intellectual exploration in the U.S. Army is an understatement. From my first days in Army boots until my last days in command, more than 38 years later, I attended courses, lectures, symposiums, and studied scholarly works on the skills and strategies needed to motivate soldiers and accomplish the mission. I wouldn't call myself an expert on this complex topic, but I will say that most Army leaders are insatiable students when it comes to the study of leadership.

Our leadership instructor was a somewhat indifferent captain, who, as I recall, was in his last assignment before leaving the Army. Nevertheless he was an effective instructor. In fact, he left me with a lesson that served me very well throughout my career. During one of our first classes the captain asked us, "What is everyone's favorite word—one single word?" We went around and around, with answers that ranged from "dinner" to "mother" to "sex." When it seemed that all the possibilities were exhausted, he gave us the correct answer—"your first name." Throughout my career I always tried to address soldiers by their first names, when appropriate. In fact, in one company of which I had recently taken command, the soldiers claimed that I stayed up at night studying rosters and memorizing their first names. But the practice served me well because it imparted the message that I recognized each soldier as a unique individual and that I cared enough to learn about them as people. I also learned that, particularly in crisis situations, the use of first names is a powerful way to gain and hold someone's close attention.

Perhaps the most fundamental lessons I learned came from the people with whom I traveled to WPI. Because we were required to attend class on the Worcester campus of WPI, it made sense for the four of us from Fitchburg State College to carpool. At first we kept each other at arm's length, because we were all quite different. Mike was a short, skinny, wiry guy who was older than the rest of us because he had served as an Army enlisted man. He soon became a kind of big brother to us. Another squad member was a painfully shy redhead with terrible acne. The third cadet was sort of your average guy, friendly, good-looking, always checking out the easiest way to get things done. Because we were from Fitchburg State College, a public university, it became clear that we were outliers at WPI—or at least perceived ourselves to be outsiders. So we soon developed an identity and bond as the bad boys from FSC. This was my first Army squad, and I soon learned that we were a tight team. If anyone messed with one of our FSC squad, they had three more of us to contend with.

Our first weekend training exercise introduced us to the best and worst of Army life. We were bused up to Fort Devens on Friday night and delivered into the care of senior year cadets, most of whom were either insufferable martinets or hopeless incompetents. Somehow we were directed to our bunks and marshaled through the mess hall. The ROTC officers and NCOs kept an eye on the chaos, but were reluctant to intervene.

Much to my delight we were trucked out to the rifle range early on Saturday morning and I wrapped my eager hands around an M16A1 rifle for the first time in my life. We had careful instruction on loading, aiming, and steady hold factors. We practiced sighting and dry firing. We sat through long safety briefings and lectures about sight adjustments. Finally after a full morning of talking about it, we assumed a good standing supported firing position in our round concrete foxholes on the firing line, ready to actually fire our rifles.

Someone handed me a magazine and I decisively slapped the shiny bronze bullets into the well of my rifle after the loudspeaker blared, "Lock and load." I released the catch and the greasy black bolt drove a single round into the chamber.

The tower voice announced, "Ready on the right. Ready on the left. The firing line is ready." Then came the order we had all anxiously awaited. "Firers, take your weapons off safe. Commence firing."

For a long moment, nothing happened, as we all hesitated, not wanting to be the first to fire. Then one brave soul squeezed the trigger and we all followed along. I held my breath as the rifle jumped slightly. I could hear the buffer spring squeak in the stock next to my right ear, but the sound and the recoil were far less than I expected. Quickly I sighted my target and fired off my three rounds as the burning scent of gunfire stung my nostrils, but it lodged in my memory as a pleasant aroma.

After checking my target and adjusting my sights, I heard a voice behind me. "How are you doing?"

I looked up and was surprised to realize that the gentle voice belonged to the meanest-looking soldier I had ever seen. He had dark deep set eyes, a long pointed nose, and pockmarked olive skin. His boots shone like glass and the creases in his starched uniform looked like they could cut your finger if you touched them. Most fearsome of all was the green beret on his head that sloped perfectly from his left eyebrow to his right ear. He squatted down behind my foxhole. "Does everything make sense to you?" he asked with hesitation. "If you have any questions, just let me know."

I stammered that I was all set and breathed a sigh of relief as he marched to the next foxhole. I didn't realize that I had just met the most important role model in my military career, perhaps the greatest mentor in my life, Sergeant First Class Al Drapeau.

The M16 range was the high point of the weekend. The low point came the next day when a self-important senior cadet took a dozen of us into his charge to show us infantry squad tactics. As we moved through the woods he somehow led us back behind the firing range impact area.

Suddenly one of my fellow first-year cadets noticed a strange hissing noise high up in the trees and asked the senior cadet what kind of insect made that sound. As we looked up, several of us realized that the hissing was caused by bullets slicing through the leaves over our heads. The senior cadet ordered us to crouch down and we sprinted as fast as we could until we were clear of the impact area.

It had been a wonderful training weekend for me—I had fired an M16, had my first experience of being shot at, and met my role model and mentor.

Many teachers, coaches, clergy, and relatives have taught me important lessons and helped shape who I have become. But no one has ever had a greater impact or been as memorable as Sgt. 1st Class Drapeau.

Those of us at Fitchburg State were delighted when the WPI ROTC leadership decided to post Drapeau permanently in Fitchburg. Not only did it mean that we had to travel to Worcester less because Sgt. 1st Class Drapeau could teach some of our classes, but suddenly we had our own wise godfather right on our own campus. We frequently stopped by the ROTC office on the Fitchburg campus to visit with Drapeau, ask for his advice, and listen to his stories. Somehow he always seemed pleased to see us.

I later learned that Sgt. 1st Class Drapeau had served in a high speed unit in Vietnam called Project DELTA , the predecessor of Delta Force and the most highly decorated unit of its size in Vietnam. Drapeau was a member of a hunter-killer team that operated deep into North Vietnamese territory collecting intelligence and conducting surgical strikes.[4] He earned four Bronze Star medals for valor among other decorations. I somehow think he was assigned to ROTC duty to allow him to take a knee from combat operations.

We were already beginning to value him when he became an instant hero to all of us on a gray spring afternoon. A senior cadet was conducting mandatory physical training in the center courtyard at Fitchburg State. We were sluggishly following his instructions for stretches, jumping jacks, and other standing exercises when it started to rain and rain hard. A mischievous smile came over the senior cadet's face as he ordered us to do pushups down in the mud. Once pushups were done, he ordered us to turn over and do sit ups in the slime and muck. Gradually we became covered with grass, rain, and mud from head to toe.

Suddenly an olive drab figure flew out of the building that held the ROTC office. Out of the corner of my eye I spotted a hatless Drapeau sprinting across the courtyard. We all stopped and watched as he called the senior cadet to attention and bellowed, "Cadet, you will dismiss this formation immediately. Do you understand me?"

The senior cadet called us to attention and dismissed us in a trembling voice. As we headed for the nearest spot to take cover from the rain, I saw the senior cadet doing pushups on the ground in front of Drapeau's boots, as the Sergeant stood with his hands on his hips. The lesson that leaders never needlessly abuse people under their command was more memorable than anything I learned in any ROTC classroom.

Over the years I've become somewhat suspicious of the veracity of veterans' war stories, but Sgt. 1st Class Drapeau's tales weren't exaggerated fables about combat heroics. Rather, I think he meant them to be parables about duty, leadership, and honor. For instance, he once told us that a local businessman came into the ROTC office late one afternoon. The man asked Drapeau about his combat experience, then made him a strange proposition. It seemed that the man represented a group of wealthy citizens who had secretly armed themselves with mortars and machine guns. They needed someone to discreetly instruct them on how to properly use these heavy weapons and they were willing to pay well. When Drapeau asked about the reason for collecting these weapons, the man explained that his group wanted to be ready when the revolution came—when poor people and minorities rose up to take over society.

"What did you tell him?" we asked breathlessly. Sgt. 1st Class Drapeau looked at us and replied slowly, "I told him he had thirty seconds to get the hell out of my office before I threw him out."

We must have looked puzzled. "One day you'll raise your right hand and swear to protect and defend the Constitution of the United States of America from enemies foreign and domestic," he said as he balled his fist. "That fine document does not allow private citizens to train secret armies intended to kill American citizens that they don't like because of the color of their skin, the place they come from, or how much money they have—Get it?"

We got it and I never forgot it.

In addition to his stories and instruction, Drapeau often invited us into his home for barbecues where we met his wife and little daughter. Although he was probably just being gracious, these visits with his family demonstrated that a warrior can still be a good husband and a devoted father.

As the end of my sophomore year of college approached, the ROTC cadre informed me that I had to make a choice; turn in my uniforms and equipment or sign a contract with the U.S. Army that would commit me to two years active duty service and six years in the reserves. At the age of nineteen, eight years seemed like an eternity. But I felt that service to defend the nation was important, I was loyal to my Fitchburg State buddies, and, believe it or not, I was growing to love the U.S. Army and what it stood for. I signed the contract with some trepidation, raised my right hand, and swore an oath to support and defend the Constitution of the United States of America.

Junior year in ROTC was somewhat more intense. Now that we were contracted cadets, the cadre had more ability to order us to attend events and training. The cadre also wanted to be certain that we'd successfully complete Advanced Camp at Fort Bragg that summer.

Junior year's courses came to an end. I received my airplane ticket to North Carolina along with orders to report to Fort Bragg in late June. Foolishly I spent the night before my flight partying into the early morning hours with some friends at Fitchburg State. They drove me to the airport with my duffel bag and a vicious hangover.

Whenever a young person proudly says something like, "I'm leaving for basic training next Thursday." I always respond with "Good for you—good luck," in my most positive voice. But inside I'm thinking, "Get ready for the worst day of your life, you poor bastard."

And so it was for me when I landed in North Carolina. I remember the blast of hot air hitting my face as I got off the airplane, just like when you open the oven door. I recall a blur of sergeants hollering, growling, seething venom as they herded us onto a bus. Arriving at Fort Bragg, other sergeants pushed us through lines as surly or bored civilians collected forms, gathered our signatures, and hurled ragged uniforms and frayed field equipment at us. Stumbling under the weight of two duffel bags, we finally arrived at our barracks, where our very own platoon sergeant bullied us through the basic tasks of making bunks, setting up lockers, and cleaning the latrine.

Throughout that first day other members of the platoon arrived—a skinny kid from Scranton, Pennsylvania, who told anyone who'd listen that he was going to be a Green Beret; a loud, smooth-talking red-haired southerner from Virginia Military Institute; Big Hank, my bunkmate, a soft spoken guy from Georgia who instantly referred to me as "Li'l Smith"; Jack from Florida, married, Christian, much more mature than the rest of us who, out of thousands of cadets, would be named the outstanding cadet for the entire training cycle. All in all, there were forty of us from across the eastern United States and Puerto Rico. By design, none of us knew one another, but we would become well acquainted over the next ten weeks. As I lay on my bunk at the end of that hellish first day, trying to get to sleep despite the airplane-engine whine of the cooling fan, I thought, "What the hell have I gotten myself into?"

In those days, ROTC Advanced Camp was designed to initiate cadets into military life, provide some training in basic military skills, and weed out those who lacked the physical or mental stamina to be officers. Accordingly, days were fast-paced, beginning before dawn with physical training and often ending after midnight. Many times we shoveled our food into our mouths standing up in the dining facility because there was no time to sit down. Leadership positions rotated so the cadre could evaluate our skills, which meant, if you were designated to be a leader, you had more responsibilities to attend to. There was constant heat, constant stress, and never enough time to sleep.

Most of us quickly learned to adapt to this new life, which was so different in very many ways. For instance, bathrooms, or latrines, were equipped with a large trough for urination, much like something from which farm animals drink, and a shower room with a dozen shower heads. Although they weren't ideal for the bashful, most of us had experienced those conditions at ballparks and in high school locker rooms.

But the latrine also offered six white porcelain toilets that were right out in the open—no partitions, no curtains, no privacy. I found this so uncomfortable that, in the first few days, I offered to take late night Fire Watch shifts after everyone was asleep just so I could move my bowels in private. However, by the beginning of the second week, the porcelain thrones became a sort of Roman Forum, where defecators would discuss training, debate politics, and share sports news—all while moving their bowels. Soldiers can adapt to anything.

Although none of us would have voluntarily chosen to be out of bed at five o'clock in the morning, I recall the beauty of forty soldiers running through the pre-dawn mist in the only coolness of the day. You became part of a powerful rhythmic machine as you clapped and sang in unison under the red, rising sun. The uplifting spirit of the formation run even affected the drill sergeants, who lost their bullying attitude for a little while, and joined in the fun of singing "jodies," or running songs, which were often obscene. As we shuffled along someone would call out the verse and the formation would repeat it as we clapped in rhythm. Here are the lyrics for one of the more acceptable jodies:

> Momma, momma, can't you see
> what the Army's done to me
> I used to drive a Cadillac
> Now I hump it on my back
>
> Momma, momma, can't you see
> what the Army's done to me
> I used to date a beauty queen
> Now I hug my M-16
>
> Momma, momma, can't you see
> what the Army's done to me
> I used to drive a Chevrolet
> Now I'm walking all the way[5]

The thought of falling out of formation never crossed my mind, even when our runs exceeded five miles, which was a distance I probably couldn't have covered on my own without stopping to catch my breath.

Above all, we learned the strength of working as part of a team. The unspoken code was that we all had each other's backs. Not only were you responsible to respond to a request for help, but you were also responsible for preventing your buddy from falling on his or her face. We were never directly taught the importance of teamwork in the Army, but we all came to clearly understand our responsibility to each other.

But the power of the team couldn't pull everyone through. Some cadets disappeared after complaining of twisted knees, sprained wrists, and other minor injuries. We soon concluded that a non-life threatening ailment was the honorable way for many cadets to say, "This isn't for me," and the Army played right along by offering the choice of another try next year or by easing them back into civilian life.

One afternoon the platoon was being punished for a dirty sink or some other mortal sin by being forced to stand in formation in the heat. Suddenly the cadet next to me, a big guy from Puerto Rico, started shouting in a mix of Spanish and English, "I can't take this shit anymore! I'm not going to take it!" Two sergeants came over, gently took him by the arms, and escorted him away. We never saw him again.

Perhaps the most valuable gift Sgt. 1st Class Drapeau ever gave me was when he paid me a visit during my second week at Fort Bragg. My platoon sergeant at the time was riding me hard. In fact, I think he had singled me out as a low performer who needed extra motivation—which probably wasn't entirely incorrect.

Drapeau took me aside and asked, "How are things going, Greg?"

"Awful," I responded. "My platoon sergeant has it out for me. He finds something wrong with everything I do. This guy is on my back from first call to lights out. I don't know what to do, Sarge."

Sgt. 1st Class Drapeau smiled at me. "Don't worry. I have a surefire way to make him stop. You really want to get him back, don't you?" He beckoned to me to come closer so he could whisper in my ear. I leaned in eagerly. "Don't—Fuck-Up." He whispered slowly. "It will drive him crazy."

Now, it may seem funny, but it worked. Maybe Drapeau talked with my platoon sergeant and told him to ease up, but I don't think so. After that conversation I focused on doing every little thing correctly and soon the platoon sergeant just ignored me and found some other target for his attention.

But more importantly, throughout my life when I felt attacked, beaten up, against the ropes, I remembered Drapeau's three words. I've always found that the best way to win is to be better than your enemies—think sharper, work harder, fight back, and never give up.

Weeks went by. We qualified with our M16 rifles, fired mortars, took our gas masks off in the tear gas chamber, and after coughing and vomiting, learned to quickly put them on again. We rappelled off hundred foot towers, crossed ravines by crawling on a single rope, and crawled under barbed wire while a machine gun fired live rounds over our heads. We also learned to clean porcelain in the latrine until it shined, make a bunk with blankets that were trampoline-tight, and shine black boots until the toes reflected like mirrors.

I remember the day we went to the live hand grenade range. We all boasted in the back of the jolting truck that we were going to throw it the farthest. When we arrived at the range, the instructor challenged us to be the first to toss a grenade into a stack of tires about twenty-five yards down range—and if anyone could do it, they'd get $25 in cash. As we tossed the light blue dummy grenades on the practice range, we bragged about what we'd buy with the cash prize.

But most of us later admitted that, when we had a real live hand grenade grasped between our two hands, the only thought we had was to pull the pin, get rid of that thing, and take cover with our faces in the dirt behind the sandbag parapet as fast as we could. I imagine that $25 cash prize went unclaimed all summer.

Looking back, the most amazing thing about Army training was that somehow it forced you to confront your worst fears. I saw people struggle with their fears of explosives, guns, heights, water, speaking in front of large groups, you name it. For me it was claustrophobia. From childhood, I always had an irrational sense of panic when I was in a tightly enclosed space. I couldn't even comfortably crawl under a car to do an oil change or ride in a crowded elevator.

Anti-armor training with the shoulder-fired Light Antitank Weapon, or LAW, consisted of hunkering down in a concrete-reinforced foxhole while a tank drove over us. The successful cadet would then pop up and click the trigger of an inert LAW pointed at the rear of the tank. I gulped when I saw the demonstration, but I figured I could choke down my fear of enclosed places for a few seconds as the tank rumbled over me.

My turn came and I nervously squeezed into the bottom of the foxhole. I began to shake as I heard the tank rumble toward me. Everything went dark when it was on top of me. Then it stopped and the engine conked out. In the quiet darkness I fought against my rising panic and reassured myself that I could handle this and that the tank would start up again. When I heard the tanker's voices complaining about the breakdown I struggled to stay calm. After what seemed an eternity, the engine roared above me. The sunlight shone on the foxhole as I fired my LAW and quickly scampered out of the hole. Just then I realized that everyone around me, including the tankers and my buddies, were laughing. The whole episode was a prank, but no one knew that it taught me the important lesson that I had the strength to overcome my greatest fear.

The ROTC Advanced Camp concluded with a 72-hour air assault operation, straight out of a Vietnam war movie. I nervously boarded the Huey with my squad for the first helicopter ride of my life and was taken aback when the crew chief directed me to sit on the deck with my boots dangling out the open door. We lifted off and I fought back the inevitable queasiness of air sickness. As we cruised over the canopy of lush green foliage just a few feet below, the beauty of the flight and the rush of cool air on my face was totally lost on me because I was obsessed with the possibility of dropping my rifle and losing it forever in the sea of green leaves below.

We hopped off the low hovering Hueys into a remote clearing, fanned out into the tree line, and formed a perimeter around the landing zone as the helicopters soared away into the blue sky. I don't clearly remember what happened during the first two days, but I seem to recall a jumble of patrols, tactical squad movements, firefights with the unseen enemy (using blank ammunition, of course), and digging foxholes again and again to defend locations that we only occupied for a few hours.

When we halted, we pulled olive drab "C" ration cans from our packs, and dined on cold entrees like beef stew, spaghetti, beans and franks, and the much maligned "chopped eggs and ham" that had a suspicious and unappetizing greenish tint. Each meal also came with smaller cans that contained fruit, candy, jelly, or drink powder—but the contents of the small cans were a mystery until you opened the "C" ration box. Trades were brisk in the "C" ration economy: a small can of cheese could fetch a can of peanut butter with a lemonade drink mix thrown in, and canned pears or a round fudge bar could even get you a date with somebody's sister. But you were a loser if your meal pack contained a coconut candy bar, orange marmalade, or hot chocolate powder, which were nearly worthless in the lively "C" ration marketplace.

These feasts were made possible by the most amazing item the Army ever issued—a little can opener, called a P-38. It was a one-inch piece of steel with a hinged half-inch cutting blade attached, which looked like an eagle's claw. To open a can, you swung the claw cutting blade out, hooked a notch on the steel arm onto the rim of the can. Then you pressed down on the claw, piercing the lid of the can. By working the claw up and down, the device almost magically traveled around the lid, opening the can. After dining, you rinsed it, folded it, and most of us attached it to our dog tag chains through a hole conveniently drilled in the steel arm. There was an urban legend that P-38 had been known to open and stab their owners in the chest when they were foolish enough to wear them with their dog tags, but most of us disregarded this unproved warning. I never knew a P-38 to malfunction and I will always assert that it is the finest item in the Army equipment inventory.

But there wasn't that much time for manipulating P-38 and dining on delicacies during this operation because we were always moving or digging. As darkness fell on our second night, the instructors called me over and told me I was now the platoon leader. I wasn't pleased about the leadership opportunity because now I actually had to think and plan about the other cadets in the platoon instead of just worrying about myself.

After receiving orders from the instructors, I moved the platoon through the woods for a mile or so into a clearing to rest for a few hours. Although it was still summer, the night was chilly. My fellow cadets wrapped themselves in their ponchos and piled on top of one another to keep warm. I remember standing guard over the sleeping mass of arms and legs with two or three designated squad leaders. When I looked up into the star-filled night sky, a warm feeling of responsibility gradually came over me along with a sense of pride—these slumbering buddies trusted me to keep them safe from the enemy, and I would do my utmost to protect them.

Just before dawn the instructors gave me new orders to assault the enemy's position at a certain location on the map. Up to this time we had only exchanged fire with the enemy, but we had never seen them. Now we had the chance to attack them. This was exciting.

I quickly awakened the platoon, issued an operations order, and moved out. As the sun began to rise on a beautiful North Carolina day, we were crouched in the woods overlooking a cluster of pup tents in a small grassy field. No one stirred among the tents. There were no sentries or fighting positions. It appeared that we had caught the enemy sleeping.

As I gave the signal to advance, each squad maneuvered quietly around the camp until we surrounded the tents. I waved my hand toward the slumbering foe and, with a whoop, our platoon kicked down the tents jamming the muzzles of our weapons into the faces of the startled occupants.

The instructors ran into the fray, waving their hands, screaming, "Cease fire, cease fire!" My platoon comrades, sleep-deprived and crazed with bloodlust, backed off, but roared and hopped about in a strange victory dance. I think we had regressed backwards through several centuries of civilization to arrive at kinship with our barbarian warrior ancestors.

Later when I recalled this incident, it occurred to me that, in a small way, it validated General Robert E. Lee's famous quote. "It is well that war is so terrible lest we become too fond of it."

After the instructors regained control, it was obvious that we had been part of someone's practical joke—the sleeping occupants of the pup tents were other cadets who had been told to bed down in a "safe" area for the night. Soon I was relieved of the mantle of leadership and it was turned over to someone sane to bring us out of the woods. But I had my first sweet taste of command—and I liked it.

In the early afternoon sunshine we squatted along the edge of the landing zone. I've rarely seen a more beautiful sight than the column of inbound Hueys, their rotors slicing through the air with the crack of that unmistakable "whop-whop" sound that precedes them. The dark green angels floated above the flattened waves of grass as we jumped up onto them. This time I savored the cool breeze that dried my sweaty face and inhaled the delicious aroma of oil and hydraulic fluid as we were carried away to safety, showers, real food, and rest on the wings of these wondrous flying creatures. I now understood how beautiful a helicopter can look to a ground soldier.

ROTC Advanced Camp was soon over and we traveled back to our final year at Fitchburg State College and the Worcester Polytechnic Institute ROTC program.

The four of us from Fitchburg State were relegated to insignificant leadership positions of no importance and we soon became disillusioned with the on-campus program, after experiencing the high tempo training of Fort Bragg. Our poor attitude must have been apparent. I recall with some embarrassment that we once booze-cruised from Fitchburg to Worcester and arrived at a mandatory formation after consuming most of a case of beer. I don't think we were drunk, but I can still remember the sense of relief after the four of us sprinted to the latrine when we heard "Fall Out."

Oddly enough, the ROTC cadre treated us with kid gloves. In a moment of weakness, Sgt. 1st Class Drapeau revealed that the Fort Bragg evaluations of his four Fitchburg cadets were far superior to those of the Worcester cadets. Although we pressed him for more information, he quickly clammed up saying, with an impish grin, that he had already said more than he should have.

In the fall I learned that fourth-year cadets who committed to entering the National Guard could be commissioned early. This was great news for me and I quickly applied for early commissioning. Drapeau was dead set against it and begged me to complete the year and serve on active duty, but my mind was made up.

On a snowy night in February 1979 I repeated the oath of office "to support and defend the Constitution of the United States from all enemies foreign and domestic." My future wife, Nora, was the only guest for the simple ceremony in the basement of the ROTC building at WPI. Little did

Cadet Smith and Ms. Nora Dougherty prepare to attend an ROTC Military Ball in 1978. Ms. Dougherty would later become Mrs. Smith (author's collection).

we know how that oath would shape our lives and our future. Sgt. 1st Class Drapeau pinned the shiny brass Second Lieutenant's bars to the shoulder straps of my dress green uniform, but he wouldn't accept the traditional silver dollar I offered when we exchanged salutes. He never explained why.

So what eventually happened to the Fitchburg State ROTC team? I lost track of one of my squad mates when he was serving in Germany, commanding an Ordnance company. My shy buddy took up weightlifting as a hobby, served as a Special Forces officer, and left the Army as a major. He then earned a Ph.D. and has a highly successful career in the corporate world. Mike, the older brother, transferred into the Marine Corps at the end of our senior year. He became a superstar in the area of military intelligence and published several important papers. He made it through Operation Desert Storm without a scratch, but was killed when his helicopter went down in a training operation.

The Marine Corps Intelligence Officer Association selects one outstanding Officer of the Year. The chosen officer receives a foot-high bronze statue, sort of like an Oscar statue at the Academy Awards. The intelligence officer statue is a likeness of Lt. Col. Michael Kuscewski.[6] I once held one of those statues and experienced a strange mingling of pride, sorrow, and nostalgia as I cradled my old friend in my hands.

Sgt. 1st Class Alfred Drapeau passed away in 2009 and is buried in his hometown of Rumford, Maine. The day I was promoted to brigadier general in 2010 was a joyous event, but I had one pang of regret. My deepest wish was that my friend and mentor could be there to share my joy. I hope he would have been proud of the results of his good work so long ago—and this time I hope he would have accepted my general's coin and a 35-year-old silver dollar.

Birth of a Weekend Warrior

I was still an ROTC cadet when I reported for my first day in the National Guard. Consequently I was told to report for duty with no insignia on my uniform. I arrived at the armory and stood behind the formation. When the company fell out to begin its scheduled tasks and training, a no-nonsense sergeant approached me and handed me a broom. It probably would have been quicker to sweep the floor, but I doggedly explained my unique status. The NCO, not sure if he was being bamboozled or not, trudged away shaking his head in search of some other loitering body who needed to be put to work.

Within a few hours, an excited buzz vibrated through the company. I could overhear snatches of conversation, but I couldn't make sense of what was going on. The company commander hastily called a formation. He explained that we were being activated to fight a flood. All personnel had two hours to go home, pack three days of clothing and personal items, and return ready to deploy to the flood zone.

As the troops dispersed, I sought out the company commander. My college dorm was a two-hour drive from the armory. There was no way I could get there and back in time. Besides, I hadn't yet been issued any field equipment or wet weather gear. He told me to explain my situation to the supply sergeant and get whatever gear I could.

The company re-formed and the commander called the platoon leaders and platoon sergeants forward to brief them on their assignments. I hung back until the leader meeting was over, then approached the commander. "What would you like me to do, Sir?" I asked, expecting that I would stay with the company headquarters.

The commander looked at me intently. "First Platoon doesn't have a lieutenant right now. Why don't you take charge of them and get them going." I stammered, "I—I'm not sure I can do that."

He shot back, "Look, Smitty, you're going to be an officer in a few weeks. You might as well start acting like one right now." With that he turned away to deal with the hundreds of other matters that needed his attention.

I found First Platoon loading up into two cargo trucks and introduced myself to the platoon sergeant. He must have thought he had been assigned babysitting duty, but he respectfully escorted me to the passenger seat in the cab of the lead truck. He also quickly briefed me on our instructions and gave me the map and operations order for the mission.

We soon departed for the flood zone, which was only about fifteen miles from the armory. Darkness was falling and it was pouring rain. After ten miles or so, the two truck drivers pulled over and the platoon sergeant informed me that we were lost. I took out the map and conferred with the drivers and platoon sergeant who made it clear that the decision was mine as to which road we would take. I made my best guess and prayed that I was right. After about five minutes we came to an area illuminated by flood lights, where a fire official waved us down with a red cone flashlight. We were in the right place after all and I breathed a huge sigh of relief.

Quickly we grabbed shovels, sandbags, and flashlights and got to work building a wall to hold back a surging river that threatened to overflow its banks. As the mission was explained to us, we needed to prevent the town's pumping station from becoming submerged or else sewage would seep into the drinking water supply.

The platoon worked like fiends in the cold, pouring rain. I grabbed sand bags and filled them alongside the soldiers. At one point the company commander called me aside and reminded me that I was an officer, not an enlisted man. I replied that I wasn't an officer yet and preferred to work with my platoon. He just gave me a half smile and walked away. Right after that, a sergeant handed me a pint of whiskey and invited me to take a swig.

After midnight the river crested and began to recede. We moved to a nearby school gym where wall-to-wall cots had been set up. The platoon sergeant saved me a spot near him, but we were too excited to sleep. I spent most of the night listening to the stories of the sergeants on my right and left. One pudgy corporal went on and on about his plans to travel to Rhodesia as a mercenary. I didn't care that it was bullshit, I was just thrilled to be accepted by the soldiers of my first command.

The next day the sun came out. We returned to the armory, quickly secured our equipment, and were dismissed. When I arrived back at my college apartment, I cracked a cold beer and sank down in a chair like an exhausted veteran. "Well, how was it?" asked my impatient roommates.

"It was awesome," I replied. "We sandbagged a flooding river and saved a town's water supply."

"Cool!" was their admiring response.

"Yah, I can't wait to see who we save next month."

It turned out that the next month's training was taken up with paperwork, equipment maintenance, and classroom training. There wasn't a flood, hurricane, or snowstorm in sight. And so, I soon came to realize that my life as a lieutenant in the National Guard was not quite as exciting as my first day on duty would have suggested.

However, in October of that year, we received word that Pope John Paul II was coming to visit Boston.[7] Hundreds of thousands of people were expected to line his travel route and attend mass on Boston Common. The National Guard was tasked to provide crowd control.

When the day arrived, we all showed up in our starched short-sleeve tan uniforms. The troops wore their green "envelope hats," while I, as an officer, wore my brand new "saucer hat," complete with gold eagle and gold chinstrap.

We loaded onto buses to stay crisp and clean for a change, and traveled to our assigned sector on Commonwealth Avenue, about four miles from downtown Boston. Although His Holiness wasn't scheduled to travel through our sector until after the mass, we were ordered to take up our crowd control positions on the street right after we ate our box lunches at noon.

There really wasn't much of a crowd, so we positioned half of the company on the street while the other half lounged around the buses in an adjacent park. The soldiers chatted pleasantly with passersby in the warm autumn sunshine. This was pretty easy duty.

Suddenly, loud rock music blared from the third floor window of an apartment building in our sector and a young college girl popped up into the window gyrating to the music. The soldiers looked up appreciatively and clapped when the music died out after a minute or so. We laughed and thought nothing of it.

About fifteen minutes later, the rock music blasted out again and a different college girl hopped up in the window to strut herself for a little while longer. This performance not only drew cheers from the street, but it started to attract the attention of the soldiers in the park area. The officers and sergeants still laughed and ordered the troops to keep it down.

The performances were repeated a few more times until, filled with apparent euphoria at seeing the Pontiff, the first girl jumped up into the window, peeled off her tee shirt, and rocked to the music with her heavenly, naked breasts bouncing this way and that. Well, this was too much for our troops, who surged toward the entrance to the apartment building. Another lieutenant ran with me to position ourselves in the doorway of the apartment building. We shoved away the first leering soldiers and threatened the others with death or worse as we commanded them to get back to their posts.

Thankfully the sergeants gained control of the situation. Moments later the Boston Police arrived to convince the young ladies that their religious zeal should probably be expressed in a more family-friendly way.

As evening fell, clouds gathered, and the rain began to fall. There were no more dancing girls. The few onlookers who hoped to get a glimpse of the Pope found drier places to be. His Holiness was delayed in downtown Boston. Finally at around nine o'clock a limousine sloshed down Commonwealth Avenue at about 35 miles per hour. We came to attention and, out of the corner of my eye, I caught a fleeting glimpse of a little old man in white through a tinted, dripping car window.

We were thoroughly soaked by the time we arrived back at the armory and our once-starched tan uniforms hung on us like sacks. But the worst part was that my new saucer hat was permanently stretched out of shape. I hope the Holy Father appreciated our service and sacrifices.

Fun at Summer Camp

In the midst of the Cold War the National Guard contributed to the war effort by deploying the entire 26th Infantry "Yankee" Division from its armories in the New England states to Fort Drum, New York, for combat training. The two week annual training period was referred to as "summer camp," and I was soon to learn that the nickname was quite accurate.

In the early 1980s the troop strength of the Yankee Division was somewhere near 10,000 soldiers. It was often said that the convoy from home stations to Fort Drum at one time stretched continuously in one long line across the roadway from Boston to Watertown, New York—a distance of nearly 340 miles. There is little doubt in my mind that this show of force ultimately led to the demise of the Soviet Union and the fall of the Berlin Wall, particularly when one considers that it would have taken several months for the division to deploy to Europe.

Not knowing what to expect at my first summer camp, I packed my Army gear and personal items into my duffel bag and threw in a box of granola bars as a last thought. Knowing that officers were required to pay for their own meals, I cleaned out my savings account and stuffed all $213 into my wallet, certain that the wad of cash would enable me to feast like a king for two weeks.

Our company was part of the Yankee Division's Supply and Transportation Battalion, which was responsible for establishing and maintaining fuel sites, or military gas stations, along the convoy route. Because we needed to be ready for the division motor move, we headed out two days before the main convoy and would arrive four days after.

My first assignment was to supervise the box lunch feeding activity at a refueling stop located at a maintenance facility along the New York Thruway. To be honest, this wasn't much of a job. I think the senior leaders only decided to assign an officer to the box lunches to prevent pilfering and wholesale theft. I was also told to observe the warrant officer in charge of the fueling operation, Chief Warrant Officer John Murray, and learn as much as I could from him.

As soon as we arrived to set up in the maintenance yard, it started to rain. With all the self-importance of a new lieutenant with an insignificant mission, I bustled back and forth as the convoy elements arrived. Were there enough brownies for all personnel? Was the mustard running out? Did anyone see that private who took two sandwiches? I wrestled with these and other matters of national security all day long.

Every now and then a staff car would arrive carrying a colonel or another high-ranking officer. I would salute smartly and prepare to brief them, but all they seemed to want to know was the location of Mr. Murray's trailer. At one point I stopped by the trailer during a break between convoy elements and found Mr. Murray and the senior sergeants enjoying a cold Budweiser. Unabashed, Mr. Murray simply asked, "Want a cold one, Smitty?"

As the cold rain fell in torrents I soon found myself soaked to the skin. By the time our team arrived back at our motel, I was coughing, sneezing, and running a fever. Out of a true sense of concern, several of the sergeants stopped by my room to offer medicinal remedies, most of which involved large quantities of strong liquor mixed with other substances like fruit juice, cough syrup, or mouthwash. Needless to say I was soon comatose on my bed.

Thankfully the sergeant with whom I shared the room tucked me into bed. All night long I had the wildest dreams involving strange animals, odd voices from my past and present, and a particularly vivid dream about people having sex next to my bed. However, I was miraculously healed when I woke up the next morning and I felt like a new man.

As I dressed and got ready to head out to the fuel site, I told my roommate about my crazy dreams. He listened with interest, then nonchalantly remarked, "Oh, yeah, my old lady stopped by last night. We figured you were too far out of it to mind if we got a little frisky." I was learning a lot about the Army.

Once all the Yankee Division vehicles had passed through our fuel site, we packed up and prepared to travel to Fort Drum. I soon learned that no one was eager to transition from motel rooms, restaurants, and on-site beer trailers to field latrines, sleeping bags, and tactical feeding (a topic upon which I will later elaborate). So I was tasked with leading the first group of cooks and mechanics to Fort Drum, but Mr. Murray and the fuel personnel would require another day to carefully break down the equipment and make the trip.

My command vehicle was a five-ton dump truck driven by a cheerful, but not very experienced corporal. Soon our small convoy was fragmented as trucks passed us and others lagged behind. I recall halting the few remaining vehicles once we had exited the New York Thruway. As one of the trucks pulled up, I approached the passenger side of the vehicle to ensure they knew the rest of the route. The co-driver or passenger rolled down the window, leaned out and vomited all over the side of the truck. Then he wiped his mouth, saluted, and said, "We're all set, Sir. Don't worry about us."

We finally arrived at Fort Drum in the late afternoon and shuttled from the motor pool to the convoy staging area to the battalion headquarters building that was now locked. By sewing together a web of rumors and partial truths, we eventually found the location where our company had established its field training bivouac.

No sooner had I stashed my duffel bag in the officers' tent than I was confronted by a frantic specialist from the company headquarters. "Sir, there's some general out here who's looking for information," the specialist stammered. "Well, can't you find the commander or first sergeant?" I asked. "Sir, they're all out of the area. You're all we've got," he pleaded.

I hastily donned my helmet and web gear and prepared to meet the general. Now I hadn't met any generals up to this point and wasn't quite ready for what I was about to face.

As I saluted the senior officer I was confronted with a short, bulldog of a man with one hand resting on his hip and one hand resting on his pistol holster. Although I couldn't see his eyes through the aviator sunglasses, I was fairly certain he was glaring at me. "Good afternoon, General," I began cheerfully. "Where's your company commander?" he barked.

"I really don't know, Sir, you see I just...." "Where's your first shirt?" I could see his temper rising. "I just arrived and I don't know where...."

"How many trucks do you have here?" Now he was really angry. "I'm not certain, General." I responded with complete surrender.

"You don't know anything, do you, Lieutenant?" He almost spit this last question at me. "Yes, Sir," I responded with shame and resignation. He stood there staring at me to ensure that my humiliation was complete, then jammed a cigar between his clenched teeth, grunted, and stormed off in his jeep.

I was considerably relieved to see him go, but I soon learned that many National Guard officers at that time affected a gruff, imperious pose to mask their lack of professional skill. They seemed to look upon intimidating junior personnel as a kind of blood sport that elevated them in the esteem of their peers and superiors. As I watched that comic-book martinet general ride off in his jeep, I resolved that I would never become a leader who took pleasure in humiliating a subordinate. I hope I lived up to that resolution.

I was finally connected with the platoon I led and gratefully set about the military tasks with which I was familiar. As a new officer who hadn't yet attended Transportation Officer Basic Course, I didn't know much about convoy operations and the technical aspects of trucking. In fact, I didn't even know how to drive a truck or a jeep.

But I knew something about setting up a defensive perimeter to defend the sector of our bivouac for which we were responsible. So our platoon spent much of the day placing fighting positions, digging hasty foxholes, positioning forward observation posts, and sighting our M-60 machine guns. I proudly developed our sector sketch and coached the machine gunners on how to write out range cards for their weapons. Some of the younger soldiers actually showed interest in the process of plotting out preplanned artillery fire coordinates. I was proud of the way the members of our platoon all pitched in despite the hot sun and warm temperatures. As I glanced at my watch and noticed that it was almost four o'clock, I estimated that we'd be able to have our defensive sector pretty well set up by supper time.

Suddenly the shrill tweet of a whistle sounded from the direction of the company command post. I watched in dismay as the soldiers in my platoon jumped up and bolted for the command post, leaving behind range cards, entrenching tools, and even the machine guns. I followed along with the deep disappointment that Napoleon must have felt after Waterloo.

As I neared the command post, I saw a swarm of soldiers jostling each other around a quarter-ton trailer that had been towed there by a jeep. The fortunate ones who could get close enough reached in and pulled out frosty cans of Budweiser with ice chips still clinging to the outsides. Hands on his hips, the first sergeant presided over this scene of joyous chaos like some kind of Bavarian brewmaster.

"Hey, only one at a time, McCarthy," he bellowed. "I'm watching you." "Slow down, Davis. If you keep chugging them you'll barf in the chow line," he warned. Wagging his finger he said, "No, you can't take Campbell's three cans to him on sentry duty, Whitney." First, he can't drink at his sentry post and second, you'd go over there behind that tree and guzzle them down.

Like a good officer, I waited until the men had their ration. Then I reached into the frigid water at the bottom of the trailer and found one of the last cans. Ice-cold beer sure hits the spot on a hot summer afternoon.

After cocktail hour, we all queued up for tactical dinner. This odd procedure required the platoon to disperse among the trees as each member approached the chow line. Once there, however, there wasn't the slightest sense of any tactical discipline—cooks shouted at each other as they clustered around the serving line and customers bunched up as they piled on their food. And, of course, the mess sergeant opened his cash box and demanded, "That will be one dollar and seventy eight cents, Lieutenant."

Following our first three night stay in the woods, the entire Yankee Division packed up and headed to the barracks area on Friday afternoon for what was called, "Middle Weekend." This two-day bacchanalian festival was an event for which many members of the National Guard planned all year. In fact I heard many soldiers confess that they eked out a little more spending money for Middle Weekend by telling their wives that they had to buy their own bullets at summer camp.

No sooner had the dusty truck engines rumbled to a halt, then out came the golf clubs, Hawaiian shirts, and coolers. Fords, Chevys, and Buicks appeared from nowhere as they loaded up with freshly showered revelers who reeked of too much aftershave. Considering that the division traveled in military convoys, it was a subject of some mystery as to how all these colorful sedans arrived at Fort Drum. The prevailing rumor was that many were loaded into twelve-ton cargo trailers then buried under piles of canvas tentage. Remarkably many wives also appeared to join their men on junkets to Ottawa or the Thousand Islands—at least they claimed to be wives. There also appeared to be a large number of younger nieces that joined their uncles for Middle Weekend.

For those who lacked the transportation, funds, or imagination to join the Friday exodus out of Fort Drum, the barracks area became a playground, albeit with a distinctively adult theme. Truckloads of beer and liquor were unloaded and quickly consumed as revelers stumbled between barracks dressed in odd combinations of military and civilian attire. Country music blared from boom boxes. One barracks was transformed into an X-rated theater as grainy black-and-white movies flickered on a bed sheet screen to the hoots, hollers, and running commentary of the enthusiastic audience.

As for me, being the most junior officer, I was assigned the job of battalion Staff Duty Officer for most of the weekend. I don't remember actually doing very much duty, but I recall being told that I must check in with headquarters every few hours and, most importantly, I had to be sober when I did so. Considering that most officers were either whooping it up in Canada or lying passed out in some hotel, there wasn't much action at headquarters and I enjoyed the peace and quiet.

When I was off duty on Sunday night, a friend invited me to join him and a group of other officers for dinner at a nearby restaurant. After a full week of Army chow, a restaurant dinner was an appealing idea. However there was one slight problem. I realized that I had to pay for my meals, but hadn't done the math all that well. Although I had cleaned out my meager savings account to prepare for Annual Training, I hadn't planned on the additional costs of eating in restaurants at the refueling site on the way to Fort Drum. By now my skimpy cash reserves were running thin. Still

I figured that, if I cut out a few meals the following week and ate granola bars when I was hungry, I could afford one nice dinner at a restaurant.

So, I squeezed into the back seat of someone's car and we all arrived at a Mom and Pop Italian restaurant just outside Fort Drum. Most of my fellow diners were young officers like me. But there were also a few older captains. I can still picture one of them, a portly guy with graying hair and a drooping mustache who sported a gold bracelet around his wrist and a neck chain with a gold medallion. He dominated the conversation as he puffed on a cigar. Because he was senior to most of us, good manners dictated that we defer to him somewhat, and he clearly enjoyed this advantage.

I watched in envy as the older captain swilled down several martinis. I sipped one Miller, "the champagne of bottled beer" after all. He eagerly wolfed down his shrimp cocktail as I passed up the appetizer. I was surprised that he still had a room for apple pie a la mode after his surf and turf entrée. My grilled chicken sandwich was enough for me.

I silently congratulated myself on my frugality as the waitress came to settle up the bill. "Will that be one check or separate?" she asked. "Just make it one check," the older captain blurted out before any of us could speak.

The waitress quickly returned with the check and handed it to the captain who studied it intently. "Let's see," he said, rubbing his greasy chin. "If we divide it evenly by seven and add a good tip, then each of us should pitch in $23—not bad."

Any protest would be unthinkable, lest the speaker be forever branded as a cheapskate. So we all dug deep and paid up. But when I got a peek at what was left in my wallet, there was only one Hamilton and a few Washingtons smiling back at me.

In the dim early morning hours of the Monday after "Middle Weekend," golf clubs were packed away, crates of beer cans were disposed of, and olive drab uniforms replaced colorful Hawaiian shirts. With throbbing heads, bleary eyes, and much regret, the Yankee Division returned to the semi-serious business of war games.

So we packed up the trucks again, reissued weapons, and headed back to the woods for three days of field training. We occupied a different bivouac site, which required new foxholes, machine gun pits, and range cards. The platoon's tactical skills were much better on this visit to the field. I was proud of them and I was pleased with my apparent ability as a leader of warriors.

On our last full day in the woods, the company supply sergeant called our platoon sergeant to pick up our last issue of ammunition. He and his assistants returned from the command post loaded down with ammunition cans full of blank M-16 rounds, belts of M-60 machine gun blanks, smoke grenades, trip flares, artillery simulators and many other pyrotechnics that produced bright flashes and loud bangs. Every soldiers' eyes glistened as they prepared to unleash the mischievous little child that lurks within all of us. As the platoon sergeant passed out this desperado's treasure to the eager recipients, he growled, "And remember, blow it all off tonight. Supply don't want nothing back."

The sun set and darkness fell as my warriors blackened their faces with charred pieces of wood or, for those who came prepared, made up their faces in elaborate designs with camouflage face paint. They settled into their fighting positions, observation posts, or machine gun pits and waited for the coming onslaught. A dozen chosen killers, like twelve deadly apostles, squatted behind the line ready to pounce as our rapid reaction force. Night set in. Each warrior silently scanned the dark forest for movement as they taped ammo magazines together end-to-end for fast loading and pinched the ends of grenade pins so they'd slide out quicker. The tension was thick in the sweaty stillness. Every cricket squeak, bird chirp, or chipmunk tweet sounded like a broken twig or the approach of a bad guy. Suddenly they were on us, a half dozen hooting and hollering mechanics with rags tied around their heads. They fired off their blanks and screamed clever epithets like "Die Yankee dogs," and "Americans suck."

Believing that this was a bona fide defensive tactical training exercise, I started to issue orders to hold our line and report up to company head-quarters. But, as the enemy marauders moved on to harass another sector of the perimeter, my bloodthirsty killers got up out of their fighting positions and began to chase them. Now, you don't need to be General Patton to know that leaving your position is just about the worst thing you can do when under attack, but apparently every member of my platoon slept through that lecture at basic training.

I tried to yell above the explosions of grenade simulators and chatter of blank gunfire, but it was no use. Soon I was all alone in my platoon sector as every last soldier chased the enemy around the perimeter. Suddenly there was a flash and a shuddering boom. The mechanics hooted and laughed with delight as their acetylene-fueled, tubular cannon-like contraption spewed a tongue of fire and shattered the night air.

Soldiers ran aimlessly through the company area shooting anything that moved in the darkness. But when they recognized that they had just pumped a full clip of blank rounds into one of their buddies, at least they would toss out a neighborly, "Oh, sorry about that." Yellow and purple smoke billowed out of grenades amidst smaller explosions and the sporadic rat-tat-tat of machine guns. A sulphuric cloud of gunpowder hung over the company area and the burning chemicals of grenades stung our nostrils. It was a tremendous waste of government funds. It was chaos. It was great fun.

On the morning after Hell Night, half my platoon combed the bivouac area to collect trash, brass shell casings, burned out smoke grenade canisters, and the other scattered debris of our play war. The other half tended to the task of dismantling our bivouac area. Considering all the labor that went into erecting tents and digging foxholes, it was truly amazing how quickly the foxholes filled in as tents came down and were packed away in the trucks.

Within hours every last duffel bag was loaded up, every cigarette butt was collected, and every foxhole was smoothed over. The trucks were lined up, engines purring, as we waited impatiently for the order to return to the barracks area. We rolled into the motor pool—a large flat sandy yard—and parked the trucks with bumpers in strict alignment, which the motor sergeants gauged with lengths of taut rope. Buses shuttled the smiling drivers up to the barracks area where boomboxes blared and cold beer flowed freely.

For the next three days we would be rear area soldiers who worked from 0800 hours to 1600 hours in clean uniforms after sleeping in beds with sheets. Our missions were the important business of washing trucks, sweeping out tents, cleaning weapons, and writing pages of meaningless reports. Other than the Company Party on the last night at Fort Drum, our off-duty time was our own.

Officers all lived in buildings called the Bachelor Officers' Quarters, or BOQs. These were white, two-story World War II vintage buildings that were identical to the barracks that housed the troops, but the BOQs were divided into two-person rooms with twin beds in them that all opened into a long hallway. There were one or two single rooms at the end of the hallway for colonels and other exalted persons.

On the first night out of the field the other lieutenants and junior officers invited me to join them on a night out in nearby Watertown. I declined, claiming that I had some work to do, but actually I was broke and could barely afford the cost of lunch in the mess hall, which was cheaper than dinner. So, there I was sitting on my bunk, polishing my boots, feeling sorry for myself and a little bit hungry.

Suddenly, the bald head and smiling, gap-toothed face of Mr. Lawlor appeared in my doorway. Chief Warrant Officer Joe Lawlor managed the bulk food supply and distribution system for the division, and so wielded considerable power. Although he probably wasn't much older than fifty, we all considered him the grandfather of the battalion, who was known for his wisdom, unfailing good humor, and perpetual sense of fun.

Mr. Lawlor teased me in a good-natured way about hanging out in the BOQ when I should be out on the town, but somehow I think he knew I was broke. In a disarming and sympathetic voice he asked, "Smitty, do you like pie?" I responded that I did.

"Do you prefer apple, cherry, or lemon meringue," he asked sweetly. "I think lemon meringue would be great," I responded enthusiastically.

"Well, you just wait here," he said with a kindly wink. "I'll be right back." I smiled, thinking how nice it was that Mr. Lawlor would bring me some pie and I returned to shining my boots.

When I looked up, Mr. Lawlor stood there with a lemon meringue pie in each hand and an impish grin on his face. Behind him lurked the massive frame of one of our captains blocking the doorway. Sensing that evil was about to transpire, I bolted for the door, lowering my head. I barreled into the captain, but bounced off his considerable bulk, landing on my bed. As I sat up, the one-two punch of lemon meringue pies hit my face and gales of laughter exploded around me. I jumped up grabbing fistfuls of pie and hurled them at my assailants.

It was "game on" throughout the BOQ. Mr. Lawlor must have had a truckload of pies in his room because hunks of sticky apple, blueberry, and lemon meringue flew through the hallway in a colossal battalion-wide pie fight. One enterprising major elevated the chaos by pulling the pin on a grenade simulator and flushing it down a toilet. There was a deep roar and water gushed out of every toilet in the building as we celebrated the achievement with howls of laughter.

But all good things must come to an end. Suddenly someone bellowed, "Attention!" We all pulled ourselves up straight and stood silently in the hallway, backs against the wall, with lumps of crust, filling, and meringue dripping off our faces.

The battalion commander, still in his dress uniform after attending a formal dinner with the post commander, gingerly stepped down the hallway, taking care to avoid stepping into any gooey piles of smashed pie. I held my breath as he stopped in front of me and looked me over from head to toe. Then he scooped something off my shoulder with two fingers and brought it to his lips. He broke the silence as he said, "Smitty, you asshole, lemon meringue is my favorite."

With that he walked to the end of the hallway, stepped into his room, and closed the door behind him. With a roar, pandemonium broke out once again as pies flew, liquor bottles appeared, and new revelers joined the fun when they returned from town. By the early morning hours the fun petered out and we all fell into our beds.

We heard that the battalion commander was called into the post commander's office the next morning. Early in the afternoon, the executive officer summoned all officers to the headquarters for a rare officers' call. He ordered us to report to the BOQ building within an hour where the sergeant major would instruct us on the proper care and cleaning of a military building. He warned us that, if the building didn't pass inspection, we would all be issued pup tents in which to sleep for the remainder of our stay at Fort Drum. We sheepishly took up our mops, brooms, and toilet brushes and returned the BOQ to some semblance of cleanliness, but I don't think the plumbing was ever the same again.

After all the surprises and shocks of my first "summer camp," I was delighted to learn that I was assigned to be the officer in charge of a small refueling site in West Lebanon, New York. That meant that I was going to get away from Fort Drum a few days early.

My fuel site team was a mixed bag of NCOs drawn from all platoons in the company. When I asked for my instructions from the company commander, he looked at me wearily and said, "Smitty, just do what Whitey tells you to do." Whitey was the sergeant in charge of the refueling mission. He was a quiet, lanky Sergeant First Class from the maintenance section with a droopy black mustache. When I first met Whitey, he looked me over with some curiosity, but he patiently answered all my questions about the operation. After I finished with my fact-finding, he half smiled and grunted, "Don't worry, Lieutenant. Me and the boys have done this before. We won't let you down."

The sky was just turning pink and purple when I arrived in the motor pool the next morning, Whitey was already in high gear as he sprinted down the line of hulking green trucks in the predawn darkness. You couldn't hear much over the growls of the diesel engines warming up as they spewed dirty black smoke out the exhaust pipes. There was something magical in the gritty stench of diesel fumes mixed with motor oil, and I grew to love it. It meant we were heading off on yet another adventure—highway pirates, free from the desk jockeys at higher headquarters, insulated from the parade ground soldiers with their shiny black boots, and exempt from most Army red tape. I settled into the relative comfort of my olive-drab Dodge Power Wagon pickup truck. Soon we said goodbye to Fort Drum and hello to the open highway.

Whitey drove the lead vehicle and I cruised up and down the column in my pickup truck, checking to make sure that none of our lumbering green tankers fell behind and that drivers maintained their intervals. The sight of the huge, dirty fuel tankers and cargo trucks with flapping brown canvas covers, evenly spaced as they climbed a hill on the highway, came to be as perfect to me as the bearskin-hatted Grenadier Guards on parade. And I must selfishly admit that I felt a thrill of pride to think that this column of massive, smoke spouting behemoths was actually under my command. I never passed an Army convoy during my long career without feeling that thrill again and again.

After a journey of several hours, we arrived at the sleepy village of West Lebanon, New York, and halted our convoy in the dry, sandy expanse of the empty raceway parking lot. Immediately the drivers jumped out of the vehicles and began running fuel hoses, placing traffic cones, and banging signs on wooden stakes to mark the convoy refueling lanes. Realizing that Whitey had the operation well under control, I drove into the town center to make arrangements for lodging and meals.

By the time I returned to the raceway, Whitey and the crew had locked up the vehicles, and designated two soldiers to sleep in the back of a supply truck to guard the equipment overnight. Seeing that the two soldiers seemed fairly happy with their assigned duty, I opted not to ask any questions about how their food and beverage needs were being met.

The rest of us enjoyed a hearty dinner at a local Italian restaurant where the owners were friendly and accommodating. Then we sacked out in soft beds with clean sheets at a homey little motel near the raceway. It wasn't elegant, but no one complained about good food and comfortable lodging at Uncle Sam's expense.

We were up before dawn the next day and on duty at the raceway as the sun rose in the sky. The first convoys arrived by mid-morning and kept coming steadily. By noon the fuel site was a swirl of choking dust and exhaust smoke accompanied by shouts over the roar of hundreds of truck engines. But spirits were high because these convoys were headed home from Fort Drum.

Shortly after noon Whitey called me aside and asked to see my timetable for convoy arrivals and numbers of vehicles. He rubbed his sweaty forehead as he looked over the numbers. "At this rate, we'll run out of fuel by mid afternoon," he warned.

"What can we do?" I asked. "For starters, we can only fill the fuel tanks in the Vermont vehicles half full," he said. "A half tank will get them home okay, but they won't like it. I still don't know if that will give us enough fuel for the tail end of the convoys."

I agreed that we should cut back on the Green Mountain trucks right away. Whitey quickly spread the word to our fuel truck operators, but in less than an hour he walked over to me shrugging his shoulders. "See that red-faced major over there?" he pointed. "He's demanding to see whoever is in charge right away." Then he added, "Sorry, Sir."

I could see Whitey watching from a distance as the Vermont major yelled and threatened me in an attempt to agree to top off his vehicles. I offered my regret at not having enough fuel. I gave him my name and unit. I even offered to send a fuel truck if any of his vehicles ran out of fuel on the way home, but I stood my ground—a half tank was all his trucks could expect. Perhaps, because I was such a mediocre young officer and used to getting my ass chewed often, the red-faced major's tirade didn't really upset me very much. I think I saw Whitey smiling as the major drove off in a swirl of dust.

It was a hot, dusty, tiring day. Halfway through the afternoon, there was a lull in convoy traffic. I thought the pause would give me a good chance to talk about our own convoy movement home with Whitey, but, when I looked across the raceway, I couldn't see any soldiers. I walked toward the trucks and hoses but no one was visible. Then I heard voices coming from behind the grandstand.

I climbed up to the top row of the stands and looked over the edge. There was a beautiful little river gurgling along near the back of the stands. In the clear rushing water bobbed fifteen lily-white asses that belonged to my whooping soldiers who were enjoying an afternoon swim—however no one had packed a bathing suit.

Whitey called out to me, "Hey, Lieutenant, why don't you join us?"

I laughed and called back, "When you can find some clothes, come on up here, Whitey. I'd like to talk with you about our trip home—unless you'd rather stay here on vacation."

But before we talked about going home, Whitey had other plans. Fifteen minutes later we were hatching a scheme to solve our fuel shortage. When a cargo truck entered the fuel site towing a trailer with a separate fuel tank, called a pod, we would wave it into a special lane. While one of our operators filled the cargo truck's fuel tank, another operator would chat up the driver to distract him or her. A third member of our special larceny squad would slip our fuel truck's suction hose into the pod and suck out whatever fuel was in there. Whitey agreed that the plan just might work and he stuck out his hand in a conspiratorial handshake, but he warned that I'd be in deep trouble if I got caught mixing fuel from different state's accounts. The plan worked well and we actually had a few hundred gallons of diesel fuel left as the sun began to set. Most importantly, no one detected our theft scheme.

Whitey approached me after the last convoy cleared our site. "We still have a few hours of daylight left, Lieutenant. The boys would like to break down the site and head home to Massachusetts tonight. I think we could make it."

"The boys have done a good job today, Whitey, but according to my timetable, we still have to wait for the trail party with the wreckers to come through," I said. "I'm afraid we'll need to spend the night here."

"Aw, come on," he protested, "the wreckers have probably taken another route or they're tied up by the side of the road somewhere. Besides, they probably have a government credit card to get fuel at any service station."

But, for the second time in one day, I stood my ground on an unpopular decision. The next hour seemed like an eternity. Our soldiers lounged in the cabs of their trucks as we waited for the trail party. The sun started to set and the grumbling and complaints grew louder. I could catch the angry glances out of the corner of my eye. I feared that I would have a real morale problem on my hands if I had kept them away from their homes needlessly.

Suddenly I heard the loud growl of heavily laden truck engines and a train of a half dozen military wreckers with broken down trucks swinging from their towing hooks limped into the raceway. As they pulled up to the refueling hoses, a sweaty captain jumped out of the lead vehicle and hugged me. "Man, am I glad to see you!" the captain gushed. "We're just about running on fumes, but I assured my people that you'd be here waiting for us."

Once the wreckers rolled out of the fuel site, we quickly reeled in the hoses, collected the cones, and pulled up the signs. There was no more grumbling. Whitey and the crew took their fuel site duties seriously. They knew it would have been a mistake to abandon the site before the wreckers came through, but there was no point discussing it.

When everything was packed, Whitey came up to me and saluted. "All our equipment is secure. We'll leave guards to sleep in the supply truck." Then he added with a smile, "Let's get an early start tomorrow, Sir. The boys are anxious to get home."

After we arrived home the next day, I reflected on what I had learned at West Lebanon. I realized that I was extremely fortunate to have a wise and experienced sergeant to guide me and hold my hand during my first real independent command. But I also learned that it's a leader's job to make tough decisions that might sometimes be unpopular. Even in the face of threats, grumbling, and complaints, good leaders stick to their guns and do the right thing.

To paraphrase from the lyrics of "Truckin'" by the Grateful Dead, the unofficial anthem of the U.S. Army Transportation Corps, "What a long strange trip it had been." Despite the many bizarre experiences of my first summer camp with the National Guard, I grew as a leader from being a clueless bystander to an only slightly shaky decision-maker. Perhaps there was some hope that I might actually become a competent Army officer.

We Ride with Pride?

After serving in the Massachusetts National Guard for over a year, and beginning my career as a high school special education teacher, I finally received my orders to report to Transportation Officer Basic Course, or TOBC, at Fort Eustis, Virginia.

Because there were only six weeks left in the school year, I was able to finish up my obligations at school for the year fairly easily. My cousin was kind enough to look after my apartment for the five months that I'd be away and forward my mail to me in Virginia. So, after bidding a tearful goodbye to my steady girlfriend, I headed off to Fort Eustis.

I arrived at the fort at nearly midnight on a warm, muggy Sunday in May. Pulling up to the sentry box to provide my ID card, I sat and waited for several minutes. Realizing that something wasn't quite right, I got out of my car and peered into the glass enclosure to see a young private peacefully asleep at the desk. As I got back into my car and drove onto the post, I smiled and thought, "I've found my home in the U.S. Army. This is definitely the place for me."

The class was made up of about forty second lieutenants, most of whom were National Guardsmen or Army Reservists. In those days, aviators were required to qualify in a non-aviation branch prior to flight school. Hard core pilots went to Infantry or Armor school, while the less gung-ho opted for Transportation School. About one third of the class was made up of "just get me to flight school the easiest way possible" future pilots.

During the first few days of TOBC the Train Advise Counsel or TAC officers—two young captains who were sort of mean-spirited den mothers—attempted to impress upon us that this was serious business. However, they knew they had a bunch of clowns on their hands after the sunglasses incident.

Those of us with poor eyesight were issued two pairs of heavy black-framed glasses, which no civilian at that time would ever wear. Some bright lieutenant found out that we could have one pair of glasses tinted in the color of our choice. In the interest of solidarity and class unity, we all conspired to have our glasses tinted red, and upon receipt of this hideous eyewear, we all wore them to morning formation. The TAC officers exploded and directed that we never wear our red sunglasses to formation again. But, they were Army issue and, although we never again staged a class-wide, sunglasses-wearing demonstration, individually we wore them throughout the duration of the course—and looked pretty strange.

The training day began at 5:30 a.m. with Physical Training, or PT. Forty groggy lieutenants assembled on the drill field wearing our new class tee shirts emblazoned with the class motto, "With Pride We Ride." The slogan seemed appropriate, but I couldn't help but think that half of the class was sort of just along for the ride anyway.

Some mornings the routine was the same-old Army conditioning drills that consisted of stretching, lunges, jumping jacks and other contortions of questionable benefit, followed by a two-mile run in formation. But most mornings we teamed up for group sports, like soccer, touch football, or a strange game called "Combat Speedball." This peculiar sport combined many of the features of soccer, football, and basketball—and most of those features were the worst ones. Basically one team attempted to place a volleyball in the other team's soccer-size goal. It was pretty simple, except that you could only advance the ball by dribbling or passing, and you could only score by kicking it into the goal. If you held the ball without dribbling, you could be tackled, as could just about anyone on the field for any reason. Teams of any size could play, which made it the perfect sport for a class of about forty lieutenants—except that it frequently resulted in flaring tempers, twisted limbs, bloody noses, and multiple bruises. Otherwise PT was an uplifting way to start the day.

After PT we showered and ate breakfast. Class began promptly at 8:30 a.m. with all of us seated in a stifling classroom that was cooled by two growling fans that looked like they had been stolen from the noses of World War II fighter planes. I recall that the curriculum largely consisted of lectures delivered from a raised platform in the front of the room, while we all fought valiantly to keep our eyes open and prevent our heads from slumping onto the tabletops. From time to time the endless drone of presentations was relieved by trips to the rifle range or motor pool or places where real soldiering was taking place. These little field trips were much appreciated.

At the end of the second week we received a pay advance of well over one thousand dollars, which to many of us was more money than we had ever possessed at one time. I invested in having much-needed repairs made to my high mileage Mercury Capri. Conversely at PT the following Monday there was an endless parade of new cars that squealed into the parking lot as my classmates disembarked from Chevy Camaros, Pontiac Trans Ams, Volkswagen convertibles, and one cherry red Triumph TR-7. One of our classmates, however, puttered up to the PT field in a brand spanking new moped. I guess there's always somebody who sees things differently.

Class usually ended at about 4:00 p.m. during the first few weeks. But most of us noted that the lectures and presentations ended earlier and earlier as time went by. With almost the entire afternoon open, many of us sharpened our golf or tennis games. I distinctly recall the honor of playing singles tennis with the Army's first female helicopter pilot. In fact, we often played together, which might be due to the fact that she beat me handily every time we faced each other on the court.

Midway through our course, the next class, many of whom were West Point graduates, arrived on post. I had never met a West Point cadet and I think it's fair to say that most of us who aren't USMA graduates are jealous of them and resent their privilege and perceived sense of entitlement. However I got along well with the lieutenant who moved into the room next to mine in the officers' quarters. Because West Pointers receive four years of back pay when they graduate, he drove a vintage Mercedes-Benz sedan and kept a careful eye on his stock investments, but he was pleasant and seemed sincerely curious about the life of a National Guardsman and high school teacher. Despite my assumption that West Pointers were spit-and-polish prigs, my next door neighbor was actually a pretty good guy.

Time went on and there were many offers and entreaties to those of us who were reservists to apply for active duty. In 1980 the active-duty Army's reputation wasn't the best after the withdrawal from Vietnam and there were many stories in the media about rampant drug abuse and lack of discipline in the ranks. There was a general push to fill up the depleted ranks of the active component and so we were subject to lectures almost every week about the wonderful opportunities that awaited us on active duty.

I became a marked man when, one day during lunch break, I stepped up onto the speaker's platform in the front of the classroom and launched into a mock invitation to my active duty classmates extolling the many advantages of the reserves. "Think of it," I continued, gesturing dramatically, "you can work at the career of your choice and live in the same place for more than a few years at a time. Most days you can wear cool, comfortable clothes instead of olive drab uniforms. You can report to the same unit where you actually might get to know your soldiers' names. And, if you're involved with a significant other, you won't have to force him or her to choose between you and their family or job or—"

Suddenly I heard a booming voice from the back of the room, "I think that's about enough, Smith. You can take your seat." Amid the shouts and laughter of my classmates, I sheepishly retreated to my chair. Although I thought I'd get a thorough ass-chewing for my little stunt, I never heard anything about it from the senior officers. I guess they actually had a sense of humor, although they hid it well.

It was probably at about this point in the class that I decided that the active-duty Army wasn't for me. It wasn't that I disliked Army life, quite the contrary, I liked it too much. But working half a day, playing tennis every afternoon, and drinking until the late hours of the night wasn't my idea of a purposeful life. I now understand that life on active duty is quite different, but that was my picture of the active component at the time. I wanted more from life—I wanted to change the world.

So I decided to return home at the end of the course, go back to my teaching job, and bring my new knowledge to my National Guard unit. I decided something else too.

I bought a round trip airline ticket to Massachusetts for the three-day Labor Day weekend. In my luggage I had a Cracker Jacks box that I had painstakingly opened and resealed. Inside it contained a very unique prize. After my longtime girlfriend, Nora, and I spent some wonderful hours getting reacquainted, I gave her the Cracker Jacks box, which was one of her favorite snacks. She laughed then opened the box, tore open the little white envelope, and held the prize in her hand. She gasped and then started to cry. I asked her to marry me as I slipped the diamond ring onto her finger. Thankfully she said, "Yes," and I've continued to be grateful for her love and support for over 40 years.

However, before I could resume my life as an educator, citizen-soldier, and husband-to-be, I had to survive one of the most bizarre training exercises I have ever experienced, which was the culminating evaluation of TOBC.

All we knew was that we'd be on a seven-day tactical exercise that would begin with a lengthy forced march. We packed our rucksacks as prescribed, strapped on our helmets and cued up on the airfield for the start of the adventure. A Chinook helicopter landed and we filed into our seats for the short flight to Camp A.P. Hill.

The Chinook set down in a grassy field and we quickly formed up in squads for a foot march into our operational area, which made no sense to us as we watched a convoy of trucks following several hundred yards behind us. After a sweaty, dusty hike we arrived in our base camp. Leaders were designated and we set about the business of consolidating a defensive perimeter—digging foxholes, sighting crew-served weapons, running phone wire, and all the other little tasks required by the field manuals. I don't remember much about the first day. Perhaps we sent out patrols, but mainly we established our area.

On the second day new leaders were selected. Shortly after noon, canisters of tear gas spewed out their choking, burning smoke in the center of the area, not so secretly thrown by our instructors. We all fumbled into our protective masks and chemical suits, called "MOPP gear" (Mission Oriented Protective Posture), and manned our defensive positions. The "All Clear" signal sounded several hours later and we thankfully emerged from our protective suits. I will always remember the cool rush of fresh air hitting my sweat-soaked face when I pulled off my protective mask and poured out the puddle of sweat that collected in the chin cup. I can also remember the sharp tang of lingering tear gas as it tickled your nostrils.

The instructors announced that we would need to be decontaminated after the tear gas attack. Accordingly we were all directed to ground our gear, turn in our weapons, and climb into the waiting cargo trucks which would transport us to the decontamination station. There was an overall sense of relief because we all knew that decontamination meant getting hosed down, which wasn't such a bad idea on this hot Virginia afternoon. As we laughed and joked in the trucks, none of us were prepared for what happened next.

The trucks headed down a dusty trail and we bounced along happily anticipating our field shower. Suddenly explosions erupted around us followed by the chatter of automatic weapons fire. The trucks jerked to a stop. Angry Marines, brandishing their weapons, appeared at the back of the truck. They unlatched the gate of the cargo truck and shouted, "Get the fuck off the truck now and put your hands on your head—Move!"

We were in a state of shock as we tumbled off the trucks. The Marines, who seemed to outnumber us, forced us to kneel in the road with our hands on our heads. As they made their way down the rows of Army lieutenants, they tied our hands behind our backs and pulled empty sandbags over our heads. All I remember during that afternoon was being pushed and prodded and shouted at. The Marines didn't seriously injure us, but they weren't exactly gentle, either.

When night fell I was hustled onto a stool in front of a field desk. An older Marine, probably an NCO or officer, questioned me.

"What's your name?" "Paul G. Smith," I replied. That was easy.

"What do you carry for a weapon?" I thought for a moment. They already know what we carry. "An M-16 rifle," I answered.

"How many officers are in your group?" I knew I couldn't answer this one correctly or else they'd be looking for anyone who escaped. "I really don't know. You see I just joined this unit recently." The lie earned me a smack on the side of the head, but they didn't follow it up.

And so the questioning continued, with me giving answers to obvious questions and evading questions that might be significant. In the end they put the sandbag over my head again and hustled me off to another area, saying, "Maybe this will help your memory and your level of cooperation."

As I knelt in the dark, I could hear an exchange next to me.

"What type of vehicles do you have in your unit?" the Marine barked. "My name is Lieutenant John Jefferson Hopkins, 034–78–6890," my classmate responded. WHACK—"Ugh."

"Where is your defensive position located?" "My name is Lieutenant John Jefferson Hopkins, 034–78–6890," my classmate replied again. THUD—"Ugh."

"What equipment were you issued?" "My name is Lieutenant John Jefferson Hopkins, 034–78–6890," my classmate said, with a little weaker voice. SMACK—"Ugh!"

And so it went on. I decided that this performance was not something I wanted to repeat. A while later I was shoved from behind and a voice with a thick, Southern accent said, "Hey, y'all, I need to get some answers here. What kind of trucks do y'all have?"

"They're just like the ones you captured us in," I responded brightly. "By the way, you sound like you're from down South—Georgia?" "Naw, Alabama… You ever been there?"

"You know I think I did drive through once—beautiful state. Wonderful farm country. Did you grow up on a farm?" I asked. "My grand dad owned a few acres that he grew some corn on…." My captor and I soon had a pleasant conversation going about farms, cars, and life in the Marines. But all good things must end during Army training.

"Hey, you seem like a decent guy," my interrogator said, "but I need to rough you up a little or I'll get in trouble."

"I understand—good talking with you."

At that he smacked me halfheartedly in the head a few times, punched me in the gut and made me walk on my knees down a gravel trail (which hurts a lot more than it sounds). Then he left me under a tree where I proceeded to moan and groan in the spirit of the evening.

After a while I felt a hand on my shoulder. "Smith, are you seriously hurt?" I continued to moan. "Smith, it's Captain Mitchell, your instructor. Do you need medical attention?" He said as he pulled off the sandbag.

"Of course not, Captain," I replied with a wink. "I'm just playing along." He chuckled and patted me on the shoulder as he pulled down the sandbag again and I resumed my pathetic moaning.

Hours went by and the area became quieter. Suddenly there was no yelling or groaning. Someone whispered behind me as he sliced the ropes that bound my hands and pulled off the sandbag. "Head straight down that path and it'll take you to the road. Stay left and you'll be at the base camp in ten minutes."

I joined my classmates as we sprinted through the darkness, eager to leave our Marine captors' embrace as quickly as we could. The freed captives soon reassembled in the former base camp and located our gear. As our M-16s were reissued, we were told, "The Marines are coming to recapture you people. If you don't hold this perimeter and they infiltrate our area, they'll take anybody they can find back into their POW camp."

The game had now changed. We all knew that our M16s with blank ammunition were nothing more than noisemakers. No, we needed REAL weapons because those USMC bastards weren't going to get us again. One lieutenant from Colorado said he knew how to make reasonably good bows and arrows from saplings and extra boot laces. Another classmate showed us how to whittle bayonets, harden them over a can of Sterno, and fasten them to our rifles with electrical tape. There was a guy who showed us how to use our belts as slings to hurl rocks at the Marines—David and Goliath style. And so it went for the entire day following our escape as we dug booby traps with sharpened punji sticks at the bottom, strung snares out of telephone wire, and sharpened our jackknives for close combat. They weren't going to take us alive.

Late in the afternoon a patrol returned with a prisoner. We lieutenants-turned-savages eagerly gathered to interrogate him with vengeance in our hearts. But the instructors soon stepped in to save him because he was actually an Army NCO who was working with them.

Night fell and we all took up our posts watching for the slightest motion, listening for the tiniest rustle or snap in the scrub brush. The humid, steamy night wore on and tension mounted. We all knew that if the Marines were coming back, it certainly would be under the cover of darkness.

Suddenly the crackle of a loudspeaker pierced the night. "Lieutenant Costello. You better be careful tonight if you plan to ever see your children again."

A squad leader in our class moved down the line to check the foxholes. This time the loudspeaker squeal came from another direction. "I wouldn't do that, Lieutenant Hall. We can see your every movement. Better stay in your foxhole where it's safe—for now."

Moments later a voice said, "I have a letter here from Billings, Montana, addressed to Lieutenant Dearborn. It's written on pink stationery with little flowers. Should I read it out loud now, Lieutenant? Perhaps I'll save it for later when we have you back in our care." On and on the loudspeakers squawked for hours. I don't know how it affected the others, but it truly made my skin crawl. Sometime after midnight the loudspeakers went silent and we started to get a sense that the much feared return of the Marines was just a hoax.

I was manning an M-60 machine gun at the main entrance to our base camp—a critical position. Perhaps it was the heat, perhaps it was the excitement of the last 48 hours, or perhaps it was the monotony of scanning the darkness, but I became very drowsy a few hours after midnight and my relief wasn't coming until dawn. I stamped my feet. I recited poems in my head. I slapped myself across the face, but I couldn't keep my eyes open. I realized that falling asleep on guard duty was a court martial offense, but I couldn't stay awake.

The next thing I knew it was light and my relief was shaking me, "Hey, Smitty, it's time to wake up." I sat up quickly and realized I was inside a sleeping bag at the bottom of the machine gun position. "How did I...," I muttered.

The smiling face of another lieutenant looked down at me as he said, "I came up to check on you last night and I found you slumped over the gun. I figured you were tired, so I started my shift a few hours early."

I realized he had also tucked me into his own sleeping bag. Now here's the thing—this lieutenant was a devout Christian from the Deep South. When I first heard him talking about going to Bible study in his Southern drawl, this sarcastic Yankee decided that he wanted no part of him. When the class headed up to the Officers' Club after class for a few beers or out to the hot spots on Friday night, this guy went to the family quarters to have dinner with his wife. I had little contact with him, and I frankly considered him too boring for my tastes.

Now, this classmate that I disregarded and disrespected had saved my ass and had done me the best favor that anyone had ever done in my brief military career. As I thanked him for his kindness, I silently smacked myself in the head for letting my prejudices get the best of me and form an unfair opinion about this guy, who was a far better man than I. Incidentally, to the best of my knowledge, he never told anyone that I fell asleep at the machine gun position.

Later that morning the instructors brought us all into the center of the base camp and conducted an After Action Review, or AAR. This is one of the best procedures the Army has ever instituted, because it requires that the entire force examine an operation and discuss what went right, what went wrong, and what could be done better. Understandably my classmates and I contended that the POW exercise was somewhat contrived, very painful, and of questionable benefit. The instructors countered that it gave us a somewhat realistic experience about what it takes to survive as a POW. They also singled me out for recognition as having particularly good survival skills as a POW, commenting on my intuition about when to comply, when to divert, and when to resist. Imagine my pride at being praised for my potential to be the best POW in our class—what a dubious honor!

The instructors admitted that the Marine captors were long gone from the area and that the instructors themselves had operated the loudspeakers with microphones from inside the base camp area. Although I wouldn't tell them, I thought the tension and paranoia caused by the loudspeakers was a very effective method of adding realism and seriousness to our efforts at perimeter defense.

After the AAR we were bused out to a building where we had about fifteen minutes to shower, throw on a clean uniform, and eat a hot breakfast. That was probably the quickest but most enjoyable shower of my life as the lukewarm water rushed over my body carrying away days of dust, dirt, and grime. I still remember how the cooks loaded our trays up with pancakes, scrambled eggs, and sausage. Because we had so little time, I poured syrup over the whole jumbled heap and wolfed it down while I was still standing. Surprisingly it tasted pretty good. To this day, whenever I taste the salty-sweet goodness of pancakes, sausage, and syrup I think of Camp A.P. Hill.

The rest of the week consisted of tactical convoy operations during which we rode in cargo trucks beside Army drivers. This seemed foolish to many of us who were licensed to drive the trucks in which we rode as passengers. Although the days were busy, there's only one incident that stands out in my memory from the convoy training.

Just as they were at ROTC Advanced Camp, leadership assignments were rotated frequently. One afternoon we were traveling through the woods in a small convoy—about ten trucks—when it became clear that we were lost. The trucks halted. The convoy commander was an older lieutenant who had come up through the ranks. In fact, he was quite proud that he had been a staff sergeant and clearly believed he was better than the rest of us. I grabbed my map from the truck and joined the group of lieutenants in front of the lead vehicle. Pointing to a nearby hillside as a reference marker, I insisted that the location I marked on my map was our present position. The convoy commander dismissed my navigation and pointed to another location on his map, which wasn't even close. I tried again to convince him that I knew where we were, but he was having none of it. Finally I threw up my hands and hopped back in my truck.

Just then one of the instructors, who had been watching and listening to our discussion on the sidelines, made a "time out" signal. He took the convoy commander's map and firmly pointed to the correct location. Then he pointed in my general direction. "Smith, get over here," I heard the instructor bark.

I raced to the front of the convoy and stood at attention as the instructor glared at me with his hands on his hips. "You know exactly where we are, don't you?" he growled. "Yes, Sir," I stammered, not really understanding what I had done wrong.

"But instead of sticking to your guns, you gave up and were ready to let the convoy move out in the wrong direction. Right?"

"Yes, Sir," I was beginning to see the light.

"You know what that causes?" he continued. "That causes missions to fail and sometimes it causes people to get killed." I studied my boots.

"When you know you have the right answer, you have an obligation to convince whoever is in command that you're right. Get it?"

"Yes, Sir."

"Now get in your truck and don't give up so easily the next time." During the course of my entire career, I never forgot the lesson he taught me.

So, at the end of the week we returned to Fort Eustis, with about a week to go before graduation. After we had been back for a few days, investigators came and interviewed us all one-by-one about the POW exercise. Apparently someone had lodged a complaint and I heard that the treatment some of my female classmates experienced had crossed the line. I believe that the exercise may have been eliminated in future courses. In the end, I learned three important lessons during that exercise.

First, I learned that I needed to guard against prejudices that can lead one to underestimate and undervalue people just because of the way they speak, their religion, or their race. I would never forget my Southern classmate's kindness and discretion after I fell asleep on guard duty.

Second, I learned that I had a duty to fight to be heard when I knew I was right. To allow my superiors to follow the path to failure was irresponsible and dangerous. "I told you so," would never be worth the cost.

Third, I learned that I would never allow myself to be taken prisoner. The last round in the clip would always be reserved.

… And, I guess I also learned that pancakes, sausage, and syrup all jumbled up was actually quite tasty.

Graduation day came at Fort Eustis. Four days later I was back in a high school classroom. I had learned many things, but the main lesson was that life in the active-duty Army wasn't for me. The smiling faces and laughter of the teenagers sitting in front of me were far more real and important than lectures and war games at Fort Eustis. Teaching was fulfilling, challenging, rewarding, and it was my best shot at changing the world.

Riot Duty

My first experience in crisis leadership occurred unexpectedly in July 1981 after I returned from Fort Eustis. The Massachusetts state legislature got into a little squabble about money matters and froze the budget. This meant that thousands of state employees received no paychecks. In response, they walked off the job in droves, and who could blame them?[8]

Now this didn't create an immediate problem at state parks, highway departments, and state offices. But at state hospitals for thousands of mentally ill, developmentally delayed, and frail elderly citizens, the situation was dire.

I received a phone call at my civilian job ordering me to report to the armory as quickly as possible with a week's worth of uniforms and personal care items. When I arrived, the armory was buzzing with activity. The battalion operations officer directed me to take the first wave of soldiers to Cushing State Hospital, which was a long term care facility for bedridden elderly patients. The trucks were loaded with soldiers as soon as they arrived, so the force I commanded consisted mostly of troops I didn't know very well.

Our trucks approached the main entrance of the state hospital and we were greeted by a mob of protesters who were waving signs and screaming obscenities. The state police eased us through the entrance without running anyone over and we quickly dismounted.

The senior NCO and I reported to the administration building where we were briefed by a haggard looking doctor and several worried nurses. Our mission was to keep the protesters from interfering with patient care or blocking the entrance to the hospital. We also needed to keep the kitchen running and assist with patient care, which meant feeding, cleaning, and changing bedpans.

One of the NCO had some cooking experience, so he took half a dozen soldiers and started work in the kitchen. Two of the other sergeants grabbed a dozen troops and followed the nurses into the wards. Together with the twenty or so remaining troops, I joined a small, beleaguered state police detail on the picket line. We formed two lines on either side of the entrance to keep the roadway open for supplies and emergency staff to get in. At first the picketers, most of whom were women, simply screamed at us:

"How do you like cleaning shitty diapers, soldier boy?" "Who's paying your fucking salary right now?" "Just wait 'til they start dropping like flies. What will you do then, G.I. Joe?"

The soldiers held back from answering at first, but the constant barrage soon wore them down. Some of the troops tried to be conciliatory, expressing sympathy for the unpaid workers, but that did little to calm down the strikers, who were becoming uglier and more aggressive.

Soon garbage, beer bottles, and other objects flew through the air from time to time. Several times we needed to push back the mob to allow food or linen trucks to get through to the hospital. My memory may be playing tricks with me, but I seem to recall that the protesters lit some sort of bonfire as darkness was falling. In short, it was becoming a hellish situation.

Night fell and I think the mob became emboldened by the anonymity that darkness provides as well as the increased consumption of alcohol. Up to this time there had been no arrests, but now, kicks, shoves, and punches were sporadically being thrown. My soldiers and I were out there with nothing but our fists to protect ourselves, and we weren't very pleased to be unarmed.

I was standing behind the line of soldiers and police doing what I could as a young officer to steady and reinforce our soldiers on the line. At one point, a drunken middle-aged man burst through the line and lunged toward me. "I want your name, you bastard," he slurred as he pulled at the nametag on my uniform.

Being a young twenty-something male, I grabbed him by the shoulders and pushed him back through the picket line saying, "I don't touch you; you don't touch me." With my final shove, I may have knocked him to the ground, but it was too difficult to tell in the darkness and chaos. Shortly after that incident, I remember one of our sergeants, a Vietnam combat veteran, turned to me and shouted, "For God's sake, Lieutenant, give me a weapon and I'll fix these mother-fuckers!" We moved him off the line, away from the insults and kicks, until he could calm down.

I later reflected that, in that instant, I had seen how the Kent State shootings had occurred. This sergeant, a patriotic American, had endured hours of verbal and physical abuse at the hands of this mob. He was a man who knew how to use weapons and he was also a man who couldn't allow someone to disrespect him without losing face. I'm certain that the volatile mix of escalating anger, mob emotions, and firepower would have resulted in deaths on this night. At the time I cursed our leaders for placing us in this situation unarmed, but, through the lens of time, I understand that they were probably wise to insist that we leave our weapons locked up at the armory.

The darkness, the noise, and the chaotic movements made it very difficult to maintain accurate situational awareness on the picket line. Suddenly I heard a scuffle behind me as several soldiers wrestled a man to the ground. The state police, with drawn weapons, quickly handcuffed the man and dragged him to their cruiser. The mob continued its jeering, but noticeably began to pull back from the picket line, probably realizing that a figurative line had been crossed and more arrests could be coming.

As the chaos subsided to a certain degree, the hospital's fire chief came up to me chuckling. "I guess I know why they make you guys officers," he said.

"Excuse me, Chief, what are you talking about?" I responded.

"That guy swung that baseball bat and it just barely missed your head," he said. "And you didn't even flinch. You just kept on walking the picket line, talking to your troops like nothing happened." The chief walked away shaking his head as I realized that the man the police arrested was the same drunken man who grabbed my shirt. Apparently he had come back with a baseball bat to settle up with me.

After an hour or so, the mob dwindled down to a handful of people who must have been assigned to some picket line night shift. I left a small squad of soldiers with the police detail and, with the rest of the picket line force, headed into the hospital. The senior NCOs had already organized around the clock duty assignments for patient care and the picket line. Off duty soldiers were free to sleep in an unused hospital ward. There were comfortable beds, spacious latrines with showers, and, best of all, a large refrigerator, which the NCOs had already stocked with beer.

Although I didn't condone drinking on duty, on this night I decided to give myself a little slack as I sipped a cold beer and cradled my head in my hands, thankful that it was still there and in one piece. It's surprising how quickly soldiers work things out and establish a routine. By the second day, we had settled comfortably into our living quarters, established a work schedule, and, most importantly, ensured that the beer refrigerator was restocked daily.

Every morning I would walk from our ward at the far end of the hospital, through the patient areas, to the administrative office. As I passed through a kind of glass enclosed courtyard, one elderly fellow would smile at me each morning and say, "Good morning, General, have we licked them Nazis yet?" After my initial startled reaction, I learned to assure him that we were beating the hell out of Hitler and would end the war soon. I also began to look forward to seeing his cheerful face each morning.

Our force at the hospital was augmented from time to time by more personnel. I was amazed to see how even senior NCOs pitched in to change diapers, empty bedpans, and feed the elderly patients. I remember one grizzled motor sergeant, who could fix any truck in the motor pool, gleefully coming out of a ward with an armload of soiled linen. He stopped me and remarked, "Hey, guess what, Lieutenant? I just had dinner with my Aunt Ethel. I haven't seen her since I was a little kid!"

Daily we sent a force to man the picket line, but after the hellish first night, cooler heads managed to bring tempers under control. After several days, it was simply one group of a dozen or so bored people indifferently holding signs casually being watched by another group of a dozen or so bored people wearing green uniforms. Gradually the two groups blended into one group as two dozen people began to mix, often sharing the newspaper and conversation.

One beautiful sunny afternoon, I decided to leave my duties inside and check on the picket line. I strolled out to the main driveway into the hospital where the picket line was usually stationed. But on this afternoon there was nothing there—no picketers, no signs, no police, and, worst of all, no soldiers! I stood there perplexed, with my hands on my hips until I heard the faint sound of giggling. I moved toward the sound, which

Massachusetts National Guardsmen stand guard at the entrance of Cushing State Hospital during the State Worker Strike of 1981 (Massachusetts National Guard Museum).

was coming from behind a row of lilac bushes. There, sitting in the grass amongst the purple blossoms, were my fine soldiers sipping cold beer in the sunshine. And even more startling, they were sitting with the protesters, who had discarded their signs and placards in favor of cans of cold Budweiser.

I was outraged. My troops were on duty, but here they were sitting in the sunshine, out of uniform, drinking cold beer with the enemy. I started forward to give them hell and set things straight, but suddenly I caught myself. I remembered that the mission on the picket line was to ensure that the roadway was open and to keep peace—the roadway was certainly open and the picket line couldn't have been much more peaceful. Heading back to the hospital, all I could do was chuckle and shake my head.

After nine days the state legislature came to its senses and agreed to pay the hospital workers. We said a fond goodbye to the patients, the workers, and the police as we loaded onto the trucks and happily headed home. It had been a long, complicated mission. Although we were at the hospital less than two weeks, I grew up a lot during that time and learned some important lessons. I learned that there are many ways to accomplish a mission—not all of them might be of my choosing or meet Army standards, but the end result is the thing that's important.

I learned that the most important thing in a crisis is to keep emotions in check. If tempers get out of control, people can get hurt or even killed. I learned that sloppy, undisciplined National Guardsmen can save lives and accomplish amazing things when they have to. I know that there were patients at that hospital that would have died without the care of those soldiers. Most importantly I learned that human nature is extremely resilient—today's enemies can become tomorrow's buddies once they see each other as fellow human beings. I also learned that it takes a lot of beer to run the National Guard.

One more thing—when Christmas time rolled around, the Company Commander received a formal envelope from Cushing State Hospital. He called me to his office and handed it to me, saying as he hid a grin, "Hey, Smitty, handle this for me, will you?" I opened the envelope and saw that it contained an invitation to the Hospital Workers' Association Christmas Party addressed to "all our friends in the National Guard." I couldn't make it, but the sergeants who went to the party said they had a great time.

The "Good Ole Guard"

The focus of my time and energies now fell squarely on my career as a special education teacher and on my new role as a husband. Before long I was nervously preparing myself to be a father. Thankfully my duties as a platoon leader in the National Guard at that time only required the basic commitment of one weekend a month and two weeks in the summer.

Life as a platoon leader was good. I was responsible for twenty or so trucks and forty or so soldiers. They knew me, I knew them and I grew to like almost all of them. In the spring and autumn, we trucked the infantry soldiers around the woods as they engaged in tactical training. In the winter we maintained vehicles and occupied our time with classroom training.

From time to time we had briefings about our mission to take our place at a strategic location in Germany, where our mission was to hold back the Soviet armored hordes. The only thing no one could explain was that it would take months for us to travel by ship to Europe with our vehicles. Would the Soviet tanks halt their surge through the gap until we arrived? I don't think any of us really took our Cold War mission seriously.

Perhaps it was an odd way of looking at it, but I reasoned that I contributed to the Cold War effort by being a part of the United States' massive trained militia. If the Soviets thought they could overrun us, they would need to contend with a half million citizen-soldiers who could put up a pretty good fight (I hoped).

We were often on alert for floods, hurricanes, or blizzards, but I don't recall any large-scale emergency response missions. However one of these hurricane alerts led to some unexpected publicity. The truck company was called to active duty in advance of a hurricane that was predicted to pulverize the New England coast. The governor was on television describing all the precautions he had taken to keep citizens safe, which included activating the National Guard, as this deluge barreled down on us. We raced to the armory, conducted hasty pre-execution checks on our trucks, and hunkered down to await the call to become heroes. We were ready to scoop infants from flood waters, carry little old ladies out of sunken trailer homes, or pile mountains of sandbags to save power plants from surging tides. The only problem was the hurricane pretty much went out to sea.

However, the unit did receive two or three bus missions to evacuate senior citizens from nursing homes that lost power, but we didn't think much of it. As we locked up the trucks, the skies started to clear, and we got ready to go home. Suddenly word traveled through the armory that there was an urgent message from emergency management state headquarters. They wanted Sergeant Frank at the headquarters building as soon as possible.

We found Frank sweeping out his bus in the motor pool. When we told him to get over to state headquarters on the double he protested that he hadn't done anything wrong. All he had done was load up his bus with senior citizens and then drove them to a public shelter. He shook his head and muttered as he got into the pickup truck with the First Sergeant who tugged at Frank's uniform in a vain effort to make him look soldierly. About an hour later, a grinning Frank sauntered into the armory with a bright, shiny Army Commendation Medal dangling from his rumpled uniform. We all gathered around him as he explained.

"They brought me into a big room and there was the governor himself," Frank explained. "I thought I was in really big trouble, but he shook my hand and thanked me for my quick actions to save the lives of the senior citizens in my bus. Then he pinned this medal on me. After that I had to stand next to the governor while photographers took pictures and reporters asked me all sorts of questions."

"What exactly happened in your bus, Frank?" the company commander asked. "Well, Sir, after my bus was full of senior citizens, I started driving down the highway," Frank said, scratching his head. "All of a sudden there was this power line in the road, sparking and twisting around like a snake. I knew I couldn't stop the bus in time, so I stomped on the gas pedal and yelled loud so everybody could hear even without their hearing aids, 'All youse old people don't touch nothin', cuz' here we go!'"

"What happened then?" the commander persisted. "I don't know," Frank said, becoming philosophical. "I heard a loud crack and there was a bunch of sparks outside the bus windows, but none of the old people got hurt. I guess everything was okay, 'cuz here I am with a new medal on my uniform." Sometimes heroes come in odd shapes and sizes, and at the most unexpected times, too.

But life in the old National Guard also had its ugly side. There were cliques and secret power alliances. Full time Guardsmen had to be particularly careful to navigate around the hidden landmines of in-groups, out-groups, and fragile egos or else they endangered their ability to feed their families. As a part-time officer I was able to remain on the sidelines and avoid entanglements. It may not have done much for my upward mobility, but it kept me out of trouble.

As an example of how outrageous things could be, I remember walking into the company office early one Sunday morning on a training weekend to find it demolished. Tables and chairs were overturned, the contents of file cabinets were strewn about, and several windows were shattered. Knowing that the NCO Club in the armory had been serving drinks until all hours the previous night, I went in search of our First Sergeant. "Don't blame the NCOs, Lieutenant," he said as he shook his head. "A certain officer and her husband had a family discussion in there last night."

I learned from reluctant witnesses that, after a few too many drinks, an officer on the battalion staff and her husband, who was a sergeant in another unit, had stepped into our company office for a private discussion. Apparently there had been some form of disagreement and mayhem had followed. Some witnesses reported that the happy couple left arm-in-arm after this destructive expression of their affection for one another. Junior soldiers were detailed to clean up the mess and put the office back in order. I urged the company commander to let me collect witness statements and prepare a complaint to be submitted to the battalion commander. The company commander called me into his office and closed the door.

"Just give it up, Greg," he cautioned. "They both have connections that go pretty high up the command chain. Any complaint you generate would get covered up and the only consequence is that you'd be a marked man. We'll clean up the mess and forget it ever happened." And so, life went on in the old guard. I worked for a few good commanders and my military life was easy. These straight-shooting leaders put the needs of the unit before their own and their example served me well in later years. Many of these fine officers ended their careers after their tours of company command, but their impact on the force lingered for decades.

I also worked for little men who viewed company command as a step to advance their careers. Life was difficult and uncomfortable because duplicity, favoritism, and self-interest drove the force under their command. Incompetent soldiers who ingratiated themselves were promoted while the skilled and talented were ignored. One of these weakling commanders once had a tantrum in a company meeting as he proclaimed, "I will be promoted to major. I will. And none of you will stop me!" Perhaps these leaders also had their lasting impact on the force in that they showed many of us what not to do as commanders.

Throughout those early years, my high school students, my wife, and my children were my focus in life. In fact, my plan was to serve out my eight-year military obligation in the easiest way possible and pack my uniforms away forever. I rumbled along happily with my platoon, with no wish to advance or take on additional responsibility. In fact, as the years went by I liked to brag that I was the senior First Lieutenant in the Yankee Division—and that may have been true. But I came to learn that sometimes life in the Army takes unexpected turns.

All good things must come to an end, and so my years as a platoon leader were abruptly halted when I was called to report to the Battalion Executive Officer. "Smitty, we have to move you into a captain's slot," he said without much enthusiasm. "Next month you'll become the Battalion Motor Officer."

"But, Sir, I like what I'm doing in the truck company," I replied. "Can't I stay where I am?"

The Executive Officer stared at me the way a teacher looks at a wayward pupil. "I don't think you get it, Lieutenant. You've been at the same rank for five years. If you don't get promoted to captain, they'll throw you out of the Army. We're only moving you to the battalion staff to save your ass. Now get out of here." And so, I became the Battalion Motor Officer of the 26th Supply and Transport Battalion, the lowliest staff officer assignment of them all. Now I was not a highly motivated officer, but I always believed that taxpayers give soldiers a day's pay for a day's worth of work. As the Motor Officer, I was responsible for the maintenance and readiness of vehicles. Although it wasn't glorious, I was going to do my job.

With the eager assistance of dedicated maintenance warrant officers and motor sergeants, who felt that they had a staff officer who actually cared about trucks, we began inspection systems, training pauses for maintenance, and relentless demands for spare parts. Although it wasn't nearly as much fun as leading a truck platoon, I threw myself wholeheartedly into my new assignment.

One of my duties as Battalion Motor Officer was to lead the trail party of wreckers and maintenance vehicles that followed the main body of the convoy. Our small detachment of five or six trucks was the last element to leave the bivouac area that the battalion was vacating and our mission was to pick up any vehicles that broke down on the route to the new bivouac site.

In the 1980s the Army became much more conscious of the tactical necessity to frequently relocate base camps and bivouacs. Gone were the days of establishing semi-permanent tent cities. Now we shifted locations every 48 to 72 hours, and the convoy movements were under the cover of darkness with blackout vehicle lights. Although officially convoy speeds were set at five miles per hour, trucks usually moved at higher speeds. Night convoys were tactically realistic, but extremely hazardous.

Before the Army made night vision devices widely available throughout the force, convoy movements in darkness were illuminated only by blackout marker lights, or as they were aptly nicknamed "cat-eyes." A vehicle's headlights were pinpoint white lights and the tail lights were small red dots. Needless to say, it was difficult to see a vehicle in the darkness and fog; rain or dust made it even worse.

I found myself leading the trail party along a dusty tank trail following the battalion convoy one night near midnight. Suddenly I made out a jeep off to one side of the trail and a tractor trailer idling on the other side. I stopped our trail party to take a look. The front end of the jeep was smashed in and the windshield was shattered. One officer was stumbling around holding his hand up to his bleeding head. Others lay on the grass. The mechanics in the trail party quickly tended to the injured occupants of the jeep as I radioed in a call for an ambulance.

I returned to the grassy area where the mechanics were trying to convince the injured soldiers to sit quietly with little success. Their injuries didn't appear to be serious after their cuts were bandaged, but several of the victims couldn't be convinced to stay seated. The officer with the head injury kept standing up saying, "You don't seem to understand. My mother is expecting me for dinner and I need to get on my way or I'll be late."

Other injured soldiers babbled about meeting their girlfriends or some other disconnected topics. At length the medics arrived and tended to the injured soldiers. When I asked about the strange conversations, the medical sergeant in charge said, "These guys are still in a state of shock. We see it all the time with trauma. When they wake up tomorrow, they won't remember what they were talking about and they may not even remember the accident." Thankfully none of the soldiers had sustained serious injury, but I hoped that I never saw people in serious shock ever again.

I now turned my attention to the tractor trailer drivers. Both the driver and assistant reported that they never saw the jeep until they collided with it head on. In fairness to the tractor trailer drivers, the road network on a blackout convoy was supposed to be strictly one-way traffic. The driver of the jeep must have slipped onto the tank trail without being aware that a blackout convoy was in progress and that he was headed in the wrong direction.

In my mind the tractor trailer drivers weren't at fault until I opened the cab to check the vehicle's mileage for the accident report I would have to complete. As I climbed into the driver's seat my boot tapped an object that clinked against another. The beam from my red-lens flashlight spotted a half dozen empty beer cans. I climbed down from the cab and ordered the two drivers to sit beside their vehicle. They didn't answer me when I asked them if they'd been drinking, but just looked down at their boots. Then I directed the maintenance sergeant to stand guard over them and called for military police. When the military police eventually arrived at our remote location it was nearly two o'clock. The military police sergeant explained that he would get them tested for intoxication, but it would have to wait until the base hospital lab opened at five o'clock.

Needless to say, by the time the drivers were tested, their blood alcohol levels were well under the legal limit. When they rejoined the battalion the next day they couldn't be punished, but they were quietly viewed with shame and they hung their heads in disgrace. In those days soldiers didn't care if someone snuck a beer in the field, but these soldiers were drivers in a truck company that prided itself on safety and professionalism. Who knows if they were drunk when they collided with the jeep? But every driver in that company knew that even a few beers can slow reaction time which probably contributed to a vehicle accident that seriously injured four soldiers.

As time went on I began to enjoy my new assignment as Battalion Motor Officer. I completed my eighth year of service and realized that my obligation to Uncle Sam was over. Maybe it was because a family with small children never has enough money and my drill check bought plenty of diapers and formula. Maybe I liked the new respect I received as a captain. Maybe I still felt a continued duty to defend our nation. A wise fellow officer once said, "As soon as you pay your bills with your drill check, they've got you."

Whatever the reason, I decided to put off my resignation from the Army, at least for a little while.

Sex and Soldiering

I walked down the line of olive drab cargo trucks as drivers raised the hoods to perform their maintenance checks. Suddenly I heard a low growling noise. One of the trucks stood untended with the driver's door open. I approached the vehicle and saw a pair of black combat boots jutting out from the end of the driver's seat. The driver's body was stretched out across the cab and I could see his hands cradling his crotch as he moaned in agony.

"Harris, what the hell is wrong with you?" I bellowed. "You should be checking out your truck."

"I can't, Lieutenant," he whined. "That new girl private kicked me in the balls." I had known Corporal Harris long enough to realize that he was a bit of a clown and an attention-getter. I also knew that, if he was really injured, he probably deserved it.

"Get up off your ass, Harris, and either go to the medics or do your maintenance checks," I barked and moved on.

A few yards away I came to the truck that was driven by a female driver who had just joined the platoon. She was the only woman and probably the first female driver to arrive in the platoon. As she balanced on the truck fender she carefully inspected the engine oil dipstick. Upon seeing me standing beside her truck, she replaced the dipstick, hopped down from the fender and saluted. She was a tall, solid young woman whose long hair was neatly braided, her boots were polished, and her uniform was creased and squared away. It was clear that she was intent on making a good impression on the first day in her new platoon.

"I just saw Corporal Harris," I said with a smirk. "Is it true that you kicked him?"

"Yes, Sir," she replied directly.

"Why would you do that, Private?"

"Lieutenant, Corporal Harris said some things to me that no one should ever say to someone else," she replied.

"Private, we can't have soldiers kicking other soldiers in their private parts, whether or not they deserve it," I said with a grin. "In the future, you need to let your squad leader handle it if someone gets fresh with you." "Yes, Sir," she responded stiffly and saluted.

Later I informed the platoon sergeant about the incident and asked him to make sure that Harris clearly understood that he got what he asked for and he was ordered to stay away from the young woman. I'm sure the platoon sergeant dealt with Harris, but neither he nor I ever thought to follow up with the female driver. Not surprisingly, several months later she was gone—transferred to another unit. I didn't realize it at the time, but I had failed as a leader to address an incident of sexual harassment.

I cringe when I remember how our Transportation Officer Basic Course class gathered in the Officers' Club at the end of the training day on Fridays. We all sat at a long table. The female lieutenants positioned themselves on one side that faced away from the corner where there was a small stage. At 6:00 p.m. the lights dimmed and the music began as a stripper stepped up onto the stage. Our class continued to tell stories and laugh as the beer flowed while onstage the young lady's outfit disappeared bit by bit. When the young woman finished her dance the catcalls of the other officers in the club drowned out all conversation. I wonder why it never occurred to me to ask myself, "How would my sister feel in this situation?" or "Would I want someone to subject my girlfriend to this?"

Years later when I was a new company commander I watched silently as a special presentation was made at a company party. Apparently the sergeants had a time-honored tradition in which they jokingly presented an officer with the "Dick of the Year" award. The award consisted of a polished wooden box that contained a foot-long rubber penis. The recipient that year was a female lieutenant who pretended that she was honored by the award and received it like it was an Oscar statuette. Later as I watched her prance around the dance floor swinging the dildo over her head to the beat of the music I should have realized that her pretended good-natured performance probably masked a deep sense of humiliation. As her mentor I should have stepped in knowing that this episode could only damage her credibility and respect as a leader.

When I became a senior commander I frequently dispensed justice to offenders, usually men, who didn't get the message that there was no longer any room in the military for sexual harassment. In many situations the facts were clear cut—the offender crossed the line of decency and respect. Consequences were meted out accordingly. But there is one case that still troubles me as I wonder whether or not justice was truly served.

The incident involved the most bitter task I've ever undertaken in the military. I found myself standing on a stateside military airfield runway in the predawn darkness as a plane touched down. It carried troops returning from an overseas combat deployment, many of whom hadn't seen their families in nearly a year. As the plane taxied toward me, I shuddered when I contemplated my duty to notify the leaders that they would be detained pending an investigation against them.

A female soldier in the unit was raped while deployed overseas. She reported the crime to her supervisors in the unit, but nothing was done. Somehow her story made its way to the higher headquarters overseas and a criminal investigation was launched. Not only was the alleged perpetrator being investigated, but the leaders in the unit were also under investigation for negligence.

The officer who commanded the unit was a friend, I might even call him a younger brother, with whom I had served for many years. We knew each other well. My heart was breaking when I saw him coming down the ramp in the glare of the harsh lights that broke through the darkness. His broad smile told me he knew nothing of what I was about to tell him. He was simply happy to be back in the USA, eagerly looking forward to his homecoming with his loving wife and beautiful children.

His face fell when I informed him as gently as I could that he was under investigation and restricted to the military base. No, he couldn't go home until the investigation was complete, although his wife and children could come to stay with him. After he regained his composure, I asked him whether or not he wanted me to inform the senior sergeants who were also under investigation, and therefore restricted to the base. He mumbled that it was better if he spoke to them.

Over the next few days I spent many hours with my friend and colleague. I wasn't part of the investigation, but I owed it to him to listen for as long as he needed to talk. He described a chaotic situation overseas in which his command was fragmented into small detachments that were dispatched across a wide geographic area. In some of these areas, he said, discipline was lax and even drunken parties had been reported. He bitterly lamented that he was unable to maintain command and control of the soldiers in his area of operations because combat conditions prevented him from traveling to many of their locations. Although I sympathized with him, there was nothing I could do but listen.

He described what I've since come to understand is an all too common condition for sexual assault. The female soldier who was victimized was a lower-ranking soldier whose job performance wasn't always the best. As such, she wasn't held in very high regard by her section leaders. We've learned that predators often target victims whom they perceive as powerless. So, when she reported that she was raped during a drinking party, her allegation was dismissed as some sort of dodge to avoid duty. Two senior sergeants in the unit, one male and one female, decided that the soldier's allegations lacked credibility. They would handle the situation unofficially and so they never informed their commander.

The victim eventually received the treatment and support she needed. The rape investigation was concluded after a few weeks. The alleged perpetrator was criminally charged. The sergeants received non-judicial punishment and letters of reprimand. My friend and colleague received a formal letter of reprimand from the general officer under whom he served overseas. This action would essentially bar him from future promotion. Shortly thereafter he retired from the military in disgust.

Did the unit fail in its responsibility to this rape victim? Absolutely. Did my brother officer receive justice? I don't know.

For centuries the business of soldiering was solely for men. Women accompanied armies as wives, laundresses, and camp followers throughout history up until the mid-nineteenth century. There were certainly female spies and heroines like Molly Pitcher, but generally women had only minor roles in military affairs. The humanitarian pioneers, Florence Nightingale and Clara Barton, organized and formalized the importance of female nurses in military medicine. When the manpower needs of World War II exceeded the supply of able-bodied men, women took on support functions in the U.S. Army as drivers, administrative clerks, and non-combat pilots. Now in the twenty-first century, women have access to all opportunities in the Army, including special operations and advanced combat specialties that had previously been restricted to men only. Women have distinguished themselves in combat and serve at all ranks, from Private to four-star General.

But we still have a long way to go.

Becoming a Commander

Because of my zeal for vehicle maintenance and equipment readiness as Battalion Motor Officer, I quickly became a pain in the ass to the other staff officers. In some battalions, I would have been marginalized or transferred out for creating too much turbulence in the staff, but the battalion commander was a thoughtful man. Realizing that he had a square peg sitting on top of a round hole, and having a company command vacancy that he needed to fill quickly, he asked me to take command of Company A, 26th Supply and Transport Battalion, which was a supply and services unit.

When he informed me of my transfer, I balked and protested vehemently—I didn't have the time to devote to company command, I wasn't qualified to run a supply company, I never attended any pre-command courses, I was a Transportation Corps officer not a Quartermaster Corps officer. In an effort to calm my anxiety, he agreed that the assignment would only be temporary until he could find a more suitable officer. In the long run, the temporary assignment was to last for nearly six years.

I assumed company command about a month before I was to lead the unit on a large-scale training operation at Canadian Forces Base Gagetown in New Brunswick. This operation, which entailed a two-day convoy to get there, would have been challenging for any unit, but for a supply company, it was monumental. The company was responsible for the bulk supply of food, fuel, and ammunition, as well as the operation of field shower points for the entire Yankee Division which probably numbered about 5,000 troops for this exercise. We would operate over a twenty-mile radius in a Canadian wilderness that we had never seen before.

My sense of panic was eased somewhat when I met with the first sergeant. Mark Loud was one of the most talented and unique soldiers with whom I ever served. We knew each other from previous interactions in the battalion, but one of those interactions was truly memorable for me.

During field training when I was the motor officer, I was standing in a clearing with 1st Sgt. Loud and a handful of NCO. Because I was low man on the staff totem pole, I didn't have a jeep, so I had to call for one to get around the battalion area, which spanned several miles. I had been waiting for nearly a half hour and had a time sensitive task to do when I saw a jeep approach. At the last minute it swerved away. Out of sheer frustration, I took off my helmet and threw it on the ground, yelling, "Fuck!"

1st Sgt. Loud looked over and calmly said, "Hey, Captain, can I talk to you for a second behind this bush?" Once we were out of sight and earshot, he poked his finger in my face and growled, "Don't you ever fucking do something like that again in front of enlisted personnel."

I shot back, "Why, did my bad language hurt your ears?"

"That's not the point," he explained. "You officers make the decisions for us enlisted people. We trust that you're in control of yourself and the situation. When you have a tantrum like that, it makes soldiers question whether or not they can trust you to know what you're doing. It makes soldiers nervous." I knew he was right. I hadn't been scolded like that by an NCO since my ROTC days, but I never forgot the lesson he taught me.

Now I was the company commander and he was stuck with me. He didn't seem overly pleased, but he didn't seem overly concerned either. A small, trim guy whose blonde hair barely met regulation standards, Mark was a philosopher-soldier who percolated energy. He chain smoked Camel cigarettes without the filters and he never stopped talking. Mark knew every soldier, had a working knowledge of each supply system, and always kept an eye on what was rumbling at higher headquarters. He assured me that the section sergeants knew what they were doing with their assigned supply system. My job wasn't to meddle in the details of their business, but to focus on the big picture of keeping the company healthy, happy, and moving in the right direction.

In the days ahead we became a great team. After briefing each other on our plans at breakfast, we each went our separate ways, rarely crossing paths. At night we compared notes from the day, highlighted concerns, and probably shared some laughs—Mark was an animated storyteller.

I have often likened the relationship between commanders and first sergeants to marriage (without the sex). When partners communicate honestly and share goals, values, and mutual trust, there's a synergy that produces good morale, operational efficiency, and cohesion in the force. If the partners are disconnected or conflicted, it's time for divorce. In my first company command, I was truly fortunate to have benefited from a wonderful marriage. I had a great partner and one of the finest first sergeants in the United States Army with whom I would have entrusted my life.

Under the tutelage of 1st Sgt. Loud we set off on our journey to CFB Gagetown in the wilds of New Brunswick, Canada. The convoy was a two-day affair that entailed an overnight stop at the University of Maine where we parked our vehicles, shuffled through the school cafeteria, and sacked out on the bare mattresses in the dorms. I don't think anyone realized that we wouldn't eat a meal under a roof or sleep on a mattress again for several weeks.

Once we left the University of Maine we saw few towns or even buildings on our northbound route. As the Maine turnpike approaches the Canadian border there are regions that have no names and are designated by tags like "B 32" that resemble Bingo squares more than locations. Once we crossed the border into Canada the roads became narrow two-lane affairs where our military vehicles almost brushed sides with speeding logging trucks.

But at last we arrived at our destination. Petersville was designated on my map as a black square, which I thought must certainly have denoted a village, or at least a military outpost. Instead we were greeted by the sight of a ragged red maple leaf flag fluttering on a crooked sapling that stood outside a low construction trailer. The civilian clerk inside pointed across a clearing and said, "Welcome to Petersville. I think you're supposed to set up your tents over there in that clump of trees."

And so we parked our vehicles and began hacking away the undergrowth to make room for our tents. One of the wonders of U.S. Army soldiers is their remarkable ability to quickly make themselves comfortable. By sundown on that first night in Canada, tents were erected, generators were humming, and the homey scent of brewing coffee was floating on the breeze from the kitchen truck.

I strolled through the company area proud of myself and my new command until my foot squished into a slimy mess on the ground. Upon closer examination, I was standing in a circle of scat about the size of a large pizza that was speckled with berry seeds. Two thoughts occurred to me—that I needed to wash off my boot as soon as I could and that I never wanted to see the creature up close that produced that amount of crap in one sitting. Well, at least I was able to clean off my boots...

Our supply company provided all the food, fuel, ammunition, field shower facilities, water purification, and other supplies to an infantry division that was operating over the 420 square miles of CFB Gagetown. Because of the far flung disposition of units, our supply sites were stretched out over a vast expanse, some as far as twenty miles from our command post in Petersville. Although I was the commander, in reality the success of these disparate operations was due to the leadership and skill of dozens of highly professional sergeants, who let me pretend that I was actually in command.

1st Sgt. Loud and I spent most daylight hours driving from site to site troubleshooting, checking on progress, and making sure that soldiers were happy and healthy. As I previously mentioned, we'd confer at breakfast to head out on our separate routes. At night we'd reconnect to share information, compare notes, and swap stories.

On the second or third day at Gagetown our unit's evaluator arrived in our company area. In those days, the regular Army sent out officers to evaluate National Guard units to ensure that we were actually training and not out trout fishing or sunbathing. Our evaluator was a ramrod straight first lieutenant from the fabled 10th Mountain Division who had recently graduated from West Point. After I gave him a quick briefing on our operations, he said, "If you don't mind, I'd like to ride along with you tomorrow." I looked at him skeptically and asked if he realized that he'd be tied up for the entire day. Perhaps he thought I was bluffing, but he replied, "I'll clear my schedule."

Sure enough, on the next morning the First Lieutenant was there with the sunrise looking like an Army-Navy store catalog model in a starched uniform, clean helmet, and stiff new web gear. We hopped into my Chevy Blazer (which had recently replaced our beloved Jeeps) and took off to check in on our far flung supply activities.

The maps for CFB Gagetown were the finest I've ever seen. Each road junction, structure, and hilltop location was noted with pinpoint precision, which eased the challenge of navigating in an unfamiliar area. After an hour of driving over pitted dirt roads we arrived at the river that provided water for our field showers and water purification sites. While I conversed with sergeants about logistics problems and personnel issues, the lieutenant received tours of our operations from proud soldiers who were only too happy to discuss the technical aspects of their processes and equipment.

And so the day flew by as we next traveled to the food storage tent complex, then the sandy valley where our soldiers skillfully stacked crates of ammunition with rough terrain forklifts. We drove to the treeless hilltop where troops carefully dispensed three different fuel types from massive tan bladders that held thousands of gallons. Later on the lieutenant looked over my shoulder as I checked the daily receiving and distribution figures for packaged products under the huge tents that covered rows of boxes on pallets. Finally we traveled to the maintenance tent location and checked in with our mechanics to get the important vehicle repair status for the day.

I asked the lieutenant if he'd like to join me for a late supper as the sun began to set and we arrived back at the company headquarters. The truth is, I had actually began to like him as the day wore on and he lost some of his stuffiness. But he declined my invitation and started to get into his vehicle.

Then he turned and said, "I just have one final question. How many years has your company been training up here in Canada?"

I looked at him puzzled. "Three days ago was the first time we ever laid eyes on this place," I replied.

"Then how come your people get around this huge area so easily?" he asked.

"I guess they just know how to read maps." He shook his head and drove off.

What I guess he didn't realize was that these National Guardsmen were much more creative, resourceful, and experienced at their specialties than he had expected. Furthermore, because equipment was so outdated and worn, Guardsmen were masters at jury-rigged repairs, making adaptations, and coming up with innovative solutions. In the world of military logistics, National Guardsmen held a clear advantage over their younger, less experienced peers in the regular Army.

As the days wore on at CFB Gagetown, we settled into a comfortable, but productive routine. Because the challenge of providing logistical support to thousands of troops in a primitive location was so ambitious, we were thankful to be unburdened by war games, repetitive reports, or foppish military protocol. Interactions with higher headquarters focused almost exclusively on food, ammunition, fuel, water, and supplies that were needed to sustain the division. It was wonderful.

Although we were co-located with Canadian Army units, we had very little contact with them. However there were some casual meetings when we swapped stories and bartered for berets, patches, and field rations. I can remember one conversation with a Canadian officer who said, "I feel sorry for you Yanks from time to time." I asked why. "Well, when we're overseas on peacekeeping, a man who injures a Canadian is regarded as an asshole." He continued, "but if he kills an American soldier, he becomes a hero." I often thought about his words later in my career.

As the days passed in my first command, my chest surely puffed out a bit as I gained confidence and pride in the belief that I could deal with just about any problem. But I hadn't reckoned on the bears.

I didn't realize it at the time, but the pizza-sized pile of scat in which I stepped was merely a reminder that we were squatters in Petersville, which belonged to its true owners—the black bear community. Every morning we found large, new, steaming pyramids of shit in our company headquarters area. At night we heard growls and rustling in the undergrowth. Bags of garbage or food were found in the woods shredded to ribbons. Soon rumors circulated about infantry soldiers up north who were mauled or had limbs torn off by angry mother bears. Thankfully these fanciful stories proved to be false.

I certainly saw the gobbled garbage and the stinking mounds of crap, but I hadn't yet laid eyes on any of our furry neighbors. In the second week I was informed that one of our cooks had been unable to sleep for nearly a week because of his fear of the bears. I was told that he was a Vietnam veteran who had begun to refer to the bears as "the VC." Apparently he lay awake at night in his sleeping bag with a meat cleaver clutched in his hand as he listened for rustling or growling.

Confidence and pride sometimes come with a dose of arrogance and my response to this situation was something I'll always regret, "Why don't you tell the cook that, if he's afraid of the bears, he can move his sleeping bag here into the headquarters tent?" I said sarcastically. "He can sleep right here next to me and I'll hold his hand all night long."

Several days later the mess steward reported that the traumatized cook had become incoherent and everyone in the mess section was afraid that he'd hurt himself or someone else. We immediately requested behavioral health support from the medical company. A few hours later, two young female enlisted personnel arrived in our area. After talking with the cook, one of them asked to meet with me. She calmly and professionally explained that the cook was reexperiencing trauma from his time in Vietnam. She recommended that he go with them to the medical company area where they could safeguard him and monitor his condition. I thanked her for her help, and, with a considerable degree of shame, agreed that the cook should go with them to the medical company. I had faced my first skirmish with post-traumatic stress, a nemesis I was to encounter many times later in my career. I had been woefully unprepared and I had been the loser.

But the bears would have the last laugh. On our last night at CFB Gagetown, I was relaxing in a tent with another officer sipping cold sodas and chatting. I was seated with my back to the tent opening. Suddenly the other officer's face froze and he whispered, "Greg, turn around, but real slowly."

There in the opening to the tent, within an arm's reach, was a massive, 300 pound black bear. He paid no attention to us, but hungrily rummaged through our trash, gobbling up all the fresh bits. The two of us froze, neither of us willing to show the obvious terror that was running through our minds. I glanced at the pistol on the other officer's belt and realized that, although I also had one at my side, we didn't have a bullet between us if worse came to worst.

After an eternity—that probably lasted about five minutes in reality—someone started up a truck engine nearby. Our furry visitor stopped his munching, perked up his ears, and bolted into the woods. We heaved a sigh of relief and chuckled, but neither of us would admit that he was scared shitless.

As I look back on it, the operation at CFB Gagetown was a commander's honeymoon. I was extremely fortunate to take command of a well-organized, confident unit that was run by experienced, professional junior officers and sergeants. Other than the bears, our Canadian adventure had been a bit of a picnic.

Shortly after we returned to home station I began to earn my pay as a commander. A National Guard company is staffed by two full time sergeants who handle day-to-day administrative business. One is the unit supply sergeant who deals with all equipment issues from boots to trucks, ensuring that soldiers have the equipment they need and that it works properly. The other sergeant attends to unit training plans as well as the individual training needs of soldiers and he or she ensures that the payroll is accurate. From time to time the two full-time sergeants confer with the commander or first sergeant, but generally the full-timers shield the part-timers from routine business.

Prior to our trip to Canada, the training NCO was a well-liked, dependable professional. As a Vietnam veteran he was widely respected, but was never known to swagger or boast about his combat experience. However during our time at Gagetown a romance developed between a young female lieutenant in the company and this training NCO.

Most of us knew about the affair but dismissed it as a casual fling. We were wrong. Weeks after our return, the training NCO informed some of the sergeants that he had left his wife and children and he was moving in with the lieutenant. Soon he was unable to complete a full day's work because of panic attacks and anxiety. I remember talking with him several times and each meeting ended with his assurances that it was just a temporary problem that he could handle. Finally he agreed to meet with a counselor, but soon he left the company on an extended medical leave upon the advice of his therapist. Although I didn't know it at the time, he was another casualty of untreated PTSD.

During this time the supply sergeant, Sergeant First Class Peter Culcasi, did his best to take up the slack by trying to manage training issues that were pressing, but he couldn't do it all. Every Wednesday I would leave work as early as possible and, weather permitting, I'd meet Pete at the tennis court near the armory. Over a set of tennis we'd discuss the problems and priorities of the week. Then we'd go to the armory and spend the next several hours developing training schedules, filing reports, and responding to training correspondence. Some Wednesdays I didn't get home much before midnight and neither did Pete.

As the weeks went by it became clear that our training NCO wasn't going to return to duty. I sent request after request to battalion headquarters to send a replacement or at least a clerk to assist Pete, who was doing two jobs. My requests received no response. Inevitably our company began to fall behind in meeting administrative training requirements and deadlines.

One night I sat in the battalion commander's monthly meeting with the other company commanders. Six captains sat silently with their backs straight in their chairs at the conference table while the battalion commander berated us about the deficiencies of our respective companies. When the topic turned to training requirements, the battalion commander cranked up the heat. Several companies were delinquent in complying with deadlines, but my company was the most egregious offender.

"So, I expect to have all delinquent training schedules on my desk by close of business tomorrow," he growled. "Isn't that right, Captain Smith?"

"No Sir." I muttered. I could almost feel a breeze as my fellow captains simultaneously gasped and held their breath.

"I don't think you heard me, Captain Smith," the battalion commander shifted his steely glare toward me.

"I can't get them done without a training NCO, Sir," I replied. "I've sent many requests—"

"I know about your personnel issues, Captain," he barked. "But I'm telling you those training schedules will be on my desk. Got it?"

The conversation was over. I wasn't going to agree to his demands, but any further argument would be pointless. I could feel the blood rushing into my face and I clenched my fists. The meeting continued but I wasn't really listening because I was too focused on plotting my next move.

Once we were dismissed, I found a vacant office with a typewriter and pounded out a memo. I signed the paper and sealed it in an envelope. Then I waited outside the battalion commander's office. The door to his office opened.

"Can I speak with you, Sir?" I asked with some formality.

"Certainly," he replied. "Come in and sit down, Captain."

I stood before his desk and thrust out the envelope. "What's this?," he asked.

"My resignation, Sir." I responded tersely.

He tore open the envelope and read it quickly. A slight smile crossed his face. "This is very well written, Smitty," he said calmly. "But I'll tell you what I think of it." Then he leaned back and tore the letter into little shreds that he piled on top of his desk.

Sitting up straight, he leaned toward me, looked me in the eye, and said, "How soon can you get those training schedules done?"

"The supply sergeant and I could probably get caught up in two weeks, but we really need some administrative help," I responded.

"We'll do our best to get someone up there to help you out," he said.

Major General Donald R. Brunelle, Commander of the 26th (YANKEE) Infantry Division, presents Capt. Smith with the Army Commendation Medal (Massachusetts National Guard PAO).

"You just do your best to get those training schedules done." That was it. I saluted and left his office. Suddenly I had one of life's epiphanies—it dawned on me that the worst thing a superior officer can do to a subordinate commander is to relieve him or her of command. I had just attempted to relieve myself of command with no success. Therefore I had nothing to lose—there was nothing any superior could do to me that really mattered. So I realized that the only responsibilities I really had were to the unit with which I was entrusted, to the missions with which we were tasked, and to the men and women who put their faith in me as their commander.

From that moment on I resolved to do whatever I believed to be the right thing for our company, our nation, and most importantly the people in our unit. Screw higher headquarters, senior officers' egos, stupid staff games, or silly regulations and anyone who dared to get in my way.

I had become a force to be reckoned with—I had truly become a commander.

More Tales of Summer Fun

Throughout the 1990s the National Guard slowly but steadily increased the professionalism and rigor of its tactical training. Because of my junior status, I wasn't aware of the factors that drove this initiative, but I can attest that it was sorely needed. Consequently, when we traveled away for our two-week period of annual training—no longer referred to as "summer camp"—we spent most of our time on tactical training in field conditions with much tougher standards. For instance, we were required to pack up our tentage and equipment and displace to new locations every 72 hours, conduct convoy movements at night under blackout conditions, and spend as long as eight continuous hours in full chemical protective gear while carrying out tactical operations. I can still feel the cascade of sweat running off my face and feel the tangy sensation of cool fresh air in my nostrils as I peeled off my protective mask after eight long, hot hours.

Gone were the days of "middle weekend" vacations. But perhaps the greatest change was the prohibition of the consumption or possession of alcoholic beverages during tactical training. I'm not so sure that soldiers stopped drinking in the field, but they certainly drank less and they did it in much more secretive ways. Not surprisingly, when we returned to the barracks area after weeks in the field, a bacchanalian celebration of alcohol in all its forms ensued as beer, whiskey, bourbon, rum, and other spirits flowed through the streets.

On the second morning in the rear area, as we made final preparations for the convoy home on the next day, I was informed that one of our soldiers was in the post hospital with serious injuries. As the battalion safety officer I was responsible for investigating the accident. So I quickly headed to the hospital. Once there we found one of our young truck drivers, Specialist Peabody, lying in a dim room, swathed in white bandages. He was a mess with stitches in his head and casts setting several broken bones. I tried to talk with him, but he was so groggy from painkillers that he made no sense. Nevertheless I expressed my sympathies, support, and offered to help him in any way I could.

Later in the day I was informed by the battalion administrative officer that I would have to complete a lengthy report because clearly Specialist Peabody had sustained an injury in the line of duty. And so, with a determination worthy of Sherlock Holmes, I set out to solve the mystery of the sad case of Specialist Peabody. After many interviews, often with reluctant or evasive reporters, I arrived at this timeline of the previous evening's events:

Capt. Smith enjoys his dinner during a field training exercise in the 1990's (author's collection).

1930 hours—Specialist Peabody arrives in the barracks area. He has been refueling tanks in the far reaches of Fort Drum and has returned from the field one day later than his buddies. He is too late for dinner and finds the dining hall closed. He is not happy.

2000 hours—Peabody's platoon buddies are not in the barracks because they have somehow found transportation to a local bar. He unloads his gear and finds a bunk on the second floor. He sadly flops down on his bunk, feeling abandoned by his buddies, and very, very thirsty.

2007 hours—A squad of Air Defense Artillery gunners from South Carolina are lounging on their bunks at one end of the barracks. They have been given bunk space in our barracks because there are only ten of them. They call out to Peabody and invite him to join them.

2009 hours—Peabody walks over to the bunks of the soldiers from South Carolina.

2010 hours—Peabody is offered a drink from a mason jar containing a clear liquid. He takes a sip. He likes it.

2011 hours—Peabody asks what this clear liquid is called. When he is told that it is "White Lightning," he comments that he is fond of this liquid and requests more.

2030 hours—Peabody continues to consume "White Lightning."
Soon he begins to sing and dance, much to the amusement of the
soldiers from South Carolina.

2105 hours—After much singing and dancing, Peabody collapses
to the floor. Upon rising up he announces that he must use the
latrine. Instead of turning left to the latrine, he turns right and
lurches toward the fire escape. The soldiers from South Carolina
call after him, but he is insistent that he must get to the latrine.

2107 hours—Peabody opens the second floor door, steps out onto the
fire escape, and tumbles over the railing. He bounces off the roof
of a van parked on the street below and lands on the pavement.

2108 hours—The soldiers from South Carolina call for an ambulance,
thinking Peabody is dead.

Later, when I shared my findings with the doctor who patched up Specialist Peabody, he responded, "Yup, that sounds about right. I was wondering why this guy's injuries weren't fatal. The flex in the sheet metal of the van's roof and the fact that he was blind drunk probably saved his life." Specialist Peabody, who was now able to sit up in his hospital bed, agreed that the facts of my report were probably correct. "The last thing I remember was having to take a wicked piss," he recalled. "Then I remember tumbling through space wondering, 'why did they take the latrine away?" Then he added this final thought, "As God is my witness, I will never touch White Lightning again as long as I live."

* * *

The lieutenant who commanded the headquarters company was one of the most talented people I've ever met. He was originally from New Orleans and joined the battalion when he enrolled in graduate school at the University of Massachusetts. No one knew much about him, but when the battalion took the yearly physical fitness test, this lieutenant finished first in the push-ups, sit-ups, and the two-mile run, handily beating out all competitors.

There was a karaoke machine at a battalion party and those who thought they could sing each took a turn. Someone challenged the lieutenant to sing. Despite repeated protests he finally took the microphone and belted out a pitch perfect Marvin Gaye tune. The audience wouldn't let him give up the microphone and he continued to croon with almost professional style for the rest of the night.

To make matters even worse, the lieutenant was well-spoken, humble, tall, slim, and handsome. In fact, he was the kind of guy that other men should hate, but he was too nice for us to resent him. He seemed to be a superior being without flaws or weaknesses, but we would soon learn about one key weakness that wasn't yet apparent.

The lieutenant owned a small dry cleaning business. At that time we wore woodland camouflage uniforms that required light pressing after they were washed. The lieutenant began to take soldiers' uniforms with him after training which he would then return cleaned and pressed at the next training event. His prices were reasonable and the turnaround time was unbeatable. As the months went by he was taking so many uniforms with him at the end of the training day that he needed to drive the cleaner's van to training.

As our annual summer training approached, nearly everyone brought their uniforms to the lieutenant to be laundered before we went into the field for two weeks. As I recall there were so many uniforms he needed to take several trips to get them all to his dry cleaning business.

Everyone arrived in a uniform for the first day of annual training, but for many it was the only clean uniform they possessed. Almost everyone looked for the lieutenant to retrieve their other freshly laundered uniforms, but he was nowhere to be seen. His detachment sergeant assured us that he had spoken with the lieutenant and he was on his way with all our uniforms. We loaded up onto the trucks and began the convoy to Camp Edwards on Cape Cod believing that we'd collect our uniforms once we arrived there.

However, after our first day at Camp Edwards there were no uniforms. After the second and third days there were still no uniforms and many soldiers were beginning to smell quite ripe. A sort of black market in uniforms now started to develop where soldiers who had more than one uniform "rented" clean ones out for a fee. This created comical situations in which soldiers ended up wearing pants that were too short, shirts that were too large with name tags that weren't their real names and collar ranks pinned on over one another. We looked like a gang of scarecrows.

But where were our uniforms? What happened to the lieutenant? After a week the battalion commander swore out a warrant for the lieutenant's arrest as an AWOL soldier. When the state police delivered him to Camp Edwards he sheepishly confessed that he had gambled away the cleaning business and its contents, including all our uniforms. He promised to try to collect what he could from the new owners once he was released, but few of us ever saw our uniforms again.

I don't know what happened to the lieutenant, because he just disappeared after annual training was over, which was good because a lot of people wanted to even the score with him. But I was kind of sorry to see him go—I liked his singing.

*   *   *

Environmental issues became a great concern in wilderness training areas during the 1990s. Although it added another layer of complication to our planning for tactical training, the precautions were long overdue. For years the military had abused the environment in training areas by burying ammunition, dumping toxic chemicals and spilling fuel. Because fuel contamination in the soil was so widespread, refueling operations began to receive special scrutiny.

During annual training at Fort Drum I received a radio message one sunny morning that a fuel tanker up in a remote forward area was in some trouble. During fueling operations, it's normal procedure to uncouple a 5,000 gallon tanker from the tractor that tows it. When it separates from the tractor, the front of the tanker rests on two metal landing legs that are cranked down to keep it level. In an unpaved area, thick wooden landing pads are set under the feet of the landing legs to prevent them from sinking into the earth because of the heavy weight of the tanker.

On this fine summer day, however, a tanker's landing legs had gradually slipped off the landing pads and had begun to settle into the earth. This prevented the drivers from safely backing the tractor under the front of the tanker to hook it up and haul it away to be refilled. I should also add that an empty or partially filled tanker is more flammable because the air-fuel mix is actually more volatile than liquid fuel on its own.

I consulted with the maintenance sergeant who, after commenting on the competence and sanity of the fuel tanker operators in profane terms, agreed to send the wrecker to remedy the situation. He explained that the wrecker crew would fashion a sling. Then, using the long boom of the wrecker, hoist the front end of the tanker so the tractor could be safely backed under it.

As we made the final coordination, the maintenance sergeant added, "You know, Sir, we might want to have a foam truck standing by just in case someone strikes a spark with all that metal moving around. Besides, the firefighter squad is probably sitting around bored this morning."

Without giving it a second thought, I radioed battalion headquarters and requested that a foam truck be sent to the map grid coordinates where the tanker was located. Little did I know that the voice that acknowledged receiving the brief radio message belonged to an excitable former Marine, who was known to be a bit of a know-it-all. Furthermore, I didn't understand that, as someone who was new to the battalion, he knew nothing about fuel operations or reasonable precautions. Also, because of the truncated way we transmitted radio messages, I was unable to explain my rationale for the request.

Hopping into my jeep with no roof or sides, I enjoyed a leisurely open-air drive through green forests, scented by honeysuckle, listening to snatches of bird songs as I made my way to the tanker's locations. I didn't realize that these were the last moments of peace I was to enjoy on this day.

When I arrived at the fuel tanker location, I surveyed the sorry sight of the long green tanker tilting to one side with its right landing leg sunk in the mud. The wrecker had arrived and its crew members were sizing up the plan of attack, shaking their heads with their customary condescending disapproval of the poor planning and stupidity that had brought them out. The fuel tanker operators stood off to the side with their heads bowed, shoulders hunched, looking appropriately ashamed. (In reality, wrecker drivers love to tackle unique engineering challenges, but they always feign a superior attitude, as if to say, "Here I am getting you out of trouble and fixing your mistakes once again, asshole.")

The sergeant in charge of the wrecker crew came over to me and said, "We'll position the boom off to the right at an angle and lift the tanker. It shouldn't be too tough to get it high enough for the tractor to back under it." Then he added, "I think we'll wait for the foam truck to get here before we rig the tanker with the sling, just to be safe."

Suddenly I heard the wail of sirens. I thought it was strange to hear police or fire vehicles in this remote area. There weren't any large military units in this training area. As the sirens grew louder, I had a feeling that they were approaching our location. I was puzzled.

Adding to the shriek of the sirens, we now heard the wop-wop-wop of a helicopter circling our location at low altitude. Now I was alarmed. Moments later a half dozen fire trucks arrived with red lights flashing. An anxious firefighter hopped out of a red command vehicle and lumbered over to me in full turnout gear. "Where's the fuel spill?" he gasped, eyes darting here and there.

When I explained the situation, the anxiety drained away from his face and he signaled to the firetrucks to turn off the flashing lights. Other military vehicles were now arriving at our location. Our battalion commander dismounted from one of them and marched over to where the firefighter and I stood. I quickly saluted and explained that the request for a foam truck was a simple precaution for our wrecker operation. The colonel breathed a sigh of relief.

Then we all turned and watched as the helicopter that had been circling overhead floated down to land in a clearing several hundred yards away. "I wonder who that is?" I asked to no one in particular. "That's the post commander," the colonel replied.

"Would you like me to go over there and brief him?" I asked, although that was about the last thing I wanted to do.

"No, Smitty," the colonel said. "There are some things colonels just have to do. But right now I wish I was a captain." After about ten minutes the colonel returned. "That wasn't as bad as it could have been," he reported. "Let's go ahead and lift that tanker."

I called to the wide-eyed wrecker sergeant and asked him to go ahead with the recovery operation as the foam truck moved into position near the tanker. Over the next half hour the wrecker crew worked their magic while firefighters, the commanding general of the post, our battalion commander, and an array of environmental monitors and military officials looked on. When the tractor successfully backed under the tanker and they were securely coupled, loud clapping and cheers could be heard echoing in the forest.

I don't believe any tow truck team had ever received such an ovation in the history of vehicle recovery. However as I drove back to company headquarters I realized that my afternoon and evening would be consumed by many pages of reports caused by my simple request for a foam truck.

*   *   *

The Army runs on rosters, paperwork, and administrative requirements. One of the greatest burdens any commander faces is the never-ending demand for lists, data, and compliance with regulatory requirements from higher headquarters. And so, during one annual training period, when our company's priority was to sharpen its tactical skills, we were haunted by the Army's requirement to have all personnel comply with DNA registration. The process was easy enough—a simple cheek swab—and the primary reason for the requirement was for our own benefit—to identify our remains if bad things happened. But my patience was worn thin by the constant call for personnel to be trucked to the rear, away from training, inevitably when I needed them most.

Finally there were only two names left on the company roster who hadn't registered their DNA—two mechanics in the maintenance section. The First Sergeant planned to get them in for testing as soon as possible. Days went by and I was annoyed to receive a threatening message from the battalion administrative officer demanding that I get the two delinquent soldiers to the clinic to get their DNA registered immediately, or else. I called for the first sergeant and asked why the mechanics hadn't gotten their DNA registered. "I've been chasing those two for days, Captain," he said. "Just yesterday I told their section sergeant to find them and get them to the clinic before they turned another wrench, but I guess he couldn't get them to go. He says they won't budge. Maybe they need to hear it from you."

Without mincing words, I told the first sergeant to bring them to headquarters as quickly as he could. My patience had run out. A few hours later two young mechanics stood in front of my desk, eyes downcast, shifting nervously from one foot to another.

"Do you know that battalion has been all over my ass because of you two?" I growled. "Can you tell me why you're different from your section sergeant, the first sergeant, the officers, me, or 150 of your fellow soldiers? Do you care to offer your reasons why you can't find the time to register your DNA?" I bellowed.

The two soldiers furtively glanced at each other. Then one of them straightened up and thrust out his chin. "You see, Sir, we don't think it's right that the Army gets to have our DNA." I hadn't expected a philosophical defense, and I was genuinely curious about their reasoning. "Why are you so concerned about giving up your DNA?"

The mechanic cleared his throat. "Well, Sir, we've talked this over quite a bit and we believe that the real reason the Army wants our DNA is to clone us." I stifled the urge to laugh and hid my face with both hands to hide my smile.

Recovering my composure, I said, "Did you ever stop to think that the Army might want to choose someone other than the two of you if they were considering the business of cloning? Perhaps they might select soldiers who were a bit taller, or stronger, who were better marksmen, had higher physical fitness scores … or maybe even were a bit smarter? I think the two of you can be fairly certain that the Army wouldn't choose your DNA for cloning."

"Now here's how we'll settle this," I continued. "You can go back to your tent and no one will bother you about DNA registration again. However, I will then code your status on the payroll as 'unsatisfactory,' and you will have volunteered your service to our nation for no pay." I let that sink in for a minute. "Or, if you'd like to continue to get paid, you can get into the pickup truck with the first sergeant right now and go to the clinic to register your DNA. You decide."

The soldiers exchanged a few whispered words, then the spokesman said, "Okay, Sir, we'll go with the first sergeant." And so the cloning mutiny was quelled. After that episode, I only hope that, if the Army really is going to clone soldiers, they carefully choose the specimens.

*   *   *

As explained earlier, when we trained at Fort Drum, our company was responsible for supplying all the food, fuel, and ammunition that the 10,000 soldiers of the Yankee Division needed to support their training. As Napoleon famously stated, "An army marches on its stomach," which was certainly true of the Yankee Division. Food was always an issue of concern—there was never enough or it wasn't the right menu—it was a constant headache. The source of the culinary discomfort was often the irascible civilian food supply system at Fort Drum, upon which we relied for bulk food delivery. The warehouse was never open when we needed it to be, or the paperwork was in error, or our soldiers were fighting with the civilians over trivial minutia.

One year, however, I realized that, after one full week of operations, there were no major complaints about food supply. The lieutenant I had placed in charge of food supply was a handsome, suave young guy who made his living as a bell captain at a swanky hotel in Boston. He had once bragged, "There isn't anything I can't get for a customer at any time of day in Boston—and I mean anything." He was a savvy operator who knew how to achieve results. But he was also a good leader who was well liked by his soldiers and fellow lieutenants. Like most of the younger officers with whom I served, I considered him a younger brother.

One night after the duty day we were both sipping beers in our quarters. "You've done an amazing job managing the food supply operation during Annual Training," I said. "I think I'm going to submit your name for an Army Commendation Medal."

"Thanks, Sir," he replied, "but there wasn't much to it."

"How did you manage to make things run so smoothly?" I asked.

"Well, we were able to get the food warehouse open when we needed it to be," he explained and paused to sip his beer.

"But that's been a problem for years," I persisted. "How did you get the civilians to cooperate with you?"

He looked up with a twinkle in his eye. "It was easy.... I was sleeping with the new warehouse manager." I paused. "Was she cute?" "Nope, but we had the warehouse open whenever we needed it."

I grabbed another beer and changed the subject. He just grinned. Nevertheless I forwarded his Army Commendation Medal recommendation to battalion, but I omitted certain details.

*　　*　　*

In the early 1990s annual training involved more and more sustained tactical training in the field. Because our supply and services company had to arrive before the maneuver brigades to set up the logistics support infrastructure, the company's annual training period extended to nearly three weeks. After two weeks in the woods, soldiers were eager to secure their rifles, ground their helmets, and shed their web gear. They couldn't wait for hot showers to wash away dust and pine needles, hot meals that could be eaten seated at an indoor table, and, most importantly, ice cold beers that would quench a fourteen day thirst.

One annual training exercise I was notified by higher headquarters that, due to an exceptionally busy training period, there were no barracks available for our company. The bottom line was that soldiers would remain in the woods until they convoyed home at the end of annual training. That meant keeping weapons and tactical gear, no hot showers, no indoor seated eating areas, and no cold beers.

I broke the news to the sergeants at our late afternoon leaders' briefing. As I expected, there was an explosion of dismay, disappointment, and downright anger. I let the grousing run for a few moments, then asked, "So what are we going to do?"

"What do you mean, Sir?" a sergeant replied angrily. "Battalion says we don't have any barracks in the rear, so I guess we're just shit out of luck."

"It's not our option to just give up," I snapped. "These folks worked hard for us for two weeks. It's up to us to solve this problem, because we can't just throw up our hands and let them down. We need to put our heads together and figure this out." My sermon was met with stony silence.

The head mechanic, Staff Sergeant Paul Simoneau, was a cheerful guy who could fix just about anything, but even he looked discouraged. Paul glanced at the flat dirt area in which we were located, sighed, and said, "Well, we have enough fucking sand around here. Maybe we should have a beach party."

There was a pause, then suddenly this gloomy crew was alive with chatter. Everyone was talking at once. I couldn't make out too much of what was said, other than that many sentences began with, "What if…" As our meeting broke up the sergeants huddled in clusters, pointing, gesturing, and conspiring. That night I convinced the battalion commander to authorize a six hour exception to the prohibition against drinking alcohol in a field environment. He agreed with my logic that, if we didn't bend the rules and allow a few beers in the field, we'd pay for it ten times over in morale issues and lack of reenlistments. We arranged for the booze truce to begin at 6:00 on the following night.

Throughout the next day I noticed a new energy in the company as soldiers scurried about lugging odd pieces of equipment through the area. I asked Staff Sgt. Simoneau about the arrangements that were being made for the beach party, but he simply smiled and said, "Just wait and see, Sir."

At 5:30 I smelled the delicious, smoky aroma of steaks sizzling on the barbecue. I shed my sweaty gear and donned gym shorts, a colorful tee shirt, and shower shoes, which was as close as I could get to appropriate beach wear.

As I walked toward the maintenance tent I could hear the tinny blare of rock music punctuated by shouts and laughter. The first thing I saw was one of the parts clerks swinging through the air on a sling suspended from the extended boom of the wrecker. When she reached her highest point, she jumped free and plunged into a 1500-gallon rubber tub filled with water. The water section sergeant noticed my grimace, but assured me that this container was an extra, and not one we used for purified drinking water.

Strange hats and bathing suits were the uniform of the night as troops gobbled up steaks, watermelon, and corn on the cob, which they washed down with cans of beer and soda plucked from barrels of ice water. Soldiers in colorful bits of clothing twisted and hopped to the loud boom box tunes on the canvas dance floor.

But the high point of the night was the arrival of the battalion maintenance warrant officer, clad only in a white speedo and his web gear, who was perched perilously on the hood of a pickup truck that rolled toward the maintenance tent. His incredible balancing act as he made it all the way across the bumpy clearing without falling off rivaled the agility of a pro surfer. It quickly became a battalion legend.

As the barbecue fires died down and the last cans of beer were plucked from the bottom of the barrels, I noticed soldiers clustering together as they whispered. I prepared myself for a time honored company tradition, and warned the other officers to stash their wallets and watches. Suddenly we were pounced upon by dozens of howling enlisted soldiers who grabbed us and hoisted us aloft. Although we all put up a half-hearted struggle, we were resigned to our

Capt. Smith (wearing a red bandana) frolics in an improvised swimming pool during the "beach party" at Fort Drum in the 1990s (author's collection).

fate. One by one we were dumped into the 600-gallon tub to the cheers of the assembled company. Our baptismal rite was complete. I wouldn't have it any other way because it meant that our family was united and strong.

Before I left the beach party to change into something cleaner and drier, I extended my soggy hand and my thanks to our sergeants, particularly Paul Simoneau. The beach party had shown agility, tenacity, and creativity. I couldn't have been prouder of them.

Serving as the commander of Company A (Supply & Service), 26th Supply and Transport Battalion was one of the most fulfilling experiences of my life. To say I enjoyed every minute of this command would be an exaggeration, but I enjoyed most of them. I took great pride in being the captain of this team of patriots, who taught me many things about teamwork, belonging, and leadership. But, like my time as a platoon leader, the Army doesn't allow officers to take root in one place. I had to move on to a higher assignment or end my military service as a captain. I figured I'd stick around and see what it was like to be a major.

*　*　*

Perhaps the strangest mission to which we were ever assigned began in the middle of the night during Annual Training on Cape Cod in July 1999. Our brand new water supply battalion was on its third day of tactical training in the sand and stubby pines of the Cape. We hadn't received any of our operational equipment to begin water purification, so all we could do was train on perimeter defense, patrolling, and convoy operations. At that time I was the Battalion Operations Officer. When I rolled out of my sleeping bag, I checked in with the staff officer on overnight duty, expecting the usual negative report. "It was pretty quiet all night, Sir, except for one strange thing," he explained. "At about 0300 the radio operator called me to listen in. There was this strange static that came in bursts over the radio."

"Could you make any of it out?" I asked. "No," the staff officer yawned and scratched his chin. "It might have been Morse Code, but it didn't seem to have any pattern." "Well, let's note it on the message log anyway," I recommended, and promptly forgot all about it.

Later that morning we received a message to send all available personnel to the airfield flight line. Helicopter observers were urgently needed. The staff quickly began organizing a plan to locate soldiers and transport them out to the airfield. "There must be a forest fire somewhere out on the Cape," I suggested to another officer. "Actually, I was just listening to the news on the radio," he responded, "John F. Kennedy, Jr.'s, airplane was reported missing overnight. They said he was headed from New York to Nantucket."

Sure enough, as the afternoon approached and we learned more from the news, it was clear that we were being called on to search for JFK Jr.'s plane out on Cape Cod Bay. By nightfall, the base gym was crowded with news trucks and reporters. We knew to steer clear of the gym, lest we get sucked into an interview by some news-hungry reporter who needed to file a story on something, because the search was producing nothing.

The weather was perfect for flying. The sky was clear blue, the humidity was low, and the temperature was in the low eighties. Perhaps that's why I volunteered to take a shift as an observer in a Hughie helicopter on the second day. The crew chief quickly briefed us on the flight line and positioned us on either side of the aircraft so we had clear sight out of the open doors. I remember that he cautioned us not to use binoculars or else we would make ourselves airsick and he didn't want to have to clean vomit out of his aircraft.

We gently lifted off from the tarmac and I felt the cool breezes drift through the helicopter as we rose up into the bright blue sky. Soon we were gliding over the deep blue-green waters of Cape Cod Bay. Back and forth we patrolled our sector, looking for any sign of wreckage. In the first few minutes, it was exciting to be skimming along in a helicopter so near the tops of the waves. The wop-wop of the helicopter main rotor blades was so loud that ear plugs were necessary and any conversation was impossible. We tapped each other on the shoulder and pointed down at every seagull or white cap wave in the distance only to shake our heads and shrug when we drew closer.

After a half hour or so, the thrill of flying soon wore off and it became intensely boring as we tried to stay alert, but all we could see was miles and miles of glittering ocean. As we passed the hour mark, the warm sunshine, gentle breezes, rocking of the helicopter, and constant humming of the rotor blades made it difficult to avoid an afternoon nap. We touched down back at the airfield with a guilty feeling of relief—pleased that the mind-numbing duty of air observer was over, but sorry that we had found no evidence of JFK Jr.'s airplane.

After three days, the search flights were suspended and it was accepted that the airplane had probably plunged into the sea in the darkness of night. Gradually the news trucks and the ravenous reporters left the base and a quiet calm returned. I overheard two soldiers talking in the mess tent after the search was over.

"It's a damn shame that the Kennedy kid and his wife and her sister were killed in that plane crash," commented one soldier. "But it was good that everybody tried so hard to find them." The other soldier squinted at him across the table. "That may be so, but do you think that they'd send that many people out looking for you and me if we were lost at sea?" There was a pause until a soldier at the end of the table asked, "Did anybody hear if the Red Sox beat the Orioles last night?"

Justice

Although I spent more than a quarter century in command assignments, I only had to use formal discipline procedures on a dozen occasions, at most. However, my first attempt at judicial punishment was a sobering and memorable experience.

My attitude toward command punishment had been shaped by an experience from my earliest days as a platoon leader in the truck company. A grizzled, loud-mouthed sergeant decided that he was thirsty one night while we were on tactical training. So he took a five-ton tractor trailer rig, uncoupled the trailer, and made a late night beer run. Being a rather vocal person, the sergeant bragged about his personal resupply mission a bit too much, and the matter came to the attention of the first sergeant.

Soon the company commander had the sergeant removed from duty and informed him that he was being charged with disobeying standing orders, which included using a military vehicle for personal business, transporting alcoholic beverages in a military vehicle, operating a vehicle that was not properly dispatched, and a host of other transgressions. Although the sergeant knew he was guilty, he wasn't going to accept his punishment like an adult and move on. Oh no, he contested the charges and consulted a Judge Advocate General, or military lawyer—JAG for short—which was his right.

Now that a JAG was involved, the punishment adjudication process became extended and carried over into our training and maintenance activities at home station. As a soldier who was innocent until proven guilty, the sergeant was free to proclaim how unjustly he was being treated by the company commander to anyone who would listen, and, unfortunately, there were many listeners. The company commander was a good, solid leader, but he must have slept through the classes on the Uniform Code of Military Justice in Officer Candidate School because he badly botched the paperwork for the charges. In the end, the sergeant's sharp-eyed JAG officer managed to have the charges dismissed because of procedural errors in the company commander's statements and records.

The sergeant was ecstatic. I remember him crowing in his raspy voice, "That captain thought he was going to fuck me over, but I beat him!" It took a long time for discipline and morale to recover in the company. I swore that, if I had to use the formal disciplinary process I would never lose.

Years later I found myself commanding a company during tactical training. At that time, forward refueling of armored vehicles was conducted in darkness. Every night we dispatched a small convoy of five thousand gallon tankers that thundered down dusty tank trails into the forward areas using only pinpoint blackout drive lights for illumination. Between the dust, the darkness, and the highly explosive nature of the load, this was a high-risk operation.

The day after the second night of operations, the platoon leader of the fuel section came to me and said, "Captain, I need your advice. I found beer cans under the trucks this morning. I told my platoon that drinking was forbidden until we returned to the rear, but somebody wasn't listening. What should I do?" I advised him to call the platoon together and inform them that drinking during such a hazardous operation was not only insubordinate, but extremely risky. They were a good platoon and I encouraged him to appeal to their professionalism and common sense.

The platoon leader came back the next morning and said, "I did what you told me to do, Sir, but I found more beer cans this morning." So much for my wise advice to appeal to their sense of reason. I told him to go back and give the platoon a serious warning that any more drinking would result in disciplinary action.

The lieutenant approached me the following day holding a paper bag. In it was an empty quart bottle of whiskey. I was furious, but more importantly, I was aware that the lieutenant and I were being tested by someone in the company. I needed to act decisively or I risked losing control of the company or worse, someone might get killed on a night convoy. I called the lieutenant and the first sergeant to the company headquarters tent later in the day and briefed them on my plan.

In the chill and pitch black of 4:30 a.m., the first sergeant and platoon sergeant turned the drivers of the fuel section out into the clearing beside their tent. I can still see the sleepy, puzzled soldiers standing in their underwear shivering in the dark. The two senior sergeants moved quickly through the tent, rummaging through duffel bags and foot lockers. Suddenly they burst out of the tent holding several bottles of liquor. "Where did you find that?" I broke the silence.

"Mooney's and Lester's foot lockers, Sir," the sergeants answered. "First sergeant, take the two of them into custody and transport them and the evidence to the Post Military Police Station."

I could hear a murmur from the rest of the platoon as they fell out of formation and went into the tent to gather their belongings. The post Military Police were every truckers' worst enemy. Not only were these two drivers in trouble, they had been handed over to the forces of evil, as well.

I spent the rest of the day consulting with the battalion legal NCO and the battalion command sergeant major. With a bit of a chuckle, the command sergeant major gently told me that I laid it on a bit thick by sending the perpetrators to the Post MP Station. In fact, the Post MP duty NCO had called battalion headquarters asking what he was supposed to do with the two knuckleheads. Although consuming alcohol in the field violated my orders, it didn't break any military laws. The sergeant major said that he would go pick them up and keep them in the battalion headquarters under house arrest. The legal NCO carefully guided me in preparing the correct paperwork and rehearsing exactly what I was to say and NOT say during the upcoming proceedings.

It was almost nightfall before I was ready to meet with the two evildoers. At the recommendation of the sergeant major and legal NCO, I was seated at a small field table with the company flag, or guidon, next to me. The table was set in a wooded clearing away from the company area for confidentiality reasons. I was flanked by the command sergeant major standing on one side and the legal NCO on the other. The sun was beginning to set and we must have looked like a dirty Holy Trinity in camouflage.

The first sergeant escorted Sergeant Mooney to the clearing. He was a big man in his late thirties, and I'll never forget that he was holding back tears as I read the charges. He waived his right to counsel, probably fearing that I'd send him back to the MP Station while we waited for a JAG to be assigned. He simply grunted an answer to most of my questions. However, when I passed the sentence of reduction in grade from sergeant to specialist, the tears rolled down his cheeks and he stammered his apology. The command sergeant major quickly plucked the sergeant's chevrons from his collar and handed him specialist's insignia. He slumped as he marched away and I thought, "Holy shit, this is powerful stuff!" I could see how this kind of power could easily become addictive.

Sergeant Lester's proceedings went essentially the same way, but without any tears. When it was all over, I shook hands with the senior NCOs and thanked them for their help. I was worn out and I was starving, but the mess tent was already cleaned up from the evening meal. Most of all, I was worried about how the unit would perceive my actions. I was afraid that I had destroyed the morale of the company. I guess it had to be done, but the humiliating predawn shakedown of mostly innocent drivers seemed a little heavy handed. Perhaps I could arrange some sort of apology. I made a note to consult with the First Sergeant in the morning.

The next morning was a bright, sunny day. I strapped on my gear over my sweaty uniform, settled my musty-smelling helmet on top of my matted hair, and headed to the mess tent. It was my morning ritual to sip a cup of coffee and talk with soldiers as they got their meals. Not only did I learn a lot of operational information, but I had a chance to gauge the company's morale. I was afraid of what I might see and hear this morning—and indeed things were quite different from the usual routine.

It started with the cooks—"Good morning, Sir, I guess you missed dinner last night. Can I set you up with a plate of eggs and some bacon we set aside for you?" Two soldiers from the fuel section trudged up until they saw me. Then they straightened up, smiled, and said, "Good morning, Sir. I think it's gonna be a beautiful day." Another cluster of soldiers walked by with their pancakes until they saw me. They stopped, smiled, and wished me a good day, reminding me that we only had four more mornings in the woods.

And so it went with smiles and greetings—no one made any reference to yesterday's ugly events, in fact they treated me with more than their usual courtesy and respect. After a while I realized that instead of resenting my use of power, most of the company actually appreciated my disciplinary actions.

When I stopped to think about it, I realized that most soldiers follow the rules. Regulations, customs, and structure can be a pain in the ass, but it's the hallmark of military culture—it's what sets soldiers apart from the civilian world. Soldiers actually feel affirmed when others who break the rules get what's coming to them, provided the punishment is fair. The soldiers in our company knew that there was drinking in the fuel section and they knew who was doing it a long time before I ever did. But now the matter had been settled. I had done my job as the commander and they seemed pleased with that. Our unit, our family, could get back to business now.

Later in my career I also learned the power of mercy. The Army had just implemented random urinalysis for drug testing. I remember opening one of the first lists of positive drug testers, expecting to see the typical handful of new recruits who came up positive for marijuana. But I was shocked when I saw the name of one of our platoon sergeants who had tested positive for cocaine.

I called him in for counseling, expecting that he would allege that his sample had been mishandled or that it was one of the half percent of false positives that we knew were possible. Instead he looked across the desk at me and said, "I fucked up, Sir. I went to a party I shouldn't have been at. I had too much to drink and I got into something I never should have touched." There wasn't much I could say. He continued. "I have a lot to lose here. I have a good marriage, two wonderful kids, and a great career in public safety."

I also knew that he was quite proud of the important position he held in his Masonic Lodge and was highly regarded in the community where he lived. It was almost certain that he would lose his job if he were discharged from the military for drug abuse and, perhaps worse, he would be humiliated within his community. "I stand to lose it all if I get kicked out." He was a proud man, but he looked at me pleadingly. "Please, Sir, I'll do anything I need to do to stay in. Please give me another chance."

Although I knew I'd have to fight with the battalion commander to make an exception, I decided to do everything in my power to save this soldier. I felt it was the best course of action for our company, and I believed that he sincerely regretted this big mistake.

So the sergeant submitted to frequent random drug testing, faithfully attended regular counseling sessions, and cleaned up his life. He was a solid, positive leader for the remainder of my time with the company. When I was transferred to another assignment, the unit had a sendoff party for me. He pulled me aside at the end of the party. "I'll never forget what you did for me, Sir," he said, looking me in the eye. "I would have been ruined if you didn't believe in me."

"No thanks needed, Sarge, it was a good investment on my part." I replied. I had learned that mercy can be as powerful as discipline.

So whatever happened to Mooney and Lester, the boozing fuel truck drivers? I know that they both straightened up enough to regain their sergeants' stripes. I don't recall much about Mooney other than that, but I clearly remember a conversation I had with Lester during Operation Desert Storm.

Our company received a warning order for mobilization. I had just spent most of the afternoon listening to several requests not to deploy because of family hardships, all of which I denied. Lester knocked on my door. When I saw his face, I prepared for another sob story.

"It looks like we might deploy, Sir, and I wanted to ask you something," the soldier stood gripping his hat nervously. "Go ahead, Lester," I barely looked up from my desk.

"A lot of these guys and girls have little kids and families," he said. "I just want you to put my name on a list of people who are volunteering to go first. I don't have a family and nobody would really miss me if I went overseas. So I guess I'm saying that you should take me first and not some of these people with kids."

I stood up and looked at him for a long moment. He shifted back and forth uncomfortably, avoiding eye contact. Then I stood up, reached out, and shook his hand. "You know what, Sergeant Lester? You're a good man." And I meant it.

As a brigade commander I had to deal with one very odd, highly public incident. Although the brigade was activated to respond to a crippling December ice storm, the situation wasn't so dire that we couldn't pause for a half hour to watch the end of an NFL football game. During a break from operations, we were gathered around a small television set in the headquarters orderly room. Of all the major sports, there's a particularly strong link between football and the military. Some of the parallels are obvious— we both wear helmets and uniforms, one side is determined to impose its will on the other side, and the players are always trying to break the rules without getting caught. Of all places, this link is particularly strong in New England, where the Patriots even share the same minuteman legacy and imagery with the National Guard.

We cheered as the final minutes of the game ticked down and the New England Patriots chalked up another victory on their way to the Super Bowl. We all laughed as a drunk fan hopped down from the stands and enthusiastically embraced Patriots linebacker, Junior Seau, dragging him down to the turf in the process. As security guards seized the fan, television cameras focused in on a close-up shot.

"Hey, that looks like one of our sergeants," a soldier shouted, pointing at the television. Everyone leaned closer to the TV screen and agreed that the inebriated fan looked an awful lot like a member of the headquarters staff. "Isn't he supposed to be on duty in the operations section?" somebody else asked. "I heard he had tickets to the game and got permission to go," someone added.

After the game we returned to the serious business of dispatching tree cutting crews, generators, wellness patrols, and shelter security teams across nearly half the state that was without electric power. When I had an opportunity, I asked the command sergeant major to look into whether or not this sergeant had been excused from duty to attend the Patriots' game.

Later that night the command sergeant major confirmed that the sergeant had indeed been given permission to attend the Patriots game and was most certainly the drunk fan who tackled Junior Seau. He added that he had already chewed out the section sergeant who had given him unofficial leave to attend the game.

We pondered what to do next. On the one hand, the sergeant was off-duty, in civilian clothes, when he committed what was really nothing more than a foolish act of rowdiness. There were no regulations in the Uniform Code of Military Justice against stupidity, or else millions of soldiers and officers, including me, would be indicted. On the other hand, the command sergeant major contended, failure to take action could pose a threat to discipline. He argued that every soldier in the brigade was aware of this very public, ridiculous action by the sergeant. Furthermore soldiers would know that he was supposed to be on duty while hundreds of them were clearing felled trees, installing generators, and knocking on doors in remote areas to check on elderly citizens without electricity. While public punishment was always a bad practice, whatever I chose to do, word would seep out to the force. The command sergeant major warned that the choice to do nothing might make the loudest statement of all.

After giving the matter considerable thought, days later I called the sergeant to my office. He arrived and stood at attention in front of my desk wearing a sheepish grin. When he saw the expression on my face he stiffened up and fixed his eyes on the wall above my head. I proceeded to read a carefully worded, one-page letter of reprimand expressing my disappointment and condemnation of his actions after the Patriots game, which I referred to as conduct unbecoming a noncommissioned officer. When I finished I asked him to sign the letter as acknowledgment of receipt.

He leaned over and picked up the pen to sign, then hesitated. "I don't mean to be a wise guy, Colonel," he said, "but I'm not sure I understand why you're punishing me. I mean, I get that what I did at the game was stupid. But I was off-duty. It wasn't like I was wearing a uniform or anything like that."

I told him to pull up a chair and sit down. "You're a section leader, right?" I began. "You have ten, maybe twelve young soldiers who report to you. When you tell them to do something, you expect them to do it. Believe it or not, they probably look up to you and follow your lead as a role model."

He silently nodded his head. "Now think about this for a moment," I continued. "One of your young soldiers is at home watching the Patriots game with his or her parents." They see you stumble out of the stands drunk and fall all over Junior Seau. The soldier turns to his or her parents and says, "Hey, that's my boss in the National Guard."

I paused to let that sink in. "Now let's look ahead," I said. "We're operating in a combat zone. You ask those young soldiers to follow you into a situation in which they're risking their lives. You assure them that you're going to bring them through safe. How much trust can they place in that drunk guy who jumped out of the stands at the Patriots game?"

He thought about this for a moment. Then slowly he picked up the pen again and signed the letter of reprimand. "You're not a bad guy," I said, "but you've got a lot of work to do to rebuild your reputation as a leader and regain the trust of your soldiers." He murmured an apology and saluted.

Not all of my disciplinary actions were so instructive, but this sergeant and I never discussed the matter again. By the time I left the brigade years later, he was considered to be one of our top section sergeants. I heard that he was eventually elected to public office and became a leader in his community. And I'm fairly certain he never tackled another member of the New England Patriots.

Unfinished Race

The United States military was formally integrated in 1948, but race relations in uniform are still as complicated as they are in American society. Because our nation's military is composed of young men and women who come from the farms, villages, and cities that make up this country they bring with them many of the prejudices, misconceptions, and half-truths about other cultures that are often found in our city streets and country roads. After all, any nation's military force is a manifestation of the society it protects.

The United States Army has long prided itself on a tradition of diversity from the Civil War on. The Army celebrates the proud legacy of African Americans who fought valiantly in the 54th Massachusetts Regiment, the famed Buffalo Soldiers, the brave Harlem Hell Fighters, and the courageous drivers of the Red Ball Express who made Patton's thrust into Hitler's Germany possible. Even the celebrated Tuskegee Airmen were technically members of the Army Air Corps. Countless soldiers of color performed heroic actions under fire. Some were recognized for their bravery, many were ignored.

When I reported to Fort Bragg for ROTC Advanced Camp in the late 1970s we were assigned bunks and lockers alphabetically in a World War II vintage wooden barracks. Along the length of the open floor bunks were stacked two-high on either side. Wall lockers in which were stored all gear and uniforms stood between each pair of bunks.

I quickly made the acquaintance of my bunk mate. Big Hank was a slow-talking, good humored, six and a half foot tall, African American guy from Georgia. He quickly dubbed me "Li'l Smith" and we gradually became friends. In typical Army fashion, I was assigned to the top bunk while he squeezed into the lower one. We dared not swap places or risk confusion and consequences.

I knew no one in our platoon. There were a few guys from other colleges in Massachusetts, but the cadets from my ROTC unit seemed to be scattered among many platoons at Fort Bragg. Although a few cadets seemed to know each other, most of us were strangers and so connections were actually much easier to make with one another because there were no existing groups. Social connections quickly reached beyond the barriers of region, race, or religion.

The platoon was made up of about forty young men and women. (The women were housed in a separate barracks.) We were all from east of the Mississippi because another ROTC Advanced Camp program was located in Kansas for cadets from the West. Nearly half of our platoon were young adults of color, mainly African American, and there were also a half dozen Latino cadets as well.

I don't recall any race-related friction during most of the training period. If anyone harbored racial prejudice they certainly had to keep it to themselves because our drill instructor was an iron-fisted Caucasian sergeant first class and our company commander was a ramrod-straight, somewhat aloof, African American captain. I don't think any of us particularly desired any individual attention from either one of them.

As the training period intensified we bonded together to help each other meet ever more demanding training tasks. No one cared if the cadet sharing his or her canteen on a ninety-degree day was black, blue, yellow, or pink. You were simply grateful for the cool water. It didn't matter where the cadet came from who was digging the other side of the foxhole as long as he or she could help get you down to armpit depth quickly. When you were dead tired on the obstacle course and a hand was extended to pull you up over the ten-foot wall, you never checked to see what color it was.

We were learning one of the most important lessons of military training: Teamwork is power—Go it alone and you fail. The mantra that was repeated over and over was, "Cooperate and Graduate!" Race, religion, gender, height, color, accent, native language, blood type, or all the other things that we choose to divide us didn't matter a bit as we struggled, sweated, and squirmed through all the challenges that confronted us during that long, hot summer.

At night while we squared away our uniforms and equipment, though, I remember an odd, allegedly comic routine between two cadets.

A Caucasian cadet, an extroverted red-haired guy from the Virginia Military Institute, would suddenly bellow in an exaggerated Southern accent, "Oh goodness, my boots are soiled and need a good shine. Where's my boy?" A short African American cadet would pantomime surprise, and then respond with wide eyes, "Here I is, Massa. Where 'dem boots of yours? I get them nice and shiny for you."

The two of them would play back and forth, leading to a chase through the barracks until they clapped each other on the back, each laughing in a seemingly good-natured way.

This scene was repeated often and I'm sure I wasn't alone as I silently cringed every time I watched this charade. Although I guess I could be accused of being an enabling bystander, I just assumed that joking about racial stereotypes was an accepted manifestation of Southern culture.

When we reached the final week of training we completed a lengthy peer rating questionnaire in which we scored the members of the platoon on their leadership qualities. Apparently this was an important aspect of a cadet's final grade for Advanced Camp that would then be used to allocate scholarship funds, award Regular Army commissions, and even assign branches, like Infantry, Quartermaster, Artillery, etc. It was a big deal for cadets who aimed to get into specialized training programs, like aviation or law school. It was also important for those who aspired to make the Army their career. As for me, I couldn't have cared less.

Soon after the peer rating questionnaire was completed, a subtle change came over the platoon. One night, the red-haired cadet from VMI called out in his "Massa" voice, but the response wasn't what he expected. "I'm not your boy, pal," his former playmate responded with a bitter edge. "You can shine your own damn boots."

On the night before graduation I walked into the dining facility, loaded up my tray with food, and looked around for someone to sit with. I always enjoyed eating with Big Hank because he was something of a Southern cuisine gourmet. He had introduced me to the proper seasoning of grits, the wonders of catfish, and he even coaxed me into eating fried okra. Ordinarily a man of few words, when it came to food, Hank could become almost lyrical in his descriptions.

As I scanned the tables I spotted Hank in a far corner. I sat down at the table with my bunkmate and two or three African American cadets from another platoon. I tried to strike up a conversation but was met with stony silence. If I had been more perceptive I would have noticed a pained, awkward expression on Hank 's face that should have warned me that I wasn't welcome. After several minutes, I got the hint and moved to another table, but I was perplexed by the chilly reception that would have been unthinkable earlier in our training cycle. Because the other cadets didn't know me well enough to dislike me, I have to believe that I was unwelcome at the table because of my skin tone.

Advanced Camp ended and, among many other things, I learned that harmonious race relations can be a fragile thing that could be easily shattered like a pane of glass at any time.

Years later I attended a two-week course for Transportation Corps officers at Fort Eustis, Virginia. Because we were only going to be on base for a short time period, all the officers in the course were housed in a rickety two-story wooden barracks, just like the one at ROTC Advanced Camp.

This time the occupants of the barracks were free to choose their bunks. I stepped into the first floor, which was prime real estate because it housed fewer bunks, which meant fewer customers for the showers and latrine. Also, there were no stairs to lug gear up and down. However, I quickly noticed the twang of country music blaring from someone's boombox and I spotted several pairs of cowboy boots and ten gallon hats. No, this Yankee wasn't going to be welcome on the first floor.

I climbed the stairs and zeroed in on the next desirable location. There was one four-bunk room at the head of the stairs that offered the luxury of some enhanced privacy and quiet. I stuck my head in the doorway and interrupted two officers who were conversing in Spanish. They greeted me cordially in English, but I decided to move on. My rudimentary Spanish language skills would never enable me to keep up.

Now I surveyed the long row of bunk beds that ran the length of the building. There were a dozen other officers making up their bunks or stowing their gear. I observed that the officers on the left side of the floor were African American and the occupants of the right side were Caucasian. Without giving it a second thought, I tossed my duffel bag on a lower bunk on the right side as I introduced myself to a round-faced, friendly white guy from Chicago.

Later that evening we reported to the classroom building for a one-hour briefing about class schedules, administrative details, and what was expected of us. After the briefing we were free for the rest of the night. Several of us brought some pizzas and cases of beer up onto the second floor of the barracks and we had a sort of block party between the two rows of bunks. Even the good ole' boys from the first floor came up. Once the beer flowed everyone mingled: Southern, Northern, Western, black, white, Latino. We were all Army officers with a lot more in common than any differences that might be noticed on the surface. It soon became apparent that the Army is a surprisingly small family and it was common to hear conversations like: "Oh my God, I was stationed in Korea at the same time. Where exactly were you posted?" "You must have known my best friend when you were assigned to the 101st. His name is ---" "I can't believe it. We were in the same Air Assault course. I remember you now."

As the evening wore on, several of us who were residents of the second floor sheepishly discussed the racial demarcation line of bunk choices. We all agreed that it was foolish that educated, mature adults who share a common profession had chosen to segregate themselves on different sides of the barracks. There was common consensus that we were ashamed of ourselves.

As I later thought about this incident I sadly concluded that our natural tendency is to band together with those who look like us, particularly in uncertain, novel situations. This tendency to cling to our own is also motivated by our fear of those who aren't like us and fueled by negative stereotypes that we might half believe are true.

Our group of intelligent, experienced Army officers had unwittingly recreated the segregation and insularity that plague our communities and serve as the foundation of polarization, inequality, and conflict. The glimmer of hope was that, once we communicated and made connections with those different from us (albeit lubricated by a few beers) we recognized that we shared common experiences, outlooks, and values. In fact, after our rocky start, I made some good friends during the next two weeks.

When it came time for me to be promoted to major, I was fortunate to be assigned as the commander of the 26th Personnel Service Company. Initially I thought that being assigned to an administrative company was some sort of punishment, but this unit was truly remarkable. The company was made up of 145 soldiers who were organized in small teams that facilitated the promotions, enlistments, retirements, evaluations, and all the bureaucratic paperwork which drove the 6,000-person Massachusetts Army National Guard. They were the most highly educated, intelligent, dedicated soldiers with whom I ever served.

Upon my arrival in the company, the unit clerk asked to review my Personnel Qualification Record with me. We quickly verified my social security number, enlistment date, spouse's name, and all the other little details in my file. When we came to my level of highest education, he said, "I see from the code on the form that you have a bachelor's degree."

"Oh, no that's incorrect. I have a master's degree in counseling psychology," I responded with more than a little pride. "We'll have to correct the error."

"Yes, Sir, we'll get that changed right away," he said as he repeated the correct code for a master's degree.

"That's pretty good, Specialist, you actually know the codes for education levels?" I responded with what I thought was a compliment.

"Well, Sir, I know the code for a master's degree. I have two of them," he said with a smile as he walked away.

I had been forewarned that this company was not your ordinary military unit. I learned precious little about personnel administration, other than what soldiers patiently explained to me. Nevertheless, the people in this company treated me like royalty and I will always consider them to be some of the finest soldiers in the Army.

Almost half of the personnel in the company were soldiers of color and half were Caucasian. Women comprised nearly half of the ranks as well as several of the key officer assignments. The previous commander, Major Cheryl Poppe, was an excellent leader and highly regarded officer who was moving up into state headquarters. (Cheryl was so widely respected that later she was appointed to be the Massachusetts Secretary of Veterans' Services.)

Half of the unit's sergeants were also leaders of color and half of the NCO's were Caucasian. The company enjoyed very high morale and esprit de corps. The sergeants were presided over by First Sergeant Jim Spillane, a remarkable philosopher-soldier who possessed exceptional intuition, a biting wit, and an iron will. The soldiers nicknamed him, "The Monsignor," because his studious, eloquent manner was reminiscent of a wizened parish priest.

The Monsignor, who knew every soldier in the company, tolerated no encroachment of behavior that even suggested sexual discrimination or racial prejudice. I think he realized that, if a hint of bigotry or sexual harassment were allowed, it could easily ignite a wildfire that would destroy the effectiveness of the company. He kept a careful eye out for any potential friction or sexual conflict and he held his sergeants accountable as well.

When I assumed command of the company I was greeted by the unit's executive officer, a good natured African American captain. From what I observed, this captain was well-liked, even beloved, by the troops. I detected that if the soldiers had their way he would have been the next commander and not some outsider Irish-American Quartermaster officer who knew nothing about personnel actions. When I asked him directly about his future, he explained that he was planning to retire within a few months because of chronic health issues. Nevertheless, he offered to help orient me to the company and support me as I assumed command. He not only guided me in my first few decisions, but I suspect he also served as a much needed cheerleader behind my back reassuring skeptical soldiers that I was going to be good for the company.

In the few months that we spent together, the captain was my adviser and guide as well as my coach. In the civilian world he was a diversity trainer for a large corporation and he gave me the full benefit of his considerable expertise.

I recall an evening when the captain and I were talking informally with a half dozen soldiers. We walked away and as soon as we were out of earshot from the soldiers, he said, "Do you realize that you addressed many of the white soldiers by their first names, but you called most of the black soldiers by their ranks and last names?"

"Really?" I replied somewhat embarrassed. "I didn't even notice that I was doing it."

"They did," he replied gently.

One morning we finished breakfast and walked out of the dining facility together. "Did you see anything odd about the KP crew today?" the captain asked.

"No, I didn't notice anything unusual," I replied.

"Everyone scrubbing pans and mopping floors was a soldier of color," he observed.

"I'm sure it was fair. It's just the way the duty roster fell today," I responded somewhat defensively.

"That's not the point," he said emphatically. "If you're new to the unit, or a visitor, or someone who doesn't understand that duties rotate, what conclusion would you draw?" I nodded, suddenly seeing the problem. "I'm sure the Monsignor's duty roster is fair," he continued, "but you don't get a chance to explain things once someone has formed an impression."

In the short time we were together the captain was an effective coach who expanded my previously limited awareness of racial and cultural issues. Most importantly he did it with gentle understanding, without criticism, judgment, or blame. I am forever in his debt.

Only one complaint of racial discrimination was brought to my attention during my time with the unit. An African American soldier who was new to the company had a conflict with his squad leader when he was directed to dig a foxhole during one of our rare tactical training exercises. The soldier felt that he had been singled out because of his race and he approached me with a request to file a formal racial discrimination complaint. When I informed the Monsignor about the request, I know he was irritated that the soldier had somehow done an end run around him, but he also understood that I couldn't refuse to hear the soldier's complaint. Accordingly I sent word to the soldier that I would meet with him in the headquarters tent at 3:00 that afternoon. In the meantime I consulted the latest regulations regarding racial discrimination grievances.

When the soldier arrived I was somewhat surprised that he was flanked by two senior African American sergeants, but he was welcome to have others present for support. I was prepared with the racial discrimination regulation on the table as I invited the soldier to tell me about his concerns.

"I want to withdraw my complaint, Major," he stammered. "I think the situation is resolved." I was puzzled and I noticed that the two sergeants struggled to suppress a smile. Then one of them nudged the soldier. "I also want to apologize for taking up your time," he added. "I know you must have other more important things to deal with." I assured him that nothing could be more important than fair treatment for soldiers in the company and told him that I was pleased that the situation was resolved. Then everyone went back to work.

Later that evening, I asked the Monsignor why the soldier's complaint was withdrawn. "It was really just a simple misunderstanding, Sir," he said somewhat mysteriously. "I wouldn't give it a second thought if I were you."

But I did give it a second thought. What I concluded was that the African American senior NCO had schooled the new soldier about how serious it was to issue a race relations complaint. They probably informed him that they had fought too hard to give the racial grievance process the importance it deserved and they weren't going to have it tossed away on trivial matters. I also suspect that the Monsignor or another Caucasian sergeant had done some nose-to-nose counseling with the section sergeant who may not have been as sensitive to the way he handed out manual labor tasks as he could have been.

But the company's proud legacy of cultural diversity was to be tested in an unexpected way. In late June 1994 America's attention was riveted on the mysterious murder of O.J. Simpson's estranged wife and a companion. Suspicion focused on the former football star and actor whom the media all but convicted of the murders, although the evidence was certainly contradictory and Simpson denied any role in the killings.

During this time the 26th Personnel Service Company was in the woods conducting tactical training on common soldier skills, a somewhat rare event for the unit. When we returned to the rear area on 17 June, officers and sergeants were billeted in small apartments that were designed to house military families during a mobilization. Each apartment contained three bedrooms that shared a kitchenette and living room with a television. We were living large indeed.

After a week in the forest training the company was in a festive mood as we all looked forward to cold beer, hot showers, and clean sheets. As officers and NCOs finished up their duties, they cracked open their beverages of choice and clustered around televisions in the common areas to catch up on the news or watch the NBA basketball championship game.

However every television network carried live coverage of what has become known as the "slow-speed chase." A warrant was issued for the arrest of O.J. Simpson but, rather than surrender to authorities, he and a friend led police on a low-speed pursuit of their white Ford Bronco SUV along the highways near Los Angeles. It was estimated that 95 million viewers watched the coverage.[9]

Already in high spirits and perhaps lubricated by a bit of alcohol, many white officers and sergeants regarded the event as high comedy. As they hurled insults at O.J. Simpson and called out caustic comments, I noticed that the television viewing audience in the apartment in which we initially gathered had become segregated.

In the course of making my rounds and checking in with the

company's leaders, I stepped into another apartment where African American officers and sergeants gathered to watch the events. Here the group watched the television with stony silence as they sipped their beers or cold drinks. There was no room for laughter or levity as they watched white America laugh at one more black man's trouble with the law.

In the morning any talk about the O.J. Simpson slow chase and murder investigation was taboo in the company. No one imposed a gag order, but everyone understood that any discussion of the murder might not end well. Thoughtful soldiers wondered how we could all see this event so differently when viewed from the position of our racial orientation. Many of us who are Caucasian were convinced of Simpson's guilt and questioned how our colleagues of color could believe that he was innocent. But we trusted their intelligence and integrity enough to know that there was something we were missing in the analysis of events. Perhaps we now know that people of color, with good reason, hold less trust in the fairness of the legal system than Caucasians, who believe in the law's impartiality.

I can't leave the topic of race in the military without discussing another event, which is far more representative of the way most soldiers regard one another. A legendary chief warrant officer, John Murray, was celebrating his last annual training at Fort Drum, New York. Mr. Murray had served for more than forty years, could fix any vehicle in the Army inventory, and had taught many of us how to drive a military truck. In short, he was a beloved and respected elder.

The sergeants in our battalion planned a retirement party at his favorite bar just outside of post, Hillbilly Heaven. When I arrived at this sprawling one-story cabin, the country western music was twanging away and the walls were thumping. As I neared the door I was joined by two of our African American senior NCO, who were in good spirits as they looked forward to honoring Mr. Murray.

The first thing we spotted when we entered the dim bar was a massive Confederate flag draped across one wall. I noticed that the bar's regular male and female patrons were also joining us for Mr. Murray's party. They were decked out in cowboy gear as they tapped their feet to the country music. There wasn't a person of color in the place. The two African American sergeants glanced at each other with worried looks. Then one of them turned to me and said, "This doesn't look like our kind of place, Sir. I don't think we're going to stick around."

Just then, John Murray, the guest of honor, spotted them heading for the door. I can clearly picture him standing in the front of the dance hall wearing a foolish blue cap with a ponytail down the back that someone gave him. He hoisted a can of Budweiser, rose up to his six foot height and bellowed, "If all of my friends aren't welcome here then none of us are staying!"

Suddenly the two reluctant sergeants were cheerfully escorted to the bar where cold beers were thrust into their hands. The rest of the night was a blur of speeches, gag gifts, and lots of beer. But I have a vivid memory of one of the African American sergeants laughing and smiling as he enjoyed a lesson in cowboy dancing from one of the local ladies.

The Army may have a complicated past and a fragile grasp on issues of race, diversity, and equal opportunity. Although it's an institution that shares the strengths and limitations of the society it defends, the Army has worked harder at stamping out discrimination than most American institutions can claim.

In the end, though, the greatest weapon the Army has in its arsenal to combat bigotry is the fierce loyalty that soldiers feel for their teammates, their brothers and sisters.

Limbo and Redemption

Company command in general and command of the 26th Personnel Service Company specifically was the best job in the Army. I distinctly remember the last field training exercise I spent with the company. They presented me with a handsome plaque and thanked me for my leadership by kneeling in unison before me, bowing to the ground, and chanting, "We're not worthy." I was tremendously embarrassed by this undeserved demonstration of gratitude, but I can assure you I was secretly flattered and deeply touched.

But all good things must come to an end and so, with little warning, the 26th Personnel Service Company was dismembered or disbanded, and all the personnel were reassigned to the detachments into which the company was splintered. That is, all the personnel were reassigned except for one major who was no longer needed to command a company that no longer existed. I was out of a job, in limbo.

After nearly eight years of company command in two different units it was time to move on. To tell the truth, though, I would have been pleased to serve as a company commander for the next twenty years, even if it meant taking a bust in rank back to captain.

Company command is the most fulfilling job in the Army when it's done right because it allows a commander to lead personally through face-to-face contact with people who are part of a large family. It's as close to parenthood as anything in the military could ever be. I don't mean to suggest that a commander acts as a parent to soldiers, but I almost shared the same sense of responsibility, pride, trust, loyalty, and affection—almost love—with soldiers that I felt for my own children. A good commander knows every member of the family and understands their strengths, weaknesses, and challenges. But command is a sword that cuts both ways—commanders may enjoy the privileges and deference that come with the title, but they are also responsible for building the power of the organization, maintaining its health, and caring for the welfare of every member of the organizational family. Command can be a heavy rucksack for some or it can be a labor of love filled with satisfaction and accomplishment. In my case, I found great reward, and even a good measure of joy, in humping the burden of command.

Later in my career as a senior officer I was always surprised and disappointed when a captain approached me and asked, "What's my next assignment, Sir? I've been a company commander for almost two years and I'm looking forward to the next step in my career." Although all officers make great contributions to the smooth execution of any operation, there's nothing like the leadership experience of company command. Any officer who wants to leave command quickly just doesn't get it.

Although I had actively dodged taking on the responsibility of company command in my early years, I eventually realized that the role of commander fit me like a well-tailored suit of clothes. There were no other roles in my life in which I felt so comfortable or so fulfilled. Command was a powerful drug to which I had become addicted. So, I was a commander without a job. Where would I be assigned?

I was briefly transferred to become the executive officer of the 26th Finance Battalion, a highly specialized unit made up of accountants and finance professionals. If I knew very little about personnel administration, I knew even less about Army finance. Economic and career disaster were narrowly averted one day when I received a phone call from Lieutenant Colonel Manny Constantine, someone I had met only once or twice, who asked, "Smitty, I'm forming a new Quartermaster Battalion. How would you like to be the operations officer?" Seconds later I was clearing out my desk. The entire Finance Battalion must have breathed a collective sigh of relief as I drove out of the parking lot.

Lt. Col. Constantine and I were the only two members of the 101st Quartermaster Battalion during our first two-week annual training period. Manny Constantine was a unique leader. He chomped on an ever-present unlit cigar, although he almost always maintained a gentlemanly bearing. He was a bundle of energy and maintained a cheerful, optimistic outlook. I once asked him if he ever lit his cigar. His only response was, "Smitty, you don't want to be anywhere nearby if I light this thing." Fortunately he never asked me for a match.

The mammoth task that lay ahead was forming and training a 600-person battalion with several million dollars worth of complex equipment. The unit was configured to purify, store, and manage a collapsible pipeline through which millions of gallons of drinking water would flow. We went to work during those first two weeks recruiting talented officers and sergeants, sketching out training plans, and making arrangements for equipment acquisition and storage.

I soon learned that Lt. Col. Constantine had little interest in learning much about the mechanics of water purification, storage, and transfer. His expertise was finance, accounting, and administration—he had no intention of becoming a water engineer. However he taught me several important lessons about senior leadership. First, he immersed himself in the process of recruiting smart, energetic junior officers and sergeants. In most cases he personally interviewed junior leaders and directly invited them to join us. He understood that he didn't need to develop technical or tactical expertise if he hired good people who could quickly learn.

Second, he was invariably enthusiastic, upbeat, and energetic to the point that soldiers tended to good-naturedly mock him behind his back. He frequently exclaimed, "It looks like another win-win for us." It took me a while to understand, but what he was doing was reinforcing a message that the key to our success was forming successful partnerships. Another one of his favorite sayings was, "You know how to eat an elephant, don't you? One bite at a time." Again, people rolled their eyes when he repeated it, but he was effectively reinforcing the message that he was looking for incremental progress, not expecting dramatic accomplishments.

Third, and most important, was something I learned when I completed the first major task he gave me. Shortly after our two-week annual training Lt. Col. Constantine called me into his office. "Smitty, can you get away from your civilian job for four days to go on a little trip?" he asked. I nodded tentatively. He had my interest.

"I want you to take a government sedan and drive down to the Quartermaster School at Fort Lee, Virginia," he explained.

"What do you want me to do when I get there?" I asked.

He leaned forward over his desk. "I want you to find out everything you can about the water business."

"Can you be more specific, Sir?" I was puzzled.

"Not really," he continued. "Think of it as a fishing expedition. I'll get you a car and cover your meals and lodging. I want you to collect manuals, talk to experts, and get all the information you can gather about the technical aspects of our battalion."

Soon I was on my way in an almost-new government sedan. After a long but leisurely drive I arrived at Fort Lee. Lt. Col. Constantine was as good as his word and I was billeted in officer's quarters that were as comfortable as any four star hotel. In the morning I met with the Chief of Fluid Logistics Training, a fellow major, and peppered him with technical questions. After about a half hour he finally came clean.

"Look, Major, I have to be honest with you," he said. "This is a new assignment for me and I'm just getting my feet wet, so to speak. My experience is mainly with fuel operations, so a lot of this stuff is really foreign to me." My disappointment must have been apparent. "But I'll see if I can help you out," he continued. "There's this retired sergeant major who knows everything there is to know about water operations. But don't get your hopes up too high. People say that he's a bit difficult, so I don't know if he'll even talk to you. Anyway, I'll call over there and see if I can get an appointment to see him."

We were in luck and received an audience with the water operations guru after lunch. I drove around the base sightseeing and shopped at the Post Exchange until the appointed hour arrived. But I knew if this interview didn't work out, I might as well turn around and drive home. As we entered the office area, it was like arriving for an audience with the Wizard of Oz. Everyone we met referred to our host in hushed tones. Soon I felt like I was about to speak with Picasso about painting, Tom Brady about passing, or the Pope about the Bible. And when it came to Army water operations, the man I was about to meet was in a comparable league.

Future Army Quartermaster Hall of Famer, John C. Marigliano sat at his desk as we were ushered into his office. He eyed the two of us like he was calculating target range as we sat across from him. He was a solid middle-aged man wearing a shirt and tie and black rimmed glasses. Although dressed as a civilian, he had a commanding military presence with his square chin thrust out and a squinting, steely-eyed gaze that penetrated right through the faint of heart. The other major introduced himself and Mr. Marigliano grunted as if to say, "I know you." The major sort of shriveled in his chair.

Then Marigliano fixed his laser look on me. "Who are you?" he bellowed. I quickly explained that I was the operations officer of a brand new water supply battalion in Massachusetts and we didn't know the first thing about water operations. I was looking for any help I could get to begin to learn the technical aspects of the water business. I basically pleaded complete ignorance, which wasn't far from the truth. But I didn't grovel before Mr. Marigliano because I figured I had nothing to lose if he threw me out of the office.

The water guru peered at me. "A new water supply battalion in Massachusetts, you say?" I'm from New York myself. Red Sox fan? I nodded and smiled. "Well I won't hold it against you," he continued. "What do you want to know?"

I pulled out a list of questions I had drawn up and started to read them off. "Whoa, whoa, Mr. Red Sox," Marigliano put up his hands. "Those are complicated questions. How much time do you have?" I told him that I had two days. "Well, then, we better make the most of your time here," he said. "Meet me here tomorrow at 0900 sharp and we'll dig into your list of questions." As we rose to leave, I glanced at the other major who looked truly astonished.

Perhaps I was so pathetic that John Marigliano couldn't help feeling some pity for me, sort of like a scruffy wandering stray dog. Maybe he just liked a challenge. Over the next two days he patiently answered all my questions, introduced me to experts in specific phases of water operations, and loaded me down with all the manuals and technical references I could carry.

When I thanked him for all his help just before I headed back to Massachusetts, he said, "When you folks are setting up your training calendar for next year, give me a call. I'd love to have an excuse to travel up to Cape Cod for a good seafood dinner." I had made the best friend our new battalion could ever hope to have. In the next few months we spoke with John often. And, yes, when he visited the battalion, we drove him to the Cape for the best seafood dinner we could find.

Why do I tell this story? Because Lt. Col. Constantine taught me a valuable lesson about empowering subordinates during this mission. He didn't dictate my activities at Fort Lee. He didn't demand deliverables. Instead he gave me the resources I needed and a description of the end-state he wanted. Then he trusted my initiative, my judgment, and my savvy to produce results, and it paid off. That was Manny Constantine's genius—the battalion he commanded soon became one of the Army's premier water supply units, but I don't think he really knew which end of the hose the water came out of. Instead of technical expertise he had a remarkable knack for choosing people with energy, initiative and smarts. Then he had the wisdom to give them what they needed to get the job done and get out of their way. He was a highly successful commander who taught me important leadership lessons about trust, empowerment, and when to leave people alone.

One final word about John Marigliano—Army water units across the globe are invited to compete in a tough competition to see who is the fastest and most technically efficient. The winning team proudly receives the John C. Marigliano trophy. Several years after I first met John, the team from our own 101st Quartermaster Battalion, Massachusetts National Guard, captured John's trophy as the best water operations team in the U.S. Army. I couldn't have been prouder and I hope John was proud too.

Under Lt. Col. Constantine's positive leadership, the 101st Quartermaster Battalion (Water Supply) flourished and grew. We learned how to operate 3,000 gallon per hour reverse osmosis water purification units, called ROWPUs. They were massive trailers that could purify even sewer water into drinking water that was as pure as Dasani or Aquafina bottled water. We mastered the intricacies of laying out ten miles of pipeline in the Tactical Water Distribution System. More importantly we discovered the tricks required to retrieve the collapsible hose line and zigzag it back into the flaking crates. We solved the mysteries of operating pumps of all sizes. We learned the importance of placing 20,000 and 50,000 fabric tanks on exactly level ground when we watched one of our first bags roll away and pop which produced an instantaneous 20,000 gallon flood.

But perhaps our funkiest piece of equipment was the semi-trailer mounted fabric tank, or SMFT. Picture a huge canvas sausage holding 3,000 gallons of drinking water strapped down onto a 12-ton flatbed trailer. The SMFT had to be filled to at least two pounds per square inch pressure, at which point it became rigid and therefore safe to travel. However, once the seal was broken, the SMFT trailer couldn't be moved until it was empty because it rippled and oozed like a baggie full of jello. I once saw a half-empty SMFT roll over the side of its trailer like a lazy blob, pulling the trailer over onto its side with it. The problem with SMFT was that customers would want water for firefighting, to fill canteens, or to bring water to multiple sites. We'd have to explain that, once we filled the first canteen or squirted the first smoldering bush, the whole trailer couldn't be moved until all 3,000 gallons were emptied. Many of our customers thought we were bullshitting them, but our standard line was, "You can't have a drop of water unless you can use all 3,000 gallons."

We were proud of our skills and confident of our ability to tackle any mission. In fact, we were eager to show our stuff when the state of New Hampshire called us to respond to a water emergency in the town of Exeter. Apparently the town's water supply had become contaminated. Public safety and health officials feared that citizens would deplete the supply of bottled water quickly and wanted our water purification equipment on site ASAP. As our ROWPUs raced up the highway to Exeter, I could see the assistant drivers nervously thumbing through the operators' manuals. As I recall, we set up the ROWPUs by the water treatment ponds and began operations, but, by the time our samples were tested and approved by state health officials, the emergency was pretty much over. Still our operators fully enjoyed their billets in the stately Exeter Inn, one of the prettiest colonial buildings in New England. I don't know what the water operations equivalent for "first blood" might be, but whatever it is, our battalion had experienced it.

Two years went by and we matured as a unit. We deployed a team to Honduras where they supported a U.S. Army engineer unit that was building schools in the jungle. The town of Webster, Massachusetts, had a water crisis and called us to purify and distribute water. It was truly a pleasure for our ROWPU to pull water out of Webster Lake, whose formal name is Lake Chargoggagoggmanchauggagoggchaubunagungamaugg, which is the longest name in the English language (or so we were told). This time we dispensed ROWPU water to customers. We were glad when the emergency was over, but everyone was a little embarrassed when it was discovered that the cause of the contamination was an excess of Canadian goose shit in the water supply.

Lt. Col. Manny Constantine was eventually promoted and moved up to the very influential and powerful position of Chief of Staff for the Massachusetts National Guard. He was succeeded in command by Lt. Col. Ray Murphy, a competent, level-headed officer who led with a calm, measured authority that was respected by soldiers and officers alike. Lt. Col. Murphy was promoted to Colonel and assumed a high level staff position at state headquarters. Then it was time for Lt. Col. Chuck Maguire to become battalion commander after serving as executive officer, or second in command, for several years. Chuck and I had served together for many years and he was like an older brother to me. In fact, although he is a few inches shorter than me, I often referred to him as "my big brother," which made him smile. Chuck was an unflappable visionary who took an analytical, almost philosophical, approach to decision-making and command.

I was fortunate to serve under three capable commanders who placed the welfare of our battalion above their own personal or career concerns. Each of them taught me important lessons—Manny Constantine showed me the importance of trust and delegation, Ray Murphy gave me a good example of balance and perspective, and Chuck Maguire demonstrated how to make sound, logical decisions. And so, after four years of interviewing new soldiers, unpacking crates of new equipment, poring over operator's manuals, planning training schedules, and correcting our mistakes, I was honored and thrilled to become Commander of the 101st Quartermaster Battalion.

End of Innocence

The high school principal with whom I worked, called me into his office on a bright, sunny morning in the second week of a new school year. "Greg, you're not going to believe this. Take a look at this video," he said as he pointed to his computer screen.

"Wow, that's a hell of an accident," I said as we replayed the video of a jetliner colliding with one of the towers of the World Trade Center. Then it dawned on me, "Oh my God, isn't that where our secretary's son works?" "She was pretty shaken up, but Kevin just called his mom and I guess he's okay," he informed me. "We found someone to cover the main office while she's watching this on a TV in the library."

For a moment I was relieved that our beloved main office secretary knew that her son was all right. Kevin Szocik was well-known and well-liked in town. A former high school football star, he had recently graduated from Fordham University and was making a name for himself in the financial industry. Then the principal sat up in his chair and pointed to the computer screen. "Holy shit, a second plane just hit the second tower. They're saying this is a terrorist attack!"

What happened next is a blur. We instantly realized that Kevin, whose office was on the upper floors of the World Trade Center, was either dead or trapped in the burning skyscraper. But our shock and grief was overridden by the immediate concerns of how to communicate the news to teachers and then how they should deal with questions and reactions from students.

Whoever was answering the main office phones called out, "Greg, the National Guard is on the line." I heard the voice of a full-time lieutenant who was the ranking officer at the battalion armory on the other end of the line. "I've locked the gates to the armory, Sir. Then I've taken the initiative to issue weapons and we're calling the brigade to request ammunition."

I recall thinking, "all we'd need is someone getting shot to make this nightmare even worse.' I replied as calmly as I could, "Good job locking the gates, Lieutenant. Don't distribute ammo or take any other defensive measures until I get there. I'm on my way." I knew that anxiety, young lieutenants, and live ammunition can be a lethal mixture.

The principal assured me that he had the situation under control at the high school and wished me luck when I told him I needed to get to the armory. I raced down the highway on a perfect sunny September day when the breeze rustled maple leaves that were just starting to turn yellow and orange and I thought, "This can't be happening. I'll wake up and this will just all be a bad dream." But the frantic reports on the car radio forced me to accept the reality that our nation was under attack. Additionally I was aware that the terrorists had launched one of their attacks from nearby Logan Airport and had probably traveled near our armory. Were there accomplices still in the area? Were follow-on attacks coming?

When I reached the armory I quickly coordinated with our higher headquarters and we executed the force protection procedures with which we would live for the next several years. It was evening before all the procedures and duty rotations were in place. I received a call from my wife who told me that our daughter wanted to come home and asked if I could go get her.

Brig. Gen. Smith kneels before a marker in remembrance of Kevin Szocik, a victim of the World Trade Center bombings on September 11, 2001 (Project 351).

It was just the previous week before when we had dropped her off at her dorm in downtown Boston. Although she tried to hide it, she had been full of the excitement, anxiety, and fear that every freshman feels when they begin this great new adventure. Now I drove through nearly deserted streets in the center of Boston. When I arrived she was relieved to see me, but I could also see the confusion, fear, and worry in her eyes. Sadly a new age of war and violence always lurking under the surface was rising from the gloom and fear of this September night. None of us knew it, but it would shape our lives.

Our battalion was planning to send a detachment to the Middle East to purify water in support of Operation Bright Star, a joint U.S.-Egyptian military exercise. Troops were scheduled to mobilize on 12 September 2001. Fortunately the exercise was postponed, but it was only delayed by a few weeks.

More immediately, the battalion was tasked with providing security at the Wachusett Reservoir and Dam in Clinton, Massachusetts, as part of a statewide critical infrastructure protection mission. Because of the confusion of the time, initially we believed that our mission was to secure the entire Wachusett Reservoir, which covers 108 square miles, with a perimeter of 37 miles. We understood that the reservoir was a critical element in the drinking water supply for three million residents of eastern Massachusetts. If it became contaminated, disaster would follow for half the state's population. But for this herculean task we were authorized funding for only 12 personnel.

We soon analyzed the mission and, after consulting a few experts, realized that terrorists would need truckloads of poisonous chemicals to contaminate the 65 billion gallons of water in the reservoir. We were reasonably assured that periodic surveillance would detect dump trucks of cyanide being discharged into the water. The more vulnerable targets were the dam itself, a concrete structure that retained the reservoir's water above the city of Clinton. If the dam were compromised, the city would be flooded. In addition, there was an important filtration and pumping facility in the area that kept clean water moving to Boston.

And so the battalion began a 24/7 security mission that would last for years through blizzards, heat waves, and holidays. When I watched the first shift change as the team coming on duty counted out their twenty .223 caliber ball live rounds and clicked them into the magazines, the reality struck home that this wasn't just another war game—it was the real thing.

Soldiers volunteered to take guard duty when they could get away from their civilian jobs and sometimes we struggled to fill shifts. I asked the officers and senior NCO to step up and take a shift during holidays and most did so cheerfully. I remember my first Thanksgiving night on guard duty. My partner, a sergeant who was a little taken aback at having to spend the night with the battalion commander, showed me the ropes. We huddled by the heater in our HMMWV,[10] which was our only source of warmth on that frigid night. Every hour one of us patrolled the top of the dam, shining a bright floodlight on the walls to check for activity or suspicious packages. When it was my turn I often thought, "Isn't it the guard with the flashlight that gets killed first in every James Bond movie?"

I have to chuckle when I compare that Thanksgiving night with the last Christmas night shift I took two years later. Our command sergeant major and I spent a pleasant night inside a warm, comfortable construction trailer as a blizzard whirled around us. By the time the shift ended I had watched three full-length action movies on the VCR, eaten a full bag of microwave popcorn, and swallowed so much freshly brewed coffee that I was jittery. How we managed to go from sitting in tactical vehicles to watching movies in a mobile Taj Mahal, I'll never know.

I can't leave the story of the Wachusett Reservoir mission without discussing the citizens of the city we guarded. Clinton, Massachusetts, is a working class mill town with strong immigrant communities. Its citizens are patriotic, proud of their city, and maybe a little hard-nosed. Beginning in the first week, hot dinners were delivered to the troops on the dam every night. Community groups, like the Rotary or Elks, signed up for each week, and as far as I know, didn't miss a night regardless of the weather. School kids made cards for Veterans' Day to express their thanks. The local Dunkin' Donuts refused to accept payment from any soldier no matter how many donuts he or she ordered.

It was common for people to stop by the dam with cookies, brownies, or cupcakes at all hours of the day. One day near Halloween I was checking in with the security team when an elderly woman teetered over toward us. She wore an old flowered dress and looked to be at least eighty years old. There was something determined in her wobbling steps that warned me to be prepared for a confrontation.

"You in charge here?" she asked in a no-nonsense manner. "Yes, Ma'am."

She peered at me through her rimless glasses and thrust out a paper bag. "Baked these last night for you boys."

"Thank you, Ma'am," I stammered.

"No, thank you, Son," she said, then turned and hobbled away. The chocolate chip cookies were delicious, but when I thought about the difficulty she must have gone through to bake them and bring them to us, they were even more precious.

However, there were times during the Wachusett Reservoir security mission when tensions rose, particularly in the early days of the mission. From time to time there was suspicious activity near the banks of the reservoir that inevitably called for heightened security measures. But perhaps the most critical event took place when a mentally ill young man peeled off his clothing and attempted to wrestle an M16 away from one of our soldiers. In retrospect, the young man was attempting to goad the soldier into shooting him, a variation of "suicide by cop." The swift, level-headed reaction of Sergeant First Class Dan Sweeney and the other soldiers on duty held the man at bay until the Clinton police arrived to take him into custody. When I reviewed the incident

I was certain that, without Sgt. 1st Class Sweeney's control of the situation, the young man would have been shot and killed by National Guardsmen.

In the end, perhaps one of our NCO summed it up best when he responded to a young soldier who complained about the long drive from his home in Boston to Clinton. "If you were someplace else near Boston, they'd be charging you property tax for standing on the ground we're guarding," the sergeant said, "but here in Clinton they serve you a hot dinner, bring you brownies, and give you all the free donuts you can eat. What are you bitching about?"

Shortly after the ground assault phase of Operation Iraqi Freedom commenced in March 2003, our battalion was notified that one of our units was alerted for possible activation. The alerted unit was the 220th Quartermaster Detachment located in Plymouth, Massachusetts, within spitting distance of the Rock and the Mayflower. The unit, which was responsible for laying collapsible pipelines, was commanded by Sgt. 1st Class Dan Sweeney, the tough, experienced NCO who prevented bloodshed in the "suicide by police" situation in Clinton. Dan looked after his 20-person water distribution detachment like his own sons and daughters. His people loved him and trusted him, but they never dared to get on his bad side. It was said that Dan Sweeney was the closest thing our battalion had to John Wayne, and I don't believe that was an exaggeration.

I accompanied them to their pre-deployment personnel screening. The atmosphere was lighthearted—probably some of the soldiers didn't take the alert very seriously. After all, we had been alerted for deployment during Operation Desert Storm and nothing came of it. However, while the soldiers passed through the medical and records review stations, I received word that the unit's mobilization orders had just arrived at headquarters.

I informed Dan about the order and asked if he'd like to announce it to his troops. He thought for a moment and then asked me to break the news to his unit. The soldiers were still laughing and joking as they huddled around me. I told them how important their water mission was in the theater of operations. I told them how proud I was of them and how they responded to the alert. Then I announced that the mobilization order had been received and informed them of the date, which was two weeks away. I'll never forget how one side of the group erupted in cheers. The other side of the group, mainly female soldiers, choked back tears. Suddenly the mood turned serious, but in the end no one asked to be excused from the deployment.

When the results of the screening were given to Dan, one of his soldiers was flagged as "non-deployable" because of dental complications. This was to later become a major reason why many reservists were unable to deploy during the Global War on Terrorism. The soldier was informed that four of his teeth were badly decayed and needed treatment. He was so determined to deploy with his unit that he arranged to have all four teeth pulled on his own and had a dentist sign off that he met standards.

The 220th would travel by convoy to their mobilization station about 300 miles away on the date of their mobilization. Because of the long distance, the convoy start time was in the early morning. Although we trusted that soldiers would report on time, we also knew that parting with family members would be emotional and tough. I decided that the unit should "lock down" in their armory by 9:00 p.m. on the previous evening.

I stood by in the armory that evening mainly going over details with Dan. But I half watched the heartbreaking scenes as mothers quietly said goodbye to their children. Lovers and spouses hugged and kissed again and again wondering if they'd ever see each other again. Older fathers and mothers choked back tears as their young adult children, barely out of their teens, left for war. We ask much of our soldiers, but we also ask much of our loved ones and family members.

The next day was cold and cloudy. The sun never really appeared and the darkness turned to steel gray as duffel bags were tossed onto growling cargo trucks. The diesel smoke mixed with the sea air that rolled in from the bay. I forced myself to cheerfully joke with the soldiers and they played along, but we weren't fooling each other. Dan and I discussed the details of the convoy and he assured me that he'd call into battalion headquarters as soon as they arrived at the mobilization station.

Then he stuck out his hand and looked me in the eye. "We better get going, Sir, or else I'll miss my start time." Then he saluted and hoisted himself up into the passenger seat of the lead truck.

A lump rose in my throat when the soldiers piled into the cargo trucks. I returned salutes or waved as the drivers passed by one-by-one. I wanted so much to go with them, but Lieutenant Colonels don't command 20-person detachments. I followed the convoy in my car for a few miles, then turned onto the highway to go to work with a heavy heart. As I drove to my job at the high school I fought back the guilty feeling that I should be with them. Lingering questions nagged me—Would "Big Army" take good care of them? Were they prepared to do the mission in Iraq? Would they all come home safely?

Under Dan Sweeney's leadership, the 220th Quartermaster Team had a successful nine-month deployment in Iraq. They mainly performed security force duties, although some personnel were detailed for a water distribution mission. However they never even saw a Tactical Water Distribution System pipeline, which was their primary mission. They all returned safely to a heroes' welcome and were honored in the Plymouth

Thanksgiving Parade following their arrival back home. Best of all, they proudly presented me with a massive Iraqi flag that they had somehow appropriated from a government building, which became a highly prized artifact in our young battalion's collection of trophies.

As the 220th was returning from Iraq, we received an alert notification for the battalion's largest unit, the 125th Quartermaster Company. The 125th was a high speed company of roughly 160 soldiers who were tasked with operating a reservoir made up of multiple 50,000 gallon fabric tanks as well as 20 miles of pipeline. The company was commanded by an irascible, tough former Marine, Captain Steve Cullinane. Steve's excitability was tempered by his sense of humor and his soldiers loved him. As I have said before, the relationship between a company commander and a first sergeant is like a marriage with the partners complementing each other and filling in for the other's weaknesses. In perfect counterpoint, First Sergeant Dave Sims was even-tempered, diplomatic, and unflappable. Dave knew his soldiers well and nicely balanced quiet discipline with care and compassion. They were a great leadership team that motivated and inspired a strong, capable company.

The 125th was quickly mobilized for deployment to Iraq. Unlike the 220th, preparing a full company for deployment required some heavy lifting. Personnel were recruited from other units to fill out the ranks of the 125th and many items of equipment were transferred or swapped out. Finally on another cold, gray morning I shook hands with Steve and Dave. Then a lump rose in my throat as the long line of trucks growled and belched and headed down the road on the long journey to Fort Dix.

When a reserve unit is activated for federal service, it reports to the higher headquarters designated on the mobilization order. That meant that the 125th was no longer under the command and control of the 101st Quartermaster Battalion. Because the 125th didn't have a specific deployment date or mission, it reported to a training headquarters at Fort Dix that was responsible for many units.

During the next few weeks I heard from Steve often. The unit was crammed into overcrowded barracks as it attempted to meet training standards for deployment. Understandably the unit wanted to get on with their mission, reasoning that the sooner they deployed, the sooner they'd come home. At one point Steve reported that he had unofficially been told that they were scheduled for deployment within days, but he was short several hundred M-16 magazines that he urgently needed to meet his equipment checklist.

When I contacted our higher headquarters to request the magazines, a senior officer told me, "I can't help you." Then he added, "Face it, Lieutenant Colonel, that unit doesn't belong to you anymore." Biting my tongue, I thought, "If they don't belong to us now, they sure as hell won't belong to us when they get back from deployment and choose not to reenlist."

I stifled my anger, then thought for a moment. Then I picked up the phone and called our unit supply sergeants. My message to each one was the same, "You can't call yourself an Army supply sergeant if you can't scrounge up 50 magazines in the next 24 hours." Two days later a sergeant was on the way to Fort Dix with 250 magazines stacked in the trunk of a car.

In spite of the magazine relief mission, the 125th wasn't called for deployment and so they continued to participate in training with decreasing urgency. From time to time Steve called with the latest deployment rumor, but nothing ever came of it.

I drove down to Fort Dix and visited their company area. When I saw the barracks area I was appalled. Soldiers slept on cots in hallways and common areas as well as in the crowded bunks. Laundry hung out to dry in most windows and personal items were stacked in every corner. I didn't fault our sergeants, but I had never seen a barracks in such disarray. Dave explained that they were doing the best they could in overcrowded conditions. I registered my complaints about the unsatisfactory conditions up the command chain, but no one listened. After all, they didn't belong to me anymore.

After six months the 125th Quartermaster Company was demobilized. Apparently there was no need for them in Iraq. They quickly packed up at Fort Dix and limped home, but there was little joy in this homecoming.

We held a welcome home ceremony and presented medals and awards. I made an impassioned speech about how willingness to serve is as important as service itself. But, when I looked at the soldiers' eyes, I could see that they were looking over my head or away from me. They weren't buying it. While none of them wanted to go to war, they felt ashamed. How were they going to explain to their neighbors and co-workers that they were called to fight, but then the Army said, "Never mind?" Months of missed birthday parties, Little League games, dance recitals, anniversaries, as well as constant worry and anxiety were all for nothing. There was no way to sugarcoat the reality.

Steve and Dave did their best to restore morale in the unit, but it took years to rebuild morale and confidence in the 125th Quartermaster Company.

After four years of battalion command, I was notified that I was to be transferred to state headquarters. The battalion honored me by staging my special request for a sendoff. On the last Sunday afternoon of my command, we formed up in the street beside the armory wearing our PT

Lt. Col. Smith receives a framed replica of the battalion flag after relinquishing command of the 101st Quartermaster Battalion (Betsy Dillbeck).

uniforms. With the assistance of the local police we ran as a battalion through the streets. I had the honor of running out front with the battalion flag carried beside me as we clapped and sang until we arrived at the Elks Hall. Kegs of ice cold beer awaited our arrival and all were invited to freely (but not too freely) partake. Toasts and cheers were offered, handshakes and hugs were exchanged, and I bid farewell to my comrades, my battle buddies, my family.

Later as I cleaned out my desk I was filled with mixed emotions. On one hand I had the honor of building and then commanding one of the Army's premier water supply battalions. I served with some of the best soldiers in the Army and I had enjoyed the trust and respect of almost every soldier in the battalion, whether or not I deserved it. To say that I had made good friends would be a weak understatement—I had gained brothers and sisters.

But I couldn't help feeling a tinge of bitterness. Together we had built a tight, proficient military force that was capable of tackling any challenge we faced. However military planners in some cubicle at the Pentagon had dismembered our powerful force and thrown us piecemeal into the Global War on Terrorism—or in the case of the 125th had made us atrophy in limbo. I likened our force to a Minuteman's musket that was primed and loaded for one deadly shot. But instead of firing at the enemy, our gunpowder was allowed to get damp and useless.

An old saying came to mind as I shut off the lights in my office, "You can love the Army, but the Army will never love you back."

Family

She glared at me across the kitchen table. Her brown eyes flashed as she shouted, "This is all your fault." I had known my wife for more than twenty-five years and I had never seen her this frustrated, distressed, and angry. We sat in silence with our adult son, each wrestling with our own intense emotions.

After an awkward quiet lapse, she continued, "If you want to throw away your life, I guess that's your decision. But don't expect me to be happy about it."

We continued to sit without speaking until I whispered to our son, "I think we need to get going." He stiffly stood and picked up his bag. My wife stepped forward, reached up and hugged him hard. I could see the tears seeping out of the corners of her eyes. Partly out of pride and partly to spare him the pain, she would hold back the sobbing until after he was gone.

I knew her heart was breaking. She had always considered the Army as a cruel rival, the other woman who lured her men away from home where they belonged. Her father was a former Army sergeant who had served in the Pacific during World War II. Her older brother was a Vietnam combat veteran who had struggled with his demons for many years after his return. Her lover and then husband was drawn away for training, emergencies, and details while she was left alone with babies to care for, excuses to be made for his absence, and nagging worries that plagued her late at night. Some might assume that she would have made her peace, or at least established a truce, with the United States Army. They would be wrong.

My son and I got into the car and drove to the end of the street. I pulled over to the side of the road. "Your mother is pretty upset," I said quietly. He nodded.

"I can take a right and drive you back to college," I said. "Or else, I can go left and take you to MEPS. It's your decision." (MEPS is the acronym for Military Entrance Processing Station.) Without any hesitation, he said quietly, "Turn left, Dad."

We tried to talk about other things on the long drive to MEPS. From time to time, though, I had to ask if he had enough money, if he was sure he had everything on the packing list, if he knew where to report when we arrived at MEPS.

I'm the proud father of two strong sons and a beautiful daughter. Our daughter and youngest son never showed more than a passing interest in military matters. But our middle son was different. As a toddler he would crawl into my duffel bag when I came home. I can picture him struggling to hold his head up as he tried on my helmet. His favorite toys were always little green plastic soldiers, tanks, and G.I. Joe dolls. I recognized the signs early on. He was going to be a soldier. He had to do it.

It was no surprise when he signed up for Army ROTC within his first few days at college. But, when he took the physical prior to signing his contract, he was medically disqualified because of a benign childhood health problem. When he received the news, he called me immediately. He was heartbroken.

I drove up to college the next day and we went to a local tavern. My ordinarily unflappable son vented his deep disappointment. He told me that serving as an Army officer was the only constant goal he had in life. As he talked, the tears began to seep out of his eyes and he quickly wiped them away. I hadn't seen him cry since he was five after a bee stung him.

I know he wanted me to tell him that I'd intervene with the medical board for him. As a colonel, I probably could have asked one of our military doctors to help. But, if my son was going to be a soldier, he couldn't stand in my shadow. He had to do it on his own. Instead I told him that some things in life just weren't meant to be. If he was determined to serve, he could apply to the Border Patrol, Federal Marshalls, or the FBI. Certainly their medical standards would be different. He dried his eyes and nodded, but he had other ideas.

Little did I know it, but a few weeks later he marched himself into the recruiting office of the Vermont National Guard. Somehow his recruiter was able to get a medical waiver for him to enlist and now he was on his way to basic training at Fort Benning. I pulled our car into the parking lot at MEPS. "Do you want me to come in with you?" I asked. "No, Dad."

We got out of the car. I reached out and shook his hand. "Be careful and take care of yourself, Nick." I wanted to hug him, but somehow I knew it would be too much for both of us. "Okay, Dad." He quickly shook my hand and turned toward the building. I knew he was nervous and eager to get on with this adventure. I think he also realized that, if he lingered, we both would melt.

I watched him walk away. Then he turned around and waved. Suddenly he wasn't a six-foot young man, he was my little boy again with a band-aid on his knee clutching a battered G.I. Joe. I got back into the car just as the tears began to flow down my face.

This was the kid who couldn't keep two socks matched. How would he keep track of an M-4 rifle? He was scared of heights. What would happen to him on a repelling tower? Suddenly I remembered the confusion, yelling, and total panic of my first day in the military and I realized that my little boy was now facing his first day of mayhem. I was certain he wouldn't survive.

Maybe the tears rained down because I worried that he wouldn't make it through basic training. Maybe I cried because I feared for his safety. But perhaps I wept because I knew that the baby I cradled in my arms, the little boy I taught to catch a football, the teenager I showed how to shave—the human being for whom I would do anything, was now on his own. He was a man.

I sobbed for the better part of a half hour. Something I hadn't done in decades. As I drove home I was ashamed of my own hypocrisy. How could I lead young men and women soldiers and yet weep like a baby when my own son joined up.

Weeks went by. Each day I half expected a phone call telling me to come pick him up, that he had washed out of basic training. But the call never came. Instead I drove through the gates of Fort Benning for Family Day on the eve of his graduation from basic training. As I walked into the company area, I passed a cluster of privates sporting stiff new berets on their shaved heads. One of the privates, a tall, skinny guy wearing square brown Army issue glasses, waved and shouted, "Hey, Dad!" Basic training had transformed my son and I didn't even recognize him.

Lt. Col. Smith and his teenage son, Nicholas, listen to speakers during a Memorial Day ceremony. Nicholas would later become a captain in the Vermont Army National Guard (author's collection).

The next day I watched with pride as my son marched across the parade field with his platoon. After graduation was over he climbed into the car and shed most of his uniform. Following a stop at McDonald's he regaled me with funny stories about the last ten weeks. We laughed and enjoyed each other for the entire three-day trip home. There were no more tears. My son was proud of himself. He was happy. He was a soldier. My son was now a member of my other family.

*   *   *

The men in black suits silently adjusted the white covering on the casket in front of the altar and positioned the candles just so. A few mourners filed into the pews, careful not to make any noise. Although it was one of the grandest houses of worship in the city, the cathedral seemed like a dim, chilly cavern as preparations were made for the morning's funeral.

Sergeant Arthur "Hollywood" Frederick sat in one of the back pews and stared straight ahead. It was strange to see him in his new dark suit, white shirt, and tie. I had never seen him wearing anything but camouflage, or maybe his dress green uniform.

Just days before, "Hollywood" had been on a forward operating base in the heat and dust of Iraq. Battalion headquarters received word that his mother had suddenly passed away and the machinery of the Army, with assistance from the Red Cross, carried the sad news to Hollywood and brought him home for the funeral as quickly as it could.

I had known Hollywood for many years and was aware that he was his widowed mother's only child. I would have reached out to him anyway, but now, as battalion commander, it was my duty to officially represent Hollywood's military family at his mother's funeral. With the awkwardness that most of us feel at funerals, I adjusted my dress uniform and walked up to the pew in which he was sitting.

"Hollywood, I'm so sorry to hear…," I said as I extended my hand. He gripped my hand, stood up, towering over me. "Hey, Sir, I was hoping you'd come," he said, a warm smile lit up his face.

"Are you okay" I stammered. "I mean do you have everything you need?" "Oh yeah," he replied, "Big Army's actually been really good to me. They got me here a lot quicker than I thought. The only thing I couldn't get was all the parts of my dress uniform, so I had to go out and buy this silly suit."

"You look great… Do you have enough money and a place to stay and all that?" I asked.

"My cousin is putting me up while I'm home and Mom was a good saver, so I've got no worries about money … the folks are gonna be lost until I get back. Nobody else on the whole base knows how to run the 10K forklift. Can you imagine that, Colonel—all those Marines and Air Force guys and nobody can drive a forklift?" He shook his head.

By now other soldiers from the battalion had arrived, and, either individually, or in small groups, they came over to Hollywood to awkwardly offer their sympathies. He greeted them all graciously and sincerely thanked them for coming.

Although only a few people outside of the battalion approached Hollywood, I noticed that the pews in the cathedral were filling up with dark-clad members of the community. "Well, I better go take a seat with the other soldiers," I said, turning toward the far corner of the church. Hollywood gently grabbed my arm. "Can you just sit here with me, Sir?" he asked in a soft voice. I settled into the pew next to him.

I looked around and noticed that the church was almost full and I was fairly certain that I recognized some of the mourners as city government officials. "Hollywood, it's really wonderful that so many people have come to honor your mother," I said. "She must have been a special lady."

"Oh, she was special, all right," he said with a hint of a smile. "You see, Sir, at one time she was the director of one of the biggest civil rights groups in the city. A lot of people in the black community looked up to my Mom and remembered the things she did."

I had met Hollywood's mother once or twice, but had no idea about her prominence in the city of Boston. "You must be really proud of her," I said. "I am." He looked straight ahead.

We sat in silence. The organ music flooded the church, drowning out the low murmur of the crowd. The funeral director marched up the aisle and stopped in front of our pew. "Mr. Frederick, it's time for the family to greet the mourners," he said solemnly with a touch of false sympathy. "Please come with me to the altar."

A look of panic crossed Hollywood's face and he grabbed my arm again. "Come on, we're going to the front of the church."

"Wait a minute, Hollywood, that's only for family members," I whispered.

"You're the only family I've got left now, Sir," he said as his grip tightened on my arm. "Let's go."

I walked self-consciously to the front of the church, side-by-side with Hollywood. Because of the obvious contrast in the color of our complexions and the difference in our height, we must have made an odd-looking pair. I knew that most of the people in that church, at least those who weren't military, were wondering why I was standing in front of the casket as a family member.

As nearly a hundred mourners filed by to shake Hollywood's hand and then mine, almost all accepted that, somehow, I was considered to be a member of this family. A few gave me a quizzical look that clearly said, "What are you doing here?," but I didn't care. After the last hand was shaken, Hollywood and I took our seats near the casket. I don't remember much about the funeral service, except that almost every politician who was present felt compelled to offer carefully prepared remarks.

When it was all over and the church was nearly empty, Hollywood took off his jacket and loosened his tie. "Am I glad that's over," he said with a sigh. "You know we can get your leave extended if you need it," I said. "There must be a lot of details you need to settle."

"No, my cousin already has most things taken care of," he said. "Besides, I need to get back as soon as I can. They'll have the equipment all tied up in knots if I'm not there to keep it straight."

"If there's anything you need…"

"I know."

"You stay safe out there," I said because I couldn't think of anything else to say. "And tell everyone over there to take good care of each other. We want to see all your smiling faces in three months when you get home."

"I will."

"I'm sorry about your Mom, Hollywood." I said, reaching out to shake his hand one last time.

He reached out and grabbed me in a bear hug. "Thanks for being my family, Sir."

Rainbow Soldiers

I often thought that we made way too much of a fuss about the sexual preferences of soldiers. Long before "Don't Ask, Don't Tell," or the repeal of "Don't Ask, Don't Tell," it was certain that military service never depended upon sexual preference. The gender of the person with whom one shared a bed has never had a bearing on courage in battle, dedication to duty, or faithfulness to one's comrades.

Although we don't celebrate it very much, the military history books are full of examples of heroes who enjoyed the company of members of the same sex. Frederick the Great of Prussia was certainly gay, and it's pretty clear that many Greek warriors participated in homosexual activities. Lawrence of Arabia may have enjoyed the company of his fellow man and it's highly likely that Baron von Steuben cultivated a close circle of male admirers. I learned early in my career that what's in a soldier's heart is far more important than who he or she sleeps with.

I met some wonderfully interesting people in the early 1980s when I was a student in the Transportation Officers' Basic Course at Fort Eustis, Virginia. Because Transportation was a lot cleaner than Infantry or Armor, many of my classmates at Fort Eustis were there to avoid low-crawling with a bayonet clenched between their teeth. There was a pervasive, class-wide atmosphere that fell far short of the "gung-ho" attitude that our instructors would have preferred.

I first met Clayton when a group of us conspired to have one pair of our issued eyeglasses tinted red, much to the frustration of our instructors. Clayton and I soon became good friends. In the civilian world he was a registered nurse in addition to serving as a National Guard officer in the Deep South. I enjoyed his biting wit that was delivered in the slow, casual manner of a true Southern gentleman. In addition to his sarcastic humor, he was also highly intelligent, tough, and capable.

Near the end of the course Clayton and I were returning to base after an evening of bar hopping in Norfolk. We stopped off at the closest bar near the base for one last nightcap. As we sipped our cold beers,

Clayton said, "I have something to tell you, Greg." I kept drinking. "Go ahead."

"I'm gay."

"That's nice, Clayton. I'm not."

We finished our beers and went back to our quarters. We never discussed the matter again and I don't believe it affected our friendship.

I haven't spent a lot of time thinking about that conversation, but I wonder if I said the wrong thing—or maybe I said exactly the right thing. I've lost contact with Clayton after more than forty years, so I guess I'll never really know.

One of the most memorable soldiers with whom I ever served was the mess sergeant in the supply company I commanded. This sergeant was flamboyantly, unashamedly gay. From time to time I had to counsel him to tone it down, but he ran a good mess section. When other soldiers first met him it was a somewhat jolting experience, but, after a little while, his constant cheerfulness and guileless good nature won almost everyone over.

I remember a drizzly, miserable morning in the woods. Soldiers hunkered down under their helmets and ponchos as they shuffled along in the breakfast mess line. The mess sergeant presided over the steamy serving line where he dished out hot eggs, pancakes, and good humor. He waved his spatula like a conductor's baton as he greeted his customers: "Good morning, Dave, did you dream about me last night?" he shouted with a wink.

"Fuck you," with a chuckle was the usual reply. "Oh, I bet you say that to all the boys!" And so it went. Maybe the banter wasn't to everyone's liking, but it boosted a lot of spirits on many crappy mornings.

As the end of the mess line approached on this drizzly morning, I fell in behind the last man, a soldier who was new to the company. The new guy tapped the shoulder of the soldier in front of him as he approached the mess sergeant, who was delivering his usual off-color morning greetings.

"Hey, is that guy a fag?" the new guy asked in surprise.

"Yup…," was the reply from the soldier next in line as they shuffled along, "but he can cook."

And that summed up how the soldiers in the company regarded the mess sergeant. He always did his job. He took good care of them and even made them laugh. No, many of them didn't approve of his lifestyle, but that was his business, not theirs. He was part of the family.

As the debate around the repeal of "Don't Ask, Don't Tell" raged in the military, I understood the arguments on both sides. But the tragedy of one of our soldiers deployed in Afghanistan made me realize that our policy needed to change.

The young woman deployed to Afghanistan with a specialized detachment. When they arrived in the country they were divided up into teams or individually assigned to headquarters elements in different sectors where they had little to no contact with other members of the detachment. This made it extremely difficult for the NCOs in the detachment to maintain contact with their soldiers and it tended to make our soldiers feel isolated.

Maybe I'm wrong, but I don't believe that anyone in the detachment knew that this soldier was a lesbian. I'm certain that no one was aware that she was involved in a complicated romantic relationship with an officer and no one knew that the love affair was coming to an end—with all the heartache that breakups bring. And I'm certain that no one was aware of her deep pain and suffering. One morning they found the soldier's lifeless body behind one of the compound buildings. There was an M9 pistol near her hand and one empty shell lying on the ground next to her.

I was her Brigade Commander, but I didn't know her well and I didn't know her family. As I offered my condolences to her family at her wake, I was received with stony silence. However when her first sergeant expressed his deep sympathy, one of her sisters exploded: "You promised to bring everyone home safely at the deployment ceremony. Well my sister didn't come home safely." She continued, "You lied to us."

I can understand the shock, the pain, and the agony when a family loses a young sister and daughter. But what they didn't understand, couldn't understand, was the deep sorrow and guilt that a military unit, a military family, feels over the loss of a soldier. Everyone asks themselves what he or she could have done to prevent this tragedy. It took many of us a lot of hours to help the first sergeant understand that, despite her sister's thoughtless words, he was not to blame for the soldier's death.

But the simple fact was that this young soldier was in agony over the end of her relationship with her lover and there was no one she could go to for help. She was a good soldier and, at that time, good soldiers weren't gay. Furthermore they didn't fraternize with officers. In desperation she chose the only way she knew to escape from the agony, and in so doing projected that pain onto countless others, some of whom were those she loved.

Although it was controversial, I was pleased to see "Don't Ask, Don't Tell" repealed. I believe the Army is healthier because of it and our society is stronger when all patriotic citizens, regardless of their sexuality, have the right to serve in its defense. General Mark Milley summed it up well when he said, "I just don't care who sleeps with whom."[11]

Public Affairs

In September 2001 the 101st Quartermaster Battalion, which I now commanded, was planning to send a water purification detachment to Egypt in support of Operation Bright Star, a multinational military exercise that's held every two years. After the attacks on the World Trade Center and Pentagon, the exercise was delayed by a few weeks, but not canceled. Needless to say, the anxiety level and attention focused on a National Guard detachment heading for the Middle East was heightened.

One of the young soldiers scheduled to go on the Bright Star mission decided to give an interview to a local newspaper. In his boasting comments he speculated that perhaps the real mission of the Bright Star team would be to hunt for Osama bin Laden and other radical Islamic terrorists. Because of the great public interest in all things related to antiterrorism and the edginess of the time, the story spread much further than it should have. No one stopped to think that a lower ranking soldier in his twenties might not be the most accurate source for military strategy.

Nevertheless the cat was out of the bag and I could foresee some real morale problems if the Bright Star soldiers and their families even half believed the story. We gave the interviewed soldier a counseling statement and ordered him not to make any more press statements, but that certainly wouldn't counteract the misinformation. I spoke with the Massachusetts National Guard Public Affairs Officer. He felt that the damage was done and saw little point in attempting to publish a statement that offered the truth behind the mission.

As the departure date for the Bright Star detachment approached, I wondered how I could best get the information out about their true mission. I called the Public Affairs Officer again and asked if he'd help me invite members of the media to the detachment's sendoff ceremony. He agreed to assist with the invitation, but made it clear that he wanted no part of facilitating the event. Undoubtedly he wanted to be clear of the blast area if things went wrong.

I called our brigade commander, Colonel Arthur Jewett, a high school athletic director and coach, to let him know what I was planning. Col. Jewett wasn't thrilled about the idea, but he didn't disapprove. I distinctly remember his final words from that conversation, "Smitty, if this goes wrong, it's your ass, not mine."

One by one we received confirmation from newspapers and New England Cable News, or NECN, that they would attend the sendoff ceremony. The responses were almost comically hesitant, as if the reporters feared that they were coordinating entry into some sort of dark cloister to witness a classified, high-security event.

The Sunday of the sendoff ceremony arrived and soldiers, families, and reporters quietly filed into the armory. Prior to the ceremony we gathered the soldiers together and encouraged them to answer questions if asked by reporters, but we gave them clear guidelines about the operational details of the mission that could not be discussed. We also assured them that they were welcome to politely decline to answer reporters' questions if they didn't want to be interviewed.

As the soldiers assembled into a formation in the armory's open area, a hush came over the onlookers. Families quietly took their seats. Reporters hung back against the walls, maintaining a respectful distance.

It was a fairly brief ceremony. Colors were presented and the National Anthem was played. The narrator read a brief description of Operation Bright Star, emphasizing the fact that it was a multinational training exercise. I offered a short speech expressing my pride and confidence in the detachment. Col. Jewett then gave an upbeat off-the-cuff pep talk worthy of his skills as a head football coach. The detachment commander said a few words, then took charge and the ceremony ended on a confident, positive note.

Reporters gingerly stepped forward to talk with Col. Jewett and me, as well as the leaders of the detachment. I encouraged them to seek out soldiers and family members who were willing to be interviewed. People made their way to the refreshments table and I noticed many soldiers and family chatting with reporters. Soon the armory was buzzing. After an hour or so the armory was clear of reporters and family members. The rest of us went back to work dealing with all the details of operations and training, equipment maintenance, and personnel actions.

Later that afternoon, someone in one of the supply rooms called out that NECN was about to air our story. We scrambled to television sets and watched a two-minute news report on the sendoff ceremony. Soldiers cackled and hooted as their friends appeared on the TV screen responding to reporters' questions. But the star of the show was Col. Jewett whose stump speech captured at least one quarter of the news story. He came across like Vince Lombardi in camouflage.

About an hour later I was called to the phone. Col. Jewett wanted to talk to me. "Hey, Smitty," the Col. said, "why don't you come over to my office after work. We can have a beer and watch the NECN news loop."

I thanked him but declined, realizing that I never managed to have just one beer with Col. Jewett. I had a long drive home and tomorrow was a work day. "Aw, that's too bad." Then he continued, "You know, I'm really glad you and I decided to invite the media to the ceremony. I think it was a great thing for the soldiers and their families."

Indeed it was … and a great thing for Col. Jewett as well.

Battalion command assignments are highly prized and typically last two to three years. I had been in command for almost four years, and so it came as no surprise when I was informed that I was going to be replaced as Commander of the 101st Quartermaster Battalion. Although I didn't want to leave another Army command that I found fulfilling, I was to be replaced by Lt. Col. Nancy Souza, a highly capable leader who had commanded a truck company in combat operations during Operation Desert Storm. The battalion would be in good hands.

I knew that Lieutenant Colonels typically were assigned to Massachusetts National Guard Joint Force Headquarters, or JFHQ, following battalion command. Rarely was the JFHQ assignment a position of any consequence. The rationale was that senior officers needed to serve a sort of apprenticeship at JFHQ to learn how the gears meshed in the big machine as they prepared for future assignments of greater responsibility. It was viewed as a sort of unpleasant rite of passage, much like the missionary year for Mormon men. However the prospect of being assigned to some cubicle where I collated reports all day seemed absolutely dreadful.

After giving it some thought, I reasoned that it might not be so bad if I could get myself assigned to the Public Affairs Office. For a long time I harbored the thought that the National Guard didn't do enough to promote the accomplishments of our soldiers and units. If citizens better understood all the good things that Guardsmen accomplished in their communities and in the world, recruiting would benefit, military families would receive more support, and even politicians would be more supportive of our budget requests. The success of the Bright Star sendoff had whetted my appetite for media engagement and I was certain I could make a positive contribution in Public Affairs.

When I made my request for a Public Affairs Office assignment to our new brigade commander, he just laughed. "If you're sure that's what you want, I'll see what I can do," he chuckled. "But I hope you know what you're getting into."

And so I reported to the Director of Public Affairs, Colonel Joe Mercuri, who owned a successful beauty supply products company in the civilian world. Col. Mercuri didn't seem overly pleased to have me in the office, but he wasn't unfriendly either. Mercuri was a somewhat odd duck, although a likable one. He referred to himself as "The Colonel" and refused to sign any document unless he was provided with a ruler to align the letters, but the soldiers in the Public Affairs section loved him. After a few weeks he called me into his office and told me that my mission was to turn our quarterly journal into a self-funded project.

The Minuteman was a full color, quarterly magazine that ran about 50 pages per issue. With a circulation of 10,000 copies, it provided news, information, and command messages to the soldiers and airmen of the Massachusetts National Guard, as well as to Massachusetts legislative and governmental leaders. Col. Mercuri explained that the budget for *The Minuteman* had been cut and it was my job to figure out how to continue publication at no cost to the government. I wasn't thrilled, but it was better than collating reports in a cubicle.

And so I immersed myself in research, advertising, crafting specifications, government bidding, and business negotiations. After six months *The Minuteman* was published by a private printer at no cost to the National Guard, but now it carried advertisements for colleges, combat boots, and sunglasses. I felt like I had passed some kind of test, and perhaps I had.

In the meantime I adjusted my ego to life at JFHQ. Lieutenant colonels who command battalions have designated parking spaces and corner offices. They're referred to as "the old man" and they reign like chieftains and warlords. When they growl, clouds gather. When they smile, the sun shines bright. Their word is law.

At JFHQ lieutenant colonels make coffee for colonels, who stir it and serve it to generals. Lieutenant Colonels create clever PowerPoint slides that colonels deliver at briefings. They set up chairs and carefully arrange place cards, then quietly suffer reprimands when the Secretary of Public Safety is seated next to his bitter enemy, the Director of the Emergency Management Agency. In short, to be a lieutenant colonel at JFHQ is like becoming a specialist again except you're never assigned to KP.

The Democratic National Convention was held in Boston in 2004. It was one of the first large-scale political events since the 2001 terrorist attacks, and so it was designated a "National Special Security Event." As such, a military Joint Task Force, or JTF, was created to coordinate all the security agencies and elements. To command the JTF, Brigadier General Gary Pappas was appointed as a Dual-Status Commander with command authority over all active-duty and reserve forces assigned to the JTF. Brig. Gen. Pappas was a highly respected Massachusetts National Guard field artillery officer who was a well-known Boston immigration attorney.

In his capacity as Dual-Status Commander, the General reported to both Governor Mitt Romney and Secretary of Defense Donald Rumsfeld, whom he was called upon to brief periodically in preparation for the DNC.

Several weeks prior to the Democratic National Convention, Col. Mercuri retired as Director of Public Affairs. With little fanfare I became the acting Director of Public Affairs. A few days before the Democratic delegates arrived, the JTF commenced operations in a large open space within the headquarters building. Each staff section and agency occupied a table with a computer and a telephone. In addition to the traditional military staff sections like logistics, personnel, intelligence, and communications, there were now stations for the Secret Service, Navy, Coast Guard, and tactical aircraft, which operated a highly classified umbrella of fighter protection over Boston. The large work space hummed with low conversations and it buzzed with anticipation and excitement.

Our Public Affairs section occupied a smaller space than many of the more critical staff elements. Our job was to field media inquiries, issue press releases, and prepare a daily summary of media reports that were of interest to Brig. Gen. Pappas and the DNC staff. We organized our small section to provide around the clock staffing and deliver a briefing at 4:00 p.m. each day.

I was a rookie when it came to fielding media inquiries, and I have to admit I was momentarily flustered when I answered the telephone for my first query. The reporter identified himself as a representative of Al-Jazeera. I remember wondering if I should respond to his questions, but I quickly reminded myself that our job was to provide accurate information about DNC security to news outlets. Although Al-Jazeera didn't always present the United States in a positive light, they were a legitimate news organization. The reporter asked questions that involved mainly open source material and I provided all the information he requested.

Later on the first day I received a very different phone call. "JTF DNC Public Affairs—This is Lieutenant Colonel Smith speaking."

"Lieutenant Colonel Smith, this is ABC News." I instantly recognized a legendary reporter's distinctive voice. We exchanged a few pleasantries. Then he said, "I'm wondering if you can offer any further information about the fighter aircraft coverage over the DNC area."

Red lights flashed and alarm bells went off in my mind. "If there were any fighter aircraft flying over the DNC, I'm sorry but I wouldn't be able to discuss it with you because it would be classified information."

There was a pause on the other end of the line. "Lieutenant Colonel Smith, if the next phone call you received was from Senator Kennedy, would your response still be the same?"

"I'm afraid Senator Kennedy would get the same answer I gave you.

Do you have any other questions?" I asked. Our conversation ended abruptly and I breathed a sigh of relief.

The main threats to security at the DNC were the activities of anarchist groups to stage disruptions and interfere with the convention. Because anarchists tend to be loosely organized, their activities were easily anticipated and security measures were put in place. For some reason, the anarchists who were operating in opposition to the DNC were particularly fond of media attention, freely discussing their numbers, locations, and planned activities with Boston reporters.

Our daily media summaries gradually attracted more attention within the JTF as we began to include more information about the anarchist threat. Soon I found that we were working in close coordination with the intelligence section. The intelligence team wisely realized that they could create a more accurate assessment of current threats by meshing open source information from the media with classified assessments from the Secret Service. This was a valuable lesson that would be helpful later in my career.

Brig. Gen. Pappas' Chief of Staff, Colonel Tom Sellars, did an outstanding job riding herd on the many staff sections and agencies involved in the JTF. Particularly in the early days he held many coordination huddles to synchronize sections, establish small working groups, and ensure that daily briefings were concise and pertinent. When I look back at all the agencies, organizations, and branches of the armed forces involved, I'm amazed that the JTF functioned so harmoniously. Tom Sellars deserves great credit for coordinating the staff sections mainly through diplomacy and humor, although he wasn't reluctant to administer a kick in the ass from time to time.

As time went by members of the various sections became friendlier, particularly in the overnight hours when events were relatively quiet. I remember chatting with a middle-aged Air Force officer whose work station was next to Public Affairs. Night after night she came and sat scanning her computer screen while she was knitting. I quietly chuckled because, with her gray hair pulled into a bun and her half glasses, she looked more like a librarian than an Air Force officer. One night after we chatted about the weather, I asked her what her job was.

"You see those two phones on the desk," she said pointing with her knitting needles. I nodded. "One of them is wired into the JTF just like the one on your desk." She paused to check her knitting. "The other one is a hotline to our fighters on standby."

"So, if we detect a legitimate threat, you scramble the fighters?" I asked. "That's about right," she confirmed and nonchalantly glanced at her computer screen. I often wondered if the bad guys realized that the can of whoop-ass that could vaporize them would begin with a call from a soccer mom taking a break from her knitting.

One night the media reported sightings of paratroopers dropping out of the sky over the DNC convention center. Where this preposterous report initiated, I have no idea, but we were deluged with media inquiries. It soon became clear that we needed to issue a press release. To give the statement force and legitimacy, I thought a statement from the JTF Commander would be appropriate. I quickly composed the press release and sent it to Col. Sellars for approval prior to sending it out. Sellars phoned me and said that Brig. Gen. Pappas wanted to see me immediately in the conference room.

Although I briefed him every day with the rest of the staff, I had never met with Pappas individually. I was surprised when he thanked me for preparing the press release so quickly and asked to review it with me. I soon realized that he was much more media savvy than I assumed and paid much closer attention to my briefings than I thought. He corrected a few words in his quoted statement and authorized me to immediately send the press release. Realizing that he understood the power of public messaging, I later arranged for Brig. Gen. Pappas to give interviews to Boston newspapers, through which he was able to correct misinformation about protester suppression and offer reassurance to citizens that they were well protected. This was the beginning of a long working relationship with Pappas that grew into an enduring friendship which continues to the present day.

After the two-week DNC I returned to my status as the part-time, or "M-Day," acting Director of Public Affairs. Although I was officially in charge, the daily public affairs business of the Massachusetts National Guard was conducted by Major Winfield Danielson, the full-time Public Affairs Officer. Win was a Ranger-qualified Infantry officer who was also highly knowledgeable about public affairs. A graduate of the Defense Information School, or DINFOS, he was smart, organized, and articulate. In all honesty Win taught me, by conversation and example, most of what I knew about the business of public affairs.

But Win had a problem. Operation Iraqi Freedom was in full swing and many of his peers were currently serving overseas. His career goal was to eventually return to the Infantry as a Battalion Commander. He was well aware that any officer who didn't have an overseas deployment under his belt would be unable to compete with his fellow Infantry officers when it came time for promotion and command assignments.

The answer to his dilemma came when there was a vacancy on an advisor team that would deploy to Iraq for six months. However when Win requested permission to transfer to the advisor team, he was told that the Adjutant General, Major General Oliver Mason, had personally rejected the request because he felt that Win's public affairs skills were too valuable to the headquarters. Win was angry and disappointed. I decided to go to bat for him and requested a meeting with Maj. Gen. Mason.

Maj. Gen. Mason was one of the most fair-minded, even-tempered, logical leaders with whom I ever served, but I soon learned that he felt that the public affairs position was too important to be without the level of professionalism that Danielson brought to the Guard. During our meeting, Mason, a former Infantry officer, easily agreed that Win needed to serve on an overseas deployment or else his career would be at a dead end. However he countered that his public affairs savvy and expertise were too crucial to allow him to deploy for six months. I fired back that we were penalizing Win for being too good at his job.

Then Maj. Gen. Mason leaned back in his chair and his eyes narrowed. "The only way I'll agree to Win's transfer to this deployment, Greg, is if you agree to come on active duty to fill in for him while he's overseas." We both knew he was calling my bluff. If there were subtitles available, under Mason's face it would have said, "Put up, or shut up, Buddy." But he was far too much of a gentleman to put it in those crude terms. I'm sure he knew that there was no way I could refuse without compromising my values as a leader. I had been outmaneuvered by the General.

I looked him in the eye. "All right, Sir. I'll coordinate the handoff date with Win and I'll let you know when I can come on active duty." He just smiled.

I coordinated my leave of absence with the school system, but because I was leaving in May with only a few weeks of classes left in the school year, it didn't create too much disruption. In short order Win was off to Iraq and I reported to JFHQ every day.

The Public Affairs Office was staffed full-time by an Air National Guard captain, a former police officer, who was highly knowledgeable, quick-witted, and professionally polished. Our office operations were managed by Army National Guard Master Sergeant Pallas DeBettencourt, an experienced, razor-sharp NCO who made certain the i's were all dotted and the t's were all crossed. Pallas was gifted with an exquisitely wicked sense of humor, which meant we spent most of the day laughing at others or one another. I was extremely fortunate to work with creative, independent professional leaders who were remarkably tolerant of my inexperience—or at least they hid it well. I probably could have stayed in my corner of the office and let Pallas run everything until Win came back, but events have a way of driving our actions.

Contrary to public perceptions, military public affairs officers very seriously understand their responsibility to provide truthful information to citizens in accordance with the First Amendment. This means that no media outlets are favored over others and no one gets a "scoop." There are also four golden rules: 1. Bad news never gets better with time. 2. Never lie or your credibility is gone. 3. Statements and media releases must be as accurate as possible in every detail. 4. If you don't give the media the information they want, they'll make it up. And you won't like the result.

To be absolutely honest, though, a military public affairs office operates somewhat like a corporate public relations operation. Public affairs offices want to promote a positive image of the military and aren't particularly eager to confess the organization's faults. And like any other business, public affairs officers work with reporters on a daily basis, so they develop friendships and have their likes and dislikes. My own favorite, and the favorite of many other public affairs colleagues, was National Public Radio, whose reporters always seemed to rise above the crowd as the most balanced, respectful, and intellectually inquisitive.

While I'm confessing, I should admit that public affairs officers also cultivate relationships with reporters. I was never shy about complimenting a writer on a positive, well-written article nor did I hesitate to invite a reporter to lunch. I also wasn't reluctant to voice my displeasure if I thought an article or segment was a "hit job." If I wanted to get a "good news" story into print—for example when a National Guardsmen saved lives at a car accident scene—I wanted to be able to talk to a friendly voice and ask for a favor. Similarly, if I had to admit that we made an error—like the night we blew up old artillery shells and woke up every baby on Cape Cod—I hoped I knew reporters well enough to ask them to go easy on us.

I learned that the media is a business run by human beings. Although they have a responsibility to report the truth, media professionals want to be treated with civility, respect, and dignity like all of us. In return they tend to handle sources fairly if they're treated well. During my time in public affairs, it was rare that I ever thought we were treated unfairly by a reporter or editor. When I hear politicians and public officials complain about mistreatment at the hands of the "mainstream media," I often think, "you reap what you sow."

The Army's initiative to embed media professionals with military units during Operation Iraqi Freedom was ingenious, but probably didn't encourage journalistic ethics or impartiality. When reporters eat, sleep, and travel with soldiers upon whom they rely for their safety, a solid bond develops, which is then reflected in reporting. The Army benefited from a wealth of positive reporting as a result of widespread embedding.

I was approached by a Boston sports announcer who wanted to embed with one of our Massachusetts National Guard units in Iraq. I received Maj. Gen. Mason's approval and then spent hours coordinating the request with military public affairs headquarters and the unit commander in

Iraq. When the final approval came through, I enthusiastically called the announcer who was pleased, but expressed concern about funding for air travel, meals, and lodging in Iraq. I researched the funding details and called him back. He was happy to hear that the Army covered all travel and living expenses, but he was worried about where he'd get a helmet and body armor. I contacted our supply room and arranged for him to draw a helmet and body armor. When I called him with the equipment arrangements, he requested that a public affairs officer escort him to and from Iraq and asked if I could accompany him. I met with Maj. Gen. Mason the next day to ask if I could take the announcer to Iraq. Mason's explosive response was to be expected—there was no way he'd allow me to go to Iraq. When I informed the sports announcer that he'd have to travel to Iraq alone, he quickly withdrew his embed request.

I should have realized it sooner, but I had been played. The sports announcer probably had no intention of actually embedding in Iraq. But the contorted effort would make for a good late night bar story when he would tell drunken admirers about the time he was planning for a Hemingwayesque journey to Iraq, but the Army let him down at the last minute.

During the time I served on active duty the Massachusetts National Guard was exceptionally busy. It seemed that every week we were coordinating a unit sendoff as troops left for deployment or we were welcoming units home from overseas duty. There were human interest stories and commendations for heroism overseas. The Base Realignment and Closure Commission threatened to close bases in Massachusetts, which jeopardized jobs and local contracts. Unfortunately during this time we also mourned our first combat fatalities.

As time passed I spent more and more time accompanying Maj. Gen. Mason to meetings with elected officials and public events. As I mentioned, Mason was a straight-shooting Infantry officer who gave me tremendous freedom to craft messages and respond to events as I thought best. The general was ordinarily a gentleman under most circumstances. However, once when I took leave for a family vacation on the coast of Maine where cell phone coverage was spotty, he was furious. Apparently he was unable to reach me for several days and he chewed me out when I finally responded to his voicemail. As I recall he ordered me never to be out of cell phone coverage for more than a few hours, and he wasn't kidding.

Although I attempted to encourage other officers and NCOs to speak to the media, in retrospect, I was probably in front of a microphone more than a public affairs officer should be. During lulls in the news cycle when I was home, friends and neighbors would sometimes say, "Hey, Greg, I saw you on the news this week." Because we were juggling so many news stories, I would often reply, "Really, what was I talking about?"

It seemed that there were hundreds of media events during this time, but one event is particularly etched in my memory. Fourteen members of the Westboro Baptist Church traveled from Kansas to Marblehead, Massachusetts, to attend the funeral of a Green Beret who was killed in action in Afghanistan. Ordinarily that might be a kind gesture of condolence, but the Westboro Baptist Church is no ordinary religious group. The antisemitic extremist sect believes that bad things occur in the United States as God's punishment for our tolerance of abortion and gay rights. To publicize their views, they often petition for the right to gather near the funerals of fallen soldiers.

I received a call the day before Staff Sergeant Christopher Piper was to be buried in Marblehead. The public affairs office at Fort Drum requested that we coordinate media for the funeral. Although this wasn't a funeral for a Massachusetts National Guardsman, they asked that we handle the event. At the time I wasn't aware of the reputation of the Westboro Baptist Church.

I must admit that, because of the short notice, my dress uniform wasn't all that squared away and I probably wasn't looking my best as I left for the funeral. When I arrived at the church I spotted the Special Forces Brigadier General who would preside over the burial. He was standing on the church steps. I saluted and introduced myself to him as I explained my role. He looked me up and down, then berated me on my appearance. Recovering my composure, I asked the General to accompany me to the area across the street from the church that was set up for the media and explained that the highest ranking officer usually offered brief remarks to the press. He grudgingly came with me, but as we neared the media, he abruptly stopped and said, "I'm not talking with some bullshit reporters." Then he returned to the church steps. Once again I found myself in front of the cameras.

At the time I harbored considerable disrespect for the general and his refusal to talk with the media, thinking, "You're a tough guy Special Forces General, but you're afraid of a few reporters." Years later, after presiding over many funerals as a general officer, I came to understand that this general's tongue lashing for me and his reluctance to speak to the media was a forgivable reaction to the grief and intense emotions that surge under the surface when called upon to bury a comrade.

As the church filled to capacity with family and friends, veterans groups, community members, and other mourners formed a large crowd on the street outside. Then the Westboro Baptist Church roared into action from their cordoned off area near the church.[12] "God hates fags!" they shrieked. "Thank God for dead soldiers!" they yelled, as the black limousine rolled up carrying Staff Sgt. Piper's widow. The crowd of mourners seethed with rage.

The Westboro Baptists waved signs that read, "America is doomed!" and "Thank God for AIDS!" and "Jews killed Jesus!" as they chanted their hatred. Several soldiers stepped toward the group and I ordered them to stand fast. I feared for the worst when members of a veterans motorcycle group moved toward the Westboro Baptist Church area and surrounded it. But the veterans turned their backs to the howling church members and formed a tight circle to prevent any attacks during this excruciating exercise of First Amendment rights.

As the funeral service neared its conclusion, many of us wondered how we could shield Staff Sgt. Piper's family from the verbal abuse of the Westboro Baptist Church. An unexpected answer came in the form of the Boston Police Bagpipe Band. When the church doors opened, the band marched down the street and positioned itself in front of the Westboro people. The Westboro Baptists began to shout at the top of their lungs, but the pipes and drums struck up the loudest Scottish tune I ever heard. Standing a few yards away from the church members, I couldn't hear a thing they were calling out. When at last the horse-drawn wagon had carried the flag-draped coffin away and the mourners were on their way to the cemetery, the pipes and drums finally stopped playing.

The Boston Police Bagpipe Band received loud and heartfelt applause from the remaining mourners and onlookers for both their quick thinking and their high volume musicianship. Later the police escorted the Westboro Baptist Church members out of town as they slithered away to their next despicable demonstration.

Operation Helping Hand

Mike Finer, a highly successful financial planner, was entertaining clients at the U.S. Tennis Open in New York when Hurricane Katrina, a category 5 hurricane, slammed into New Orleans. As Finer, a major in the Massachusetts National Guard, flew home on August 30, 2005, he had no idea that he would soon be called to duty. When the levees breached and the situation in New Orleans became more desperate, the call went out across the country for National Guard troops.

On the Friday before the Labor Day weekend, Maj. Finer was notified that he was to command a 600 soldier task force that would proceed to New Orleans as quickly as possible. In keeping with the minuteman legacy of the Massachusetts National Guard, Finer's task force was alerted, mobilized, armed, and supplied with a week's provisions over the holiday weekend. On Sunday night the force was assembled at Camp Edwards on Cape Cod as soldiers prepared to board aircraft the following day.

I accompanied Maj. Gen. Mason to Camp Edwards as he checked on the final details of the task force's preparation. In what I believe was his finest hour, Mason gathered groups of soldiers around him and asked them to take a knee. In plain speech he dispensed unvarnished, direct advice, but more importantly, he expressed his gratitude and sincere pride in them from the heart for stepping up to help out New Orleans. The image of Mason surrounded by young kneeling soldiers who were motivated and inspired by his words was military leadership at its finest.

Maj. Finer's task force conducted vital search and rescue missions in the flooded neighborhoods of New Orleans. They also retrieved corpses from the stinking flood waters. When soldiers began to rescue dogs from the flooding, Finer had the wisdom to organize the effort. Soon Massachusetts troops were working with the ASPCA to save stranded pets. Shortly thereafter the *Worcester* (MA) *Telegram and Gazette* ran a front page story on pet rescues that gained national attention. Back at JFHQ our public affairs office fielded a flood of positive contacts either praising the pet rescue effort or requesting further information.

After nearly a month Maj. Finer's task force arrived back in Massachusetts, stiff from a 72-hour railroad journey from New Orleans. Although they had saved many human lives and helped identify the deceased, most reporters just wanted to hear anecdotes about the pets they saved. But the Massachusetts National Guard's response to Hurricane Katrina wasn't nearly finished.

The first evacuation of 107 residents of Louisiana, including families with small children and senior citizens, landed on the tarmac at Camp Edwards on September 8, 2005. Many had been in the stinking flood waters of New Orleans only hours before. Most had only a vague idea of the location of Cape Cod, but they were happy to be in Massachusetts, away from the devastation of New Orleans. One traveler later described Camp Edwards as looking like Disney World to him and he compared New Orleans in the aftermath of the hurricane to the depths of hell.

Prior to the New Orleans residents' arrival at Camp Edwards, Governor Mitt Romney pledged the assistance of the Commonwealth of Massachusetts to shelter homeless residents of New Orleans who had been displaced by the devastation of Hurricane Katrina. Romney designated the military base at Camp Edwards as the location in which the people from Louisiana would be received and housed.

The Massachusetts National Guard had to scramble to prepare suitable living quarters for a large group of people that would include family groups, babies, toddlers, and wheelchair-bound senior citizens. The full time staff at Camp Edwards worked tirelessly to transform a barracks square into the "Camp Edwards Village." In preparation for the arrival of the people from New Orleans, a task force of state government agencies soon converged on Camp Edwards.

Media attention was intense. Our public affairs office was flooded with media inquiries so that it soon became clear that we needed to schedule daily press events. I offered a tour of Camp Edwards Village to a throng of television and print reporters on the day before the arrival of the group from New Orleans. As I escorted the gaggle of reporters through the dining facility, someone asked, "How do you plan to refer to these people—Refugees? Evacuees?"

In one of the only moments in my life that I can claim inspiration, I thought for a moment and responded, "We'll refer to them as our guests." The term "guests" stuck like glue after the television news ran that night. From that day on, our New Orleans visitors were referred to as guests by reporters, in official statements, even by Governor Romney in his statements. Although I may be claiming too much credit, I believe that using the term, "guests," helped to frame our relationship with our visitors in the weeks to come.

When the guests arrived, they were greeted by an army of social service organizations, state government officials, and community representatives. The outpouring of generosity for these unfortunate people was truly amazing. The population of Camp Edwards Village soon grew to 235 guests[13] and it became apparent that, although there was a vast array of support, we hadn't anticipated many of the challenges we would face. Within the first few days we needed to arrange a wedding, deal with a wide range of medical requirements, adjust housing accommodations to meet the needs of families with small children, as well as many little, but important, personal details.

We soon learned that people with money in New Orleans had already taken care of themselves. Our guests were generally people who lacked resources, family support, or connections. In most cases, they arrived at Camp Edwards with nothing but the clothes they wore. One man told me that when he got off the airplane his pants were still wet from New Orleans flood waters.

The initial objective of the government and social service agencies was to meet the comfort needs of our guests. But the ultimate goal was to help them join family members or eventually resettle into permanent homes and jobs. Of all the social service agencies that supported the Camp Edwards Village, the superstars were the Salvation Army. While many other organizations enforced their restrictions and processes before delivering services, the Salvation Army representatives delivered quick, personal services with few questions asked. Although there was always a Bible on the desk, I never knew them to preach while they achieved results for people in need.

Because of the relentless media attention, I stationed myself at Camp Edwards and slept in military quarters there. I began each day having breakfast with different groups of guests in an effort to learn more about them. In the late morning I would greet media representatives and welcome them to the Camp Edwards Village, reiterating the rules and guidelines to ensure that guests' privacy was respected. After I escorted reporters off the base in the late afternoon, I attended a daily interagency meeting for all government organizations.

During the first week after our guests' arrival, I greeted over 40 print reporters and television news crews each day. Standing on the hood of a HMMWV I offered mundane instructions about refreshments and restrooms, as well as warnings about staying out of living areas and respecting guests' rights not to engage with the media. Then the horde of reporters would descend on the village.

I recall one scrawny reporter from the *Boston Globe* who repeatedly muttered, "That's what you think," as I gave my late morning spiel. At the time I thought that maybe I wasn't hearing him correctly. But later in the week, a distraught guest asked to speak with me. Pointing out the mischievous *Boston Globe* reporter, the guest said, "Colonel, I want you to know that guy just offered me some money for pictures of dead bodies from Katrina." The man continued, "I didn't want to sell him any, but he kept on bothering me and even followed me into our rooms. I don't think that's right."

I agreed with our guest and assured him that I'd take care of the matter. Storming over to the reporter I told him that he had ten minutes to get off the base for violating our rules. He blubbered and protested, asking me what I'd do if he refused to leave. With a sly grin, I assured him that there was nothing I'd like better than to help our Military Police remove him from the base. After I watched him get in his car and drive off, I called the editorial office of the *Boston Globe* to inform them of the dismissal of one of their reporters. The editor on duty assured me that she would deal with him. But somehow I felt that maybe he had been sent to work around our limits.

In all fairness, the *Boston Globe* sent other reporters to Camp Edwards Village and these people were intelligent, sensitive, and professional. I met many great reporters and good people during the media feeding frenzy at Camp Edwards Village. I particularly enjoyed chatting with one reporter who was often on site. He impressed me as a regular guy and a proud young father who liked talking about his kids. Perhaps because he usually dressed in shorts, a tee shirt, and sandals I had the impression that he was a local reporter or a freelance writer. It was with considerable surprise a week later when I heard his voice on the national broadcast of National Public Radio.

One incident reminded me that reporters are just like any other workers. Late one Friday afternoon I received an ugly call on my cell phone. The producer of a Boston television station was screaming at me for forcing his crew off base. I rose to the bait and hollered back that I had bent over backwards to accommodate his news truck on late broadcasts. After we both vented, he hung up on me.

I walked over to the station's news truck and explained what had just taken place with their producer.

"But, hey, this has nothing to do with how we feel about you down here. You folks have been great," I assured the young reporter and her cameraman. The two of them looked at each other sheepishly. "We're really sorry, Colonel," the reporter said, hanging her head. "We didn't mean to cause any trouble."

"What are you talking about?" I was puzzled. "Well, you know the traffic on a Friday afternoon can be really awful," she explained. "We just figured that, if we called our producer and told him you kicked us out, we could get ahead of the traffic and get home quicker." I asked that she explain the situation to her producer, but I just had to chuckle as I walked away.

In the first few days of Operation Helping Hand there was a halo of generosity and compassion that floated over Camp Edwards Village. Governor Romney and his wife hosted a gourmet barbecue featuring live music under a tent in the village. Players from the New England Patriots visited to toss passes to the children and sign autographs. The social services area overflowed with donated food, clothing, and comfort items. And, of course, elected officials visited in large numbers as they posed for the news cameras.

Once the Hurricane Katrina guests were safely housed in the Camp Edwards Village, the second phase of Operation Helping Hand began and things became complicated. Although many communities across Massachusetts offered to host families and small groups to help them rebuild their lives, most of the guests remained in the village. Increasingly the afternoon interagency meetings became prickly—the clear message being that the village shouldn't become too comfortable. At the same time, guests became aware of shortfalls in services, bristled against restrictions about their freedom to come and go on an active military installation, and expressed concerns about their ability to have a voice in the affairs of the village, which was becoming their community.

Most of the guests were people of color, but almost all members of the interagency team managing the village were Caucasian. Although I never detected overt racial tensions, the potential for cultural misunderstanding loomed large. Governor Romney wisely asked the Rev. Jeffrey L. Brown, a highly respected Baptist minister from Cambridge, to step in as "Mayor." As soon as he arrived, the Reverend Brown was everywhere, troubleshooting gaps in services, mediating disputes, and dispensing a unique sense of warmth and peace as he gained the trust of both residents, state officials, and social service volunteers.

For some reason, the Reverend Brown and I began to work together closely. We hosted group meetings at night during which guests were able to voice their concerns, recommend improvements, and sometimes, just vent their frustrations. Although I'm not certain that Baptists recognize sainthood, the Reverend Brown's compassion, sincerity, and remarkable ability to soothe and reassure convinced me that he was as worthy of canonization as anyone enshrined in the Vatican.

The Reverend and I conferred at least daily during which he asked me to help address programmatic issues and the concerns of individual guests. Generally these were simple tasks, but I was startled by one of his requests in particular. He explained that there was a growing conflict between the Urban League and the Boston chapter of the NAACP over which organization would be the primary advocate for the guests. The Reverend Brown explained that, unless someone mediated the situation, there would be unhealthy competition for the loyalty of our guests, which would fracture the village.

When he said, "I think you're the best person to mediate between the two organizations," my jaw dropped. "You understand, Reverend… I'm white," I stammered. He smiled. "Yes, I understand that, Colonel. But I can't facilitate the meeting because I'd be perceived as being biased. I've had too many interactions with both organizations to be considered impartial. I need you to do this."

There was no way I could refuse him, so I gulped and agreed to facilitate the meeting. Several days later I nervously shook hands with two professional gentlemen in business suits—one who represented the Urban League and one who represented the NAACP. Although both men were polite, there was palpable tension.

I fully expected the meeting to end abruptly with either gentleman rejecting my legitimacy as a mediator regarding an issue that affected people of color, but I opened by thanking each organization for their services to our guests. Then I quickly followed up with our concern that competition between the organizations would be unhealthy for all involved, particularly our guests. I invited each representative to state his position, which they did clearly and without animosity. It soon became apparent to me that each organization could take responsibility for different aspects of service delivery. Although I don't recall the details, I proposed a division of advocacy—for instance, the Urban League would deal with housing issues, while the NAACP would focus on employment concerns. To my great relief, the approach seemed to make sense to both parties and we spent the rest of the meeting laying out the lines of responsibility. We ended the meeting by exchanging business cards and warmly shaking hands. Although I was initially uncomfortable and reluctant to facilitate the meeting, I learned two important lessons.

First, I learned that, for the most part, the military is a trusted, honest broker in our society. The representatives of these two powerful African American organizations were willing to accept a Caucasian Army officer as a mediator in a dispute because of my military status. I was unknown to them and carried little credibility, but they trusted my integrity because of the uniform I wore. The U.S. military would only continue to be trusted as a values-based organization if it continuously enforced and lived up to those values.

Second, the very success of this meeting forced me to confront my own hidden racial bias. Why would I assume that representatives of African American organizations would reject well-meaning assistance from a white person? Did I have so little faith in people of color that I would assume that they would automatically distrust a person who wasn't black? My foolish fears going into the mediation meeting caused me to think hard about my incorrect assumptions.

Before the winter snow arrived the last guests of Camp Edwards Village had moved out to resettle permanently in new communities. Many of them were welcomed into Bay State communities where they currently live. Some even became New England Patriots fans.

However, long before the village closed I was troubled by an intense, burning indigestion one day when I went home. The painful sensation wouldn't go away, so my wife drove me to the emergency room. I was surprised when the doctor explained that the pain wasn't in my stomach, it was in my heart. My bad habits had caught up with me and I was out of commission for the next month as I recovered from a mild heart attack.

Heroes

During my time in uniform I met some of the best people in America. Not everyone with whom I served was among the best, but there were those who were truly exceptional. I had the good fortune to serve with real, honest to goodness, bayonet between their teeth, John Wayne type warriors who accomplished incredible feats of bravery. I certainly can't count myself in that category—and I mean them no disrespect—but my heroes were the soldiers who quietly embodied solid values in their own way, without fanfare or recognition. They profoundly touched those around them and made them better soldiers, better citizens, better men and women.

With deepest apologies to the many good people with whom I served and aren't mentioned here, I want to single out a few soldiers and one officer who made me a better man because I had the privilege to know them.

"My Stars!," was how Hattie reacted to almost every situation she encountered. Then she got to work and made it better. She was a staff sergeant who served as the Chaplain's Assistant for the 101st Quartermaster Battalion. We never had a chaplain for more than a few months, but that was fine with us, because we had Hattie to pray for us and care for us. We didn't really know much about her, other than that she was born in the Deep South and sometimes our Yankee ears had difficulty deciphering what exactly she was talking about, particularly if she was excited. But that was okay, because the warmth, compassion, and sincerity she communicated nonverbally was loud and clear.

When we traveled to the field, a pickup truck had to be assigned to carry Hattie because she needed extra cargo room for the big black trash bags she lugged out to the bivouac site. The trash bags didn't hold her personal equipment and supplies—they were filled with blankets, hot cocoa packets, popcorn, extra socks, pillows, and such things to make sure that her fellow soldiers were comfortable and cared for.

One chilly, dark night on a field exercise, I decided to walk the battalion perimeter to ensure that the fighting positions were manned and alert.

As I approached a critical crew-served M60 machine gun position, I was startled by an unfamiliar voice. "Halt! Who goes there?" chirped a high voice with a distinct Southern twang followed by the evening's challenge.

"It's the battalion commander," I added after giving the password. "My Stars!, what are you doing up at this hour, Colonel?," Hattie asked. "You need your sleep."

I jumped into the dirt foxhole next to her. "Sergeant Hattie, why are you in this fighting position? You know Chaplain's Assistants aren't assigned to guard duty."

"I hope I didn't break any rules, Sir." It's just that Private Nelson was so tired after all the work he did today, and he isn't sleeping well at night, so I said, "You climb into your sleeping bag and get a good night's sleep and don't you worry about your guard duty shift."

I wished her a good night and moved on to the next fighting position not knowing whether to be pleased or angry. On one hand, she probably had no idea how to fire the M60 because her job precluded her from training on crew-served weapons. On the other hand, how could I argue with one of our most treasured Army values—selfless service.

Hattie never seemed to age and we had no idea how old she was, other than that she had an adult son who was a high school principal. She was very proud of him. When it came time for the Army Physical Fitness Test, Hattie was out there on the track with soldiers who were probably less than half her age. I won't say that she had the fastest time, but she certainly wasn't the last one to complete the two-mile run. The ovation she got when she crossed the finish line would make you think she won the Boston Marathon.

I guess the day Hattie became my greatest hero wasn't a day she'd like to remember. She had traveled home by bus to visit her ailing mother— Hattie never had a drivers' license. On the way back to New England her trip was delayed by a vicious winter storm. Hattie ended up spending that Friday night sleeping in a cold bus terminal in Memphis. Now she was present at the unit's training assembly on Saturday morning with a high fever and a deep cough. The NCOs begged her to call her husband to take her home, but Hattie would have none of it. Ordinarily she was a person who was cooperative and pleasant to everyone, but not this day. Finally, I decided to give it a try as her commanding officer. I found her in her office, wrapped in a blanket, trying to fill out a report in the midst of a pile of used tissues. She started to stand up when I came in, but I insisted she sit.

"Hattie, you look like this cold has really gotten the best of you," I began in a soothing voice.

"I'll be all right, Colonel. Don't you worry about me," she responded, not looking up from the paperwork.

"We're all worried about you, Hattie. Won't you please let us call your husband to take you home?" I pleaded.

"No, Sir," she replied, still looking at the report on the desk. "I intend to finish this duty day."

"What if I ordered you to go home, Sergeant?" I asked in my best official tone of voice. "Would you go then?"

"No, Sir," she said, "because that would be an unlawful order. No soldier needs to abide by an unlawful order." Then she looked at me directly and I could read the determination in her eyes. "I traveled for two days by bus through a snowstorm to be here today. Do you know why, Sir?"

I didn't dare try to answer. She continued, "Because I have never failed to do my duty and I never will."

That was it. I knew that I couldn't convince her to go home, and frankly I didn't want to. As I stood to leave the office, I asked, "Please go right home after formation, Hattie. And please take care of yourself, you mean an awful lot to many of us in this unit." I heard her cough, but I thought I caught a barely hidden smile as I walked away.

*   *   *

I think all of us carry around a role model or two in the back of our minds. Someone whom we admire, that we've specially selected to be that compass azimuth that points the way. Military command can be a lonely place, which makes it particularly important to have a solid, ethical role model.

Although he was never aware of it (and he'd be as embarrassed as hell if he ever read this), I've been fortunate to have Colonel Frank Labollita with me in some pretty dark hours to help me make the tough decisions in my life. But we certainly didn't start off on the right foot.

Lieutenant Colonel Labollita took command of the battalion in which I served as a Second Lieutenant and he was almost instantly worshiped like a rock star. Perhaps it was because he took command from a priggish, aristocratic officer who never made any connection with the troops, but it was more likely because he had a plain-spoken, direct manner that radiated warmth tempered with strength. As a lowly platoon leader I had little direct contact with the battalion commander, but I shared the troops' admiration for our new leader.

However, I worked directly for a company commander who had a low opinion of my abilities, and the feeling was quite mutual. Suddenly it was announced one morning that our company commander was being transferred. He hastily spent the morning completing paperwork, cleaned out his office, and was gone by late afternoon with little fanfare.

I was delighted that the company commander was moving on, but my joy was short-lived when I opened a manila envelope in my mailbox. Inside was an Officer Evaluation Report in which the departing company commander attacked my competency, leadership, character, appearance, and everything except my table manners. But what was far worse was that the evaluation was endorsed by Lieutenant Colonel Labollita. I was furious.

I marched across the armory to the battalion commander's office and knocked on the door. I could feel my cheeks burning. He opened the door and then sat behind his desk. "What is it, Lieutenant?" he asked.

Silently I laid the report on the desk in front of him. "Have you seen this OER, Sir?" I asked through gritted teeth.

He glanced at the report and his brow furrowed. "That's my signature in the block, so I guess I reviewed it," he said, rubbing his chin.

"If you stand by these comments, then you'll have my resignation by the end of the day," I growled.

"Wait a minute, Lieutenant," he said, regaining control of the situation. "You barge in here challenging my evaluation. I think I need a few minutes to read this over a little more carefully. Now you march yourself out of here and wait until I send for you this afternoon."

I stewed for the rest of the day, fairly certain that I was going to end the day by resigning. Yes, I had worked hard to become a U.S. Army officer, but this was a matter of honor. If that company commander had been in the building I probably would have challenged him to a fight.

Late in the afternoon, a sergeant came and told me to report to the battalion commander's office. Lieutenant Colonel Labollita waved me into his office and motioned for me to sit on the couch. He sat at the other end. "I looked over this OER carefully and I agree that it's a bit harsh," he began. "Did your company commander review this with you before he left?"

"No, Sir." I replied. "He should have discussed this with you before submitting it to me. If I had been more alert, I probably would have asked him to restate some of these comments." He paused and looked me in the eye. "But can you honestly tell me, Lieutenant, that you've done your best as a platoon leader?"

I looked at the floor. He asked in a firm but quiet voice. "Have you always been as prepared as you should have been to lead training? Did you show initiative to take some of the burden off the company commander? Did you do your personal best on the PT test and the rifle range?"

I shifted on the couch. Labollita continued. "You're a good junior officer, but you have to admit there's room for improvement. I'm not going to change this OER, because you need to show me that you're better than this. Now you're getting a new company commander and a fresh start. Prove to me that your last company commander was wrong and you'll never see another OER like this." He stood and we shook hands.

As I turned to leave his office he said, "One more thing, Lieutenant—don't ever challenge me like that again." I never did challenge him again but I also never received another Officer Evaluation Report like that again. Perhaps I had a bitter aftertaste from my first real interaction with Lieutenant Colonel Labollita and I think that maybe we avoided each other to some degree.

Years passed. Colonel Labollita was now my brigade commander and I was a company commander in my first operation providing supplies and support to the Yankee Division at Canadian Forces Base Gagetown. Nothing was quite right in the dense forests of New Brunswick—between liters and kilos, bears and coyotes, divisional supply was a bit of a pick-up game. Our water purification site was ten miles from our fuel dump, which was eight miles from the company headquarters. Supply activities ranged over dozens of miles, 24 hours a day. The problems and challenges were non-stop. I worked with a great team of smart, resourceful NCO, but I was in charge, and I loved it.

One morning just after sunrise, the biggest colonel I ever saw loomed in the door of our headquarters tent. He gruffly introduced himself as the commander of the Division Support Command of the 10th Mountain Division and asked me to brief him about the logistics support that my company provided.

I took him to our map with the tactical overlay and walked him through all of our food, fuel, water, ammunition, shower, maintenance, and self-defense activities. He asked several questions and, after I answered each one, he responded flatly with, "That's what you say." Finally the interrogation ended. He grunted and sped away in a waiting command vehicle. I was too busy with real world problems to think much about the morning's interview. Later in the day word got back to me that the colonel from the 10th Mountain Division, who was our brigade's evaluator, was singing the praises of our supply company. Based on my interaction with him, I thought that was highly unlikely.

The next day I was out at the river where our soldiers were purifying water. I noticed that Colonel Labollita's command vehicle was there. I greeted him and saluted. He smiled at me, puffed on his cigar, and beckoned to me to walk with him. "Our chief evaluator colonel from the 10th Mountain was pretty impressed with your little show over there yesterday," he said. "In fact, he told me I was very fortunate to have such a sharp captain running the supply company."

I was somewhat caught off guard and muttered my thanks. Col. Labollita turned away from me slightly. "I want you to know, my son, sometimes dishonest people throw up smokescreens in front of you." He continued, "and sometimes senior leaders get their heads stuck so far up their asses that they can't see the truth."

I wasn't sure that I understood what he was getting at. He turned and looked me in the eye. "You did good, kid." Then he shook my hand, hopped in his vehicle, and drove away.

When I thought about it I came to realize that, despite the intervening years, he had never forgotten our dispute over the negative OER and that he had just delivered the closest thing he could get to an apology. Some fools think that an apology is a sign of weakness, but, after that brief conversation, during which he had the strength to admit that he was wrong, face-to-face, man-to-man, my admiration for Colonel Labollita as a leader knew no bounds. I would have followed that man into the jaws of death if he asked me to.

There was one more moment when Colonel Labollita showed me how to lead. In those days, the regular Army would pounce on National Guard units to conduct unannounced comprehensive training evaluations. Our unit was informed on Thursday that the evaluation team would be there on Saturday morning and they would spend two full days inspecting all aspects of training. Our brigade had not done well. In fact, the last four units had failed their inspections miserably. It was rumored that one more failure would cost Colonel Labollita his brigade command.

As soon as I received the phone call notifying us that we were next on the chopping block, I called in the lieutenants and platoon sergeants. We worked all day and night on Friday, scouring records, perfecting training plans, and rehearsing training presentations. If we were going down, we were going down with a fight.

A poker-faced regular Army major arrived on Saturday morning and began his silent note-taking. He offered little feedback as to how the evaluation was proceeding. Colonel Labollita visited the armory on Sunday and called me aside. "How do you think it's going?" The concern in his voice was clear. "I really don't know, Sir. I can't get a read on this major," I said.

Knowing how important the outcome was to Colonel Labollita's career, I braced myself for a stern pep talk, or perhaps a threat to my own career. Instead, he put his hand on my shoulder, looked me in the eye and said, "Whatever the outcome is, I know that you did your best to pull this off and I'm grateful."

If I would have followed him into the jaws of death at Gagetown, I would have battled dragons bare-handed after he thanked me for trying to save his career. What were the inspection results? We passed by the slimmest margin, but we passed.

I'm sure there were celebrations and congratulations, but I really don't remember them. However, I never forgot how Colonel Labollita made me feel, or what it taught me—that praise and gratitude can be far more powerful motivators than harsh words or threats in dark times.

Perhaps more important than the lessons he taught me, Colonel Labollita became enshrined in the back of my mind. Whenever I was faced with a difficult leadership decision, I would pull him out of his niche and ask, "What would you do, Colonel?" and he always had the right answer.

*   *   *

Two unlikely heroes in my memory were once the ugliest drunks I've ever met.

Brig. Gen. Smith (right) offers his longtime mentor and friend, Brig. Gen. Frank Labollita, a token of appreciation (Massachusetts National Guard PAO).

During my first few months in the National Guard I was shuttled from assignment to assignment. One Saturday the battalion was training on Cape Cod and I was assigned to ride there in a pickup truck with Sergeant First Class Peter Culcasi, whom I'd never met before. We started down the road when suddenly Sergeant Culcasi pulled over to the side of the highway into a rest area. Reaching behind the seat he pulled out a bottle of whiskey, uncapped it, and took a good long swig. Then he offered it to me. I declined, but said a silent prayer that we would arrive safely at Cape Cod. When I told other lieutenants about the incident, they laughed—Pete Culcasi was well known as one of the battalion's worst drunks.

Years later as I took command of Company A, 26th Supply & Transport Battalion, I was introduced to our full time supply sergeant, who would oversee the accountability of supplies and equipment for which I was financially responsible—Sgt. 1st Class Peter Culcasi. I was told that Sergeant Culcasi hadn't had a drink in years, that he had sobered up on his own, cold turkey. I was skeptical.

However when the only other full time sergeant became medically disabled, Pete Culcasi took on the responsibility of working two jobs and he never complained. Every Wednesday I'd come to the armory after work. Pete and I would discuss current business over a set of tennis. Then we'd roll up our sleeves and work into the night preparing training schedules, reports, and inventories. We soon became close friends, but he never discussed his sobriety. He carried that company single-handedly through some dark and trying times and I owe him a deep debt of gratitude.

I first saw Sergeant First Class Buck bellowing that he'd fight anyone in the battalion during a party. I'll never forget the image of the slobbering mechanic with his belly hanging out over his belt holding a can of beer in each hand. Everyone in the vehicle maintenance section knew that Buck could fix anything with wheels, but you stayed away from him when he was drinking.

Years later, when I took command of Company A, I met the unit motor sergeant—Sgt. 1st Class Buck. Needless to say, I was concerned that this angry drunk was responsible for keeping our trucks running and supervising other mechanics. Like Pete Culcasi, I was told that Buck was a new man, but I wasn't buying it. He was to prove me wrong.

Buck was no parade ground soldier, but he had lost weight and his taste for alcohol. I soon realized that he was one of the most capable, dependable leaders in our company. So when First Sergeant Mark Loud moved on, I asked Buck to take on the top job, company first sergeant, and I never regretted it. Buck brought a father's calm wisdom to the job, balanced with an unwillingness to put up with anyone's shit.

I once watched him instructing a nervous trio of soldiers performing their first helicopter sling load operation. This requires a team of four to crouch near a pallet of supplies wrapped in a net while a helicopter hovers just over their heads. Then they fasten the net to the cargo hook on the airframe of the helicopter and exit the rotor wash circumference to either side of the helicopter. It looks more dangerous than it is, but the team must never move toward the tail of the helicopter where the invisible spinning tail rotor would chew them up into little pieces.

As 1st Sgt. Buck patiently guided this raw, green crew through the hookup, one panicked soldier lurched toward the tail rotor. I watched in horror, but I swear Buck's right arm grew to twice its length as he lunged, grabbed the soldier by the collar, and yanked him back to safety. Buck will always be a superhero in my eyes.

When the flood of alcohol washed over the company during parties, Buck and Pete sat together sipping cans of iced tea with a look of "Been there, done that." They never appeared to miss their boozing days, but I think they kept each other in check, just in case the temptation became too great.

So why are Sgt. 1st Class Pete Culcasi and 1st Sgt. Buck my heroes? Because they had the incredible strength of character to conquer a powerful addiction, redeem their reputations, and become outstanding leaders. They taught me the power of resurrection if anyone is willing to confront their weaknesses head on … and don't we all have our share of shortcomings if we have the guts to admit it?

Opportunity Knocks

The doctor ordered me to take it easy for a month after my heart attack. That meant no work, no travel, mild exercise, and a tasteless, bland diet. Colleagues from both the military and high school visited, phoned to ask how I was feeling, and sent cards wishing me a speedy recovery. I even received a large handmade "Get Well card" from the guests at the Camp Edwards Village.

Despite all the good wishes from my friends, I was intensely ashamed and uncomfortable being an object of pity because of a health crisis that, if I were totally honest, I had brought on myself. Many of us who are over-worked might fantasize about stepping away from it all for a few weeks, but I learned that the sidelines can become sad and lonely after a while. Once my wife and kids headed off to school in the morning, I had little to do but read, go for a walk, and cruise daytime television stations in search of intelligent life. I eventually started writing a novel, but even that couldn't cut the silence and sinking feeling that the world was passing me by.

Near the end of my recuperation, Win Danielson returned from Iraq and resumed his duties as full time public affairs officer at JFHQ. My leave of absence from school expired and my doctor agreed to allow me to return to work on a part time basis. Soon I was back at school full time and it seemed like I had never been away.

I soon returned to my duties at Joint Forces Headquarters as the part-time Director of Public Affairs. The people in the Public Affairs section welcomed me back warmly, but I detected a certain hesitancy from them, or perhaps I was just projecting my expectation that soon I'd be called to the chief of staff's office and informed of my fate. I resigned myself to the near certainty that I would be pronounced medically unfit for military duty and that my career would soon end. Making my peace with retirement as a lieutenant colonel, I reminded myself that I was lucky to make it to captain.

Sure enough, the phone rang in my office after lunch one day. Maj. Gen. Mason said he was coming down to my office to talk with me in ten minutes. I thought it was very kind and thoughtful of the Adjutant General to come to my office and deliver the news of my retirement in person.

Mason stepped into my office, closed the door behind him, and sat in the chair on the opposite side of my desk. "So, how are you feeling?" he asked. "Well, Sir, I feel a whole lot better than I did a few weeks ago."

"If you're feeling up to it, Greg, I'd like you to take on a new assignment."

"I'm always up for a challenge, Sir." I replied a bit puzzled. "What did you have in mind?"

"I want you to take over as Commander of the 51st Troop Command," he said with a grin. I was speechless. Maj. Gen. Mason was not only telling me that I could continue to serve, but he was offering me an important command assignment that carried a promotion to colonel with it.

"Yes, Sir… Thank you," I stammered.

He stood and shook my hand. "You had us all worried, you know." Then he continued, "Get with the chief of staff to figure out a transition timeline. Go over to the troop command and do your own command assessment. Then set up a meeting with me to talk about your command priorities." He turned to leave, then looked at me and said, "Welcome back, Greg."

I assumed command of the 51st Troop Command, Massachusetts National Guard, on February 1, 2006. Before I describe the adventures of the 51st, some explanation is in order. A Troop Command in the reserves is a brigade-size organization, which usually comprises about 2,000 soldiers. It is technically not a brigade, which has a unified, permanent structure. Rather, a Troop Command is a bit of a hodge-podge command that cobbles together different elements. In this case, the 51st was made up of a Military Police Battalion, an Engineer Battalion, a Chemical Company, a Public Affairs Detachment, and, if memory serves correctly, the Army Band. The 51st headquarters also had sole ownership of Camp Curtis Guild, a 680-acre military base in the Boston suburbs.

Within the Army there are numerous branches, or corps, that reflect the special missions of soldiers and units. There are the big ones, like infantry, artillery, aviation, engineers, military police, or medical. Then there are smaller, specialized ones like chemical, transportation, finance, ordnance, or quartermaster. These branches all have their own subculture within the Army. Sometimes they operate like professional families, other times they act like rival gangs or cults.

So it was my job to lead this patchwork of military subcultures. Maj. Gen. Mason met with me to give his guidance. He didn't seem to have any particular concerns, but I noted that he didn't have many positive things to say about the command either. Without the general spelling it out, I could see that my task was to improve the readiness and effectiveness of the units within the 51st. It also became clear why Mason had chosen me, a Quartermaster officer, to lead this amalgamation of engineers, military police, chemical, finance, and even public affairs soldiers. I had no past history, no favorites, no enemies, and hopefully no prejudices against any of the military gangs in the 51st.

On my first day of command I parked my old, dented Toyota Tercel in the prominent parking space reserved for the commander in front of the square two-story brick headquarters at Camp Curtis Guild. As I learned later Command Sergeant Major Dave Costa looked out the window and remarked, "Hey, some asshole just parked his shitbox in the commander's space. I can't wait to see him get his ass kicked."

I was off to an auspicious start. As an outsider coming into the 51st, I was at both an advantage and a disadvantage. On the plus side I had no baggage, no skeletons, no unpaid personal debts, no preconceived notions. On the minus side, I had no allies, no dependable assistants, and no trusted advisors to start off my time in command.

However I was extraordinarily fortunate to find two solid, dependable leaders within the headquarters. The first was the full time administrative officer and second-in-command. This lieutenant colonel was a business-like, detail-oriented administrator who demanded results from subordinates. His desk was always immaculate—clear of any paperwork, post-it notes, or even a paperclip. I never saw him lose his temper or treat anyone with disrespect, but, when he issued an order he expected it to be carried out on time, or else.

The second was Command Sergeant Major Dave Costa, the highest ranking enlisted man in the 51st. Dave was a Vietnam combat veteran who was highly respected, and perhaps feared, by soldiers. Not exactly the warm and fuzzy type, he was nevertheless extremely insightful into the ways soldiers would react to potential orders or circumstances. While Dave wasn't reluctant to give credit where credit was due, he had a critical eye for situations and circumstances that needed improvement. Both of these men soon became reliable and discrete advisors who weren't reluctant to deliver bad news, prevent me from making poor decisions, tell me when I was wrong, and even admit when they were wrong. In time we developed a deep bond of mutual trust and became close friends.

The two battalion commanders in the 51st were as different as their military gangs. The grizzled commander of the 101st Engineer Battalion was an Army civilian contractor who worked with Special Forces units. He was a straight-shooting man of few words, just like the heavy equipment operators, carpenters, and bomb disposal techs he commanded. I'll never forget his first briefing during which he read through the first three slides of the PowerPoint presentation of his annual training plan. Then he stopped abruptly, turned to me and said, "Look, you can read. Why don't you look these slides over and ask me about anything you don't understand." We often disagreed and argued, but I liked his bulldog advocacy for his people and I respected his "no bullshit" style. Years later I was pleased to pass command of the brigade to him.

In stark contrast, the commander of the 211th Military Police Battalion was a polished, rising star in the Massachusetts National Guard. Lt. Col. Brian O'Hare was a well-known Massachusetts State police sergeant in the civilian world who was impressively well-connected. An Iraq War veteran, Brian had also distinguished himself during the 2004 Democratic National Convention when he commanded the elite Rapid Reaction Force that was poised to respond to any crisis. Already selected for the prestigious one-year Army War College fellowship at Harvard University, there was no doubt that Brian was being groomed to become a future general, which probably meant he would replace me as commander of the 51st when he completed the Harvard program.

Despite his impressive credentials as a superstar, when I first met with him I found him to be respectful, gracious, and cooperative. But within my first two weeks in command he requested a major change to his training schedule, which I told him I would consider. The administrative officer informed me that the request couldn't be funded on short notice, so I informed Brian that his request wasn't approved and I told him my reasons.

About two days later I received a phone call from Brig. Gen. Pappas, Land Component Commander, and my boss. The conversation with Brig. Gen. Pappas started off in a friendly way, but soon the general expressed his concern that I needed to more aggressively support challenging training for the Military Police battalion. I could read between the lines: Brian had gone over my head to appeal my decision to Brig. Gen. Pappas, who had listened to his complaint. Now Pappas was telling me to rethink my position. I could see that Lt. Col. O'Hare was going to be a complicated subordinate to deal with, but I had no idea how complicated he would eventually become.

On February 28, 2006, FBI agents swooped in to arrest an alleged pedophile, known only as "Ranger 1777," who was on his way to hook up with a fictional 14-year-old boy for a sexual encounter that had been arranged online. When the FBI agents confronted "Ranger 1777," and took him into custody, they identified him as Massachusetts State Police Sergeant and National Guard Lt. Col. Brian O'Hare.[14]

The news struck the Massachusetts National Guard like an earthquake and the aftershocks reverberated throughout the force. No one knew what to believe—was the proud, accomplished officer we all knew actually a sexual predator, or was this some strange case of mistaken identity? Upon the advice of our Judge Advocate General officers, I had the unenviable task of contacting Brian directly and informed him that he was not to set foot on National Guard property until the charges had been adjudicated. I don't remember that phone call well, other than that it was stiff, awkward, and uncomfortable for both of us.

I pondered what to do next. Clearly the Military Police battalion would be in chaos and I needed to ensure that an acting commander was put in place immediately. Should I send a letter to MP leaders or did this situation require face-to-face communication? I remembered a quote I had heard that went something like this—the right thing to do is usually the hardest thing to do.

I knew that I had to face the MP community in person. I set up a meeting with all MP officers and senior NCOs at their headquarters on the following day. Because I had been in command for a little over one month, this would be the first time I would meet most of them.

I was reminded of my status as an outsider when I approached the MP headquarters building. The parking lot was jammed with cruisers, K-9 cars, SUVs bristling with antennas, unmarked cars with rows of lights, and every other conceivable law enforcement vehicle in the state. Somehow I found a parking space for my battered Toyota. The array of police rolling stock did nothing for my self-confidence, but I reminded myself that, as their commander, it was my job to answer their questions and map out the way ahead.

A hush came over the armory when I stepped inside. I shook hands with the senior officers in the battalion then asked them to call everyone together in a large conference room. The room quickly filled up with police officers of all shapes and sizes. Soon it was dead quiet.

I can't recall exactly what I said, but I know I recounted my conversation with Lt. Col. O'Hare and stated that everyone is innocent until proven guilty. Then I launched into what I expected from them as leaders. First, Major Rich Johnson, the full time administrative officer, would be the acting battalion commander and I expected them to obey his orders. Next, I didn't want speculation or extensive discussion about Lt. Col. O'Hare with soldiers. Certainly they would have questions, but those questions should be addressed quickly with only known facts. Finally I urged them to focus on the missions, training, and readiness challenges ahead. I reminded them that the battalion was a strong team that didn't depend on any one individual for its power. I invited their questions and answered perhaps a half dozen hushed inquiries, but I really had no more information than they had from watching news reports on Boston TV stations.

Ultimately the meeting was a success. Although I provided no new information or unique guidance, I gave them a chance to gather as a team to share collective concerns. I also showed them that I wasn't afraid to face them in a difficult time, offer what little information I had, and honestly admit that there was information I didn't have. I learned that, although it can be awkward and uncomfortable, effective leaders must communicate with soldiers face-to-face during tough times and reassure them that the situation is under control—there is no substitute. I also made a fortunate choice in placing Major Rich Johnson (who is now a Major General) in command. Rich, who was widely respected, took charge of the battalion and moved ahead with training and operations.

One year later, Brian O'Hare was sentenced to five years in federal prison for soliciting a minor for sex. When I look back on this tragic affair that ruined an accomplished law enforcement professional, distinguished military officer, devoted husband, and loving father, I think of the ancient Greek fable of Icarus, who flew too close to the sun and plummeted to earth. I remind myself of the lesson the fable illustrates.

If my intention upon taking command of the 51st was to focus on training and readiness, my hopes were soon dashed. During this time it seemed like every unit in the command was either serving in Iraq or Afghanistan, returning from deployment, or scheduled to deploy in the near future. And events on the home front were soon to drive us in other directions.

In May 2006 heavy rain storms struck the New England coast, producing what became known as "The Mothers' Day Flood." Water levels reached historic proportions in communities along the Merrimack River that had not been recorded since the disastrous flooding of 1938. Governor Mitt Romney quickly declared a state of emergency and activated the National Guard.[15]

I accompanied Maj. Gen. Mason on a damage assessment helicopter flight over the area and was struck by the sight of rooftops popping up on the surface of what appeared to be a massive lake. The 51st Troop Command carried the main effort of the National Guard response because we held the heavy equipment assets to shore up flood containment structures and we had hundreds of military police personnel to assist local law enforcement with traffic management and, to a lesser degree, anti-looting protection. In addition, our headquarters was located a mere eight miles from flood damaged areas. Gradually the waters subsided and soldiers returned to their civilian lives. They had performed well during this crisis and I was proud of them.

Following a foiled terror plot to plant bombs on airliners at Heathrow

Airport, the terrorism alert was heightened at Logan Airport in Boston on August 10, 2006. Terrorism alerts were taken seriously at Logan, from which one of the World Trade Center bombing aircraft took off on September 11, 2001.[16]

Authorities immediately called for National Guard military police from the 51st. We were tasked with providing troops around the clock, seven days a week. Shortly after the start of the security mission I visited Logan to assess the situation and check in with our soldiers. The TSA personnel with whom I spoke were grateful for our assistance because they said the presence of military personnel created a greater level of order and cooperation from passengers. Perhaps it was respect for the U.S. Army uniform, or perhaps it was the visible presence of a large, black 9 mm pistol on every MP's hip. Whatever the reason, I was pleasantly surprised when several air travelers stopped to thank me as I walked through the airport, saying that they felt safer and more secure because of the National Guard presence.

The barracks at Camp Curtis Guild had once been used to house troops, but there simply weren't enough funds to maintain them in good condition. However, now we needed to house military police personnel who lived long distances from Boston. Maintenance personnel were able to get two barracks up to speed with new mattresses on the bunks and working showers, but, admittedly, they weren't pretty. For Army National Guard soldiers who are used to sleeping in tents, the accommodations were just fine.

At one point the Air National Guard sent a detachment of 20 security police to augment the Logan security force. I was surprised that, after briefing the major who was in charge of the force, he returned to my office with an irritated expression on his face. Drawing stiffly into a position of attention he said, "Colonel, I need to inform you that the living conditions in those barracks are unacceptable for Air Force personnel. I cannot permit them to stay here."

I thought about his comment for a moment, then calmly replied, "I hope you have a safe trip back to your air base, Major."

Perhaps this wasn't my best moment as a commander, but it first made me aware that, although Army and Air Force personnel both wear U.S. flags on their uniforms, their professional cultures can be quite different. This awareness was helpful later in my career when I commanded joint task forces with personnel from different services.

I visited Logan Airport frequently during the security mission. I soon learned that the pride and excitement of rushing into Boston to secure the airport evaporates quickly for young MP. Simply put, standing in one place, visually scanning passengers for signs of concern, soon becomes mind-numbing monotony once the crisis has passed. Although I advocated strongly to release the MPs from this mission when the threat level subsided, it was months before we could stand down the mission. I was later to learn that once troops are committed to an emergency, it can be extremely difficult to get civilian officials to release their grasp on them.

The Land
of "Not Quite Right"

In early 2007 my boss, Brigadier General Tom Sellars, invited me to a meeting at State Headquarters about the newly launched State Partnership Program. Under this highly effective initiative, each state National Guard organization is paired with at least one foreign national partner for training assistance. The intent is for U.S. personnel to gain overseas experience while projecting American principles of rule of law, respect for individual rights, and positive civil-military relations. Massachusetts had recently formed a partnership with the Republic of Paraguay, which up until 1989 was ruled by the brutal dictator General Alfredo Stroessner. Brig. Gen. Sellars had recently returned from a high-level coordination visit in Paraguay and freely shared his impressions. I listened with some interest, but really didn't think it had much to do with me.

However as the meeting progressed the general began to discuss future initiatives. Then he said, "The Paraguayans are looking for us to provide a training course in peacekeeping operations at their officers' academy in May. Is anybody interested in a South American vacation?" At this point the room fell silent and everyone seemed to search out some detail of interest in the floor tile while carefully avoiding eye contact with Brig. Gen. Sellars.

Sellars broke the silence. "Hey, Smitty, you're a teacher. This should be right up your line." In the military when your boss suggests that you do something, there's only one correct response. "Yes, Sir. Where can I get the details?"

The meeting broke up moments later. The general walked me out of the conference room. "Our liaison officer will coordinate with you soon about the visa process, human rights training, hostage rescue precautions and what the Paraguayans are expecting for training." Then he smiled and put his hand on my shoulder. "You're gonna like this place, Smitty. It's got a few security problems, but don't worry—if a U.S. Army colonel gets sent back in a body bag, it's really bad for tourism." We both laughed, but I wasn't looking forward to this mission.

When I got into the hallway I asked another officer if he knew where I could find a world map. He asked me why I needed it. I replied, "I just agreed to go to a place, and I have no fucking idea where it is."

And so I began one of the most fulfilling, and ultimately frustrating, adventures of my military career that would span more than five years. Perhaps a few basic facts about Paraguay are in order[17]—Its land area is comparable to California and its population numbers a little over seven million, 90 percent of whom are Roman Catholic and mestizo—an ethnic mix of native Indian and European ancestry. The country is sandwiched between Argentina, Brazil, Bolivia, and Uruguay—all of whom consider it a backward, impoverished cousin. These nations have not always been the best neighbors. In the late nineteenth century Argentina, Brazil, and Uruguay attempted to overrun and carve up Paraguay during the War of the Triple Alliance. (In fairness, Paraguay started the war.) In the 1930s Paraguay fought a more successful war against Bolivia for possession of the arid, barren, barely inhabitable Chaco region. (Both countries erroneously thought it held vast oil reserves.)

For most of its history Paraguay was ruled by ruthless, brutal dictators. In 1989 the last autocratic strongman, General Alfredo Stroessner Matiauda was deposed and democracy was instituted. During the twentieth century the country was a refuge for German utopians, including Nietzsche's sister, as well as an undisclosed number of ex–Nazis, of whom Josef Mengele is the most well-known. Blonde-haired European Mennonites have also established self-contained colonies throughout the country.

I soon learned that most relationships in this poor country are about economic gain. Corruption is rampant, from police on the take to government ministers fattening their bank accounts. Initially I was flattered to receive red carpet treatment, but I gradually came to the realization that I was seen as the conduit to U.S. aid—in short many government officials saw dollar signs on my forehead.

However I was fortunate to meet true Paraguayan patriots who understood that corruption and government bureaucracy smothered their nation, but they still held a deep love for the beauty of the land and the strength of their people. In particular, Rafael, a devoutly religious former sergeant major in the Paraguayan Army, served as my driver, guide, and bodyguard during all of my trips to Paraguay. Rafael often took me off the beaten path, into city slums and small villages, and frequently into people's homes.

We took each other's measure on my first trip. We were staying in a primitive guest house outside Asunción. After 22 hours in an airplane I was anxious to stretch my legs. So I told Rafael that I was going out for a jog in the morning. He said, "No, Colonel, that's not wise." I just smiled.

I trotted down a red clay road with lush greenery on either side before sunrise the next morning. I waved to campesinos on horseback as they passed. Soon I heard the growl of a vehicle engine behind me. I stepped to the roadside and motioned for the car to pass, but it just crept along behind me. Growing somewhat alarmed, I stopped and turned around to see the serious face of Rafael behind the steering wheel of our SUV. I learned that he meant business and I think he grudgingly respected my determination. Over the course of our travels we became good friends and he accompanied me on all eight of my trips to his country.

When I would ask him to take me to a particular barrio or village, Rafael would say with a smirk, "I don't think the U.S. embassy would be too happy if they knew you were going there, Colonel."

I'd respond, "That's not what I asked you, Rafael. Do you know how to get there?"

Then he'd chuckle and say, "Okay, Colonel, but don't tell anyone where we went." But I think he understood that I wanted to better understand the culture, social conditions, and most importantly, the people of this complex nation.

Most of the time we traveled in relatively safe areas, which was good because U.S. military personnel aren't permitted to be armed in the country. However in later years we encouraged the Paraguayan military to sponsor medical clinics and other civic improvement projects in San Pedro Department. The Paraguayan People's Army, or Ejército del Pueblo Paraguayo, a shadowy communist insurgent group, travels freely within this region with the support of the people. The intent was to win "hearts and minds" by providing badly needed health care to the campesinos and improving infrastructure to demonstrate that the government could deliver a better life for them than the EPP could.

Once when we loaded up our vehicle to travel into the contested area and inspect a clinic site, I saw Rafael loading ammunition cans into the SUV. When I asked him what was in the cans, he just said, "Don't worry about it, Colonel." Later that afternoon a Paraguayan Army officer who was traveling with us handed me a well-worn old Browning Hi-Power pistol. All he said was, "Maybe you should have this with you." I knew we were in deep shit.

When we returned to Asunción after several days we read in the newspaper that an EPP camp in the jungle, within several hundred yards of a clinic site we had recently visited, had been taken by Paraguayan police and military forces after a sharp firefight. Allegedly the military had discovered written plans, one of which involved the capture of a U.S. Army general, but this could have been a fabrication to leverage increased U.S.

Col. Smith confers with the leaders of the Paraguayan Multirole Engineer Company during their preparations for United Nations service in Haiti (author's collection).

security funding. Whatever the veracity of the report, I became a bit more cautious about my travels and surroundings during future missions.

There were many excellent U.S. State Department personnel in Paraguay, and Ambassador Liliana Ayalde deserves special mention for her grace and diplomatic skill. However, other State Department people stayed within the orbit of the embassy in Asunción and its social circle. I suspect that some of them didn't know a single Paraguayan other than the people who mowed their lawns and cleaned their pools. We sensed a certain tension and mistrust with some State Department folks that seemed to say, "Take off your combat boots before you step onto the embassy carpet. Don't plan to stay long and, for God's sake, don't break anything while you're here." Many of them seemed to be biding their time until they could be posted to Dublin, Brussels, Paris, or any embassy with more prestige and influence. However Ambassador Ayalde was revered by Paraguayans and was warmly received wherever she traveled. Moreover she treated U.S. military personnel with respect. I was humbled and amazed at one social function when the Ambassador offered to interpret my conversation with a Paraguayan senator who regaled me with tales of the mythical Chaco petroleum deposits.

With Rafael as an expert guide, our team traveled throughout the country trying to encourage the Paraguayan military to modernize, improve civil-military relations, and support the principles of democratic government. We were proud of our efforts to help train a United Nations peacekeeping company that served with distinction in Haiti. But ultimately we were unable to accomplish half of what we intended. An insidious culture of institutional corruption squelched progress, diverted money away from where it was needed, and the U.S. foreign aid cycle was a fickle roller coaster that often failed to honor our commitments.

The Republic of Paraguay presented me with the "Medalla de Honor de CECOPAZ" or Medal of Honor for Peacekeeping, for which I am deeply grateful. I'm only aware of one other recipient—Ban Ki-moon, Secretary General of the United Nations. I clearly recall the surge of pride I felt as the Paraguayan military band played the "Star Spangled Banner" in my honor, albeit slightly off key. But perhaps a greater honor was bestowed late one afternoon when Rafael and I came up on a hillside that overlooked a

Col. Will Tyminski (left) and Col. Smith gather with Paraguayan school children outside Escuela Santa Rosa de Lima in Asunción, Paraguay. Assistance to this school in an impoverished area was an initiative of the State Partnership program (author's collection).

field of deep green grass rippling in the gentle breeze. The road we traveled glowed in the sunlight like a bright red ribbon as it stretched to the horizon and four hump-backed Brahma cows grazed peacefully.

"My God, what a beautiful country," I muttered.

Rafael turned and looked at me solemnly. "It is your country now, General."

Operation Big Ice

My wife and I woke up to the sound of loud, sharp cracks—almost like gunshots—in the darkness outside our bedroom window on 11 December 2008. Looking into the woods I could barely make out silvery tree limbs bowed over under the weight of a heavy ice coating. Every several minutes I heard a loud bang followed by the swish of a broken tree limb as it plummeted to the snowy surface. Oddly enough, I was able to log onto my computer to check e-mail messages before the screen went dark. Little did we know that we wouldn't see lights in our house again for nearly two weeks.

It wasn't long before I received the alert phone call from the brigade headquarters. Governor Deval Patrick had declared a state of emergency and activated the National Guard.[18] Thankfully I had my son's four-wheel drive Jeep Cherokee to roll over fallen trees and drive over lawns to avoid tangled brush as I made my way to the main roads and down the highway to headquarters.

For the first several hours of the emergency the entire brigade staff was composed of Major Christine Hoffmann, Sergeant First Class Greg Jasinskas, and me as we dispatched missions to the command's subordinate units across the state. Gradually other brigade staff members arrived at the headquarters, but Maj. Hoffmann and Sgt. 1st Class Jasinskas would always boast that the headquarters ran most efficiently when it was just the three of us. (Maj. Hoffmann would later be the first female officer to rise to the powerful position of chief of staff for the Massachusetts National Guard. Sgt. 1st Class Jasinskas would later take his own life.)

Our initial assessment was that the ice storm would cause fallen tree limbs that would lead to temporary power outages. We anticipated some requests for chainsaw teams to clear roads and military police details to direct rerouted traffic, and we received a moderate number of mission requests during the first day.

On my way home that evening I decided to check on a community shelter in a nearby city that had requested a squad of soldiers to provide security. Folding cots were set up in the classrooms and hallways of a middle school and the cafeteria was staffed with volunteers serving up hot meals to citizens who had been forced to leave their frigid homes. I talked with the police chief about his concerns for the safety of the odd mix of displaced families, senior citizens, and street people, many of whom were drug addicts and those with mental health issues. The chief doubted the ability of his limited police staff to maintain safety in the shelter while responding to requests for assistance across the city.

Later as I toured the shelter I was struck by the sight of a mother and father who were huddled in a corner with their two small children, as they politely attempted to resist the persistent inquiries of an unkempt older man who clearly had mental health issues. At length a military cargo truck growled outside the entrance to the school and a half dozen young soldiers jogged into the school with helmets fastened and rucksacks on their backs. I briefed a sergeant about what I had seen and asked him to keep a special eye on the family in the corner. As the soldiers made their way through the shelter, I could almost feel the tension and fear dissipate. The cavalry was here.

On the following day my boss, Brig. Gen. Sellars, invited me to join him on a helicopter flight over the areas hardest hit by the ice storm to assess damage. I was surprised by the normal vehicle traffic and lack of damage as our Blackhawk lifted off in eastern Massachusetts. But as we climbed into the hills of central and western Massachusetts, we were dazzled by what lay below us. The bright sunshine sparkled off tangled trees coated with thick ice so that the entire landscape glittered like a silvery kaleidoscope. Later we touched down in a field next to the Ashby Fire Department, which was a mere ten miles from my home. I realized that my family was in the heart of the disaster zone.

Our assumption was that the relief effort for the ice storm would follow the pattern of a winter blizzard, which was an initial surge of mission requests that gradually tapered off over several days. However, widespread power outages and plunging temperatures increased requests for assistance. Town officials who believed they had enough resources for a few days and people who thought they could ride out the emergency in their homes until power was restored now realized that they needed to take shelter where there was warmth and hot food. It was also becoming apparent that the critical need was power restoration, but electrical crews couldn't reach downed power lines unless roads and pathways were cleared of fallen trees first.

Because of the expanding demand for chainsaw crews, traffic control, community shelter security, generator delivery, and other missions, the task force under my command was considerably beefed up beyond our brigade. Lt. Col. George Harrington and the 1–181 Infantry Battalion joined us and Lt. Col. Arthur Elbthal added his 182nd Infantry Battalion to the fight. The two versatile commanders swapped M-4 rifles for chainsaws and dispatched road clearing crews across the state. The 104th Fighter Wing and the 102nd Fighter Wing sent Air Force security personnel to help with military police missions. The 212th Engineering Installation Squadron deserves special credit for their heroic efforts to scale an icy mountain in western Massachusetts and restore the operation of a radio signal repeater which was critical for emergency communications throughout a wide swath of the Berkshire Hills. The Connecticut National Guard also sent a company of sawyers—specially trained chainsaw troops—whose skills were in high demand.

A daily routine, or battle rhythm, started to emerge during which I presided over morning and evening task force briefings, then back briefed the Adjutant General, Maj. Gen. Joseph Carter, and the Joint Task Force Commander, Brig. Gen. Sellars, at State Headquarters by conference call. In between I raced around the disaster area to coordinate with local officials, confer with subordinate leaders, and check in on missions. Although we constantly stressed safety, particularly with chainsaw use, I was always impressed by the ingenuity of soldiers and airmen who figured out better and quicker ways to clear roads, plan wellness checks, or direct traffic. I was also struck by the inadequacy of the cold weather gear issued by the military and often found myself talking to troops decked out in snowmobile suits, orange hunting gear, and other warm articles of clothing. But this was no parade. If soldiers were warm, dry, and accomplishing the mission, I was satisfied.

Lt. Col. John MacPherson, commander of the 211th Military Police Battalion, suggested that we move our task force headquarters out of the brigade's base in eastern Massachusetts, to the National Guard Maintenance Facility at Fort Devens. This was a brilliant recommendation because it placed our command and control center squarely in the disaster area, which gave us better situational awareness and response time. Within hours the staff displaced to Fort Devens and we soon had a smooth running operation with communications, mission status boards, and a briefing schedule. Most importantly they were prepared to staff the operation around the clock for as long as necessary.

While central and western Massachusetts struggled to recover, the storm had little impact on eastern Massachusetts. I was scheduled to give a speech at the Wreaths Across America event at the National Cemetery on Cape Cod. I asked Maj. Gen. Carter if someone else could give the speech because of my operational duties, but he assured me that the task force staff could survive in my absence and urged me to give the speech as planned. When I arrived at Cape Cod I was amazed to see green grass, warm sunshine, and very little awareness that the other half of the state was still buried under tangled tree limbs and had no electricity. However I was pleased to give the speech and hoped that my father and mother, who rested under a stone marker in the National Cemetery, were proud of me that day.

We were surprised that assistance requests actually increased as the first week of the mission drew to a close. Because falling temperatures made the situation more desperate for residents in unheated homes without electricity, there were increased demands for local shelter security and wellness checks in remote areas. In addition the chainsaw crews continued their work during daylight hours to give power restoration crews access to downed lines.

Brig. Gen. Sellars often told me that the most important thing in a relief operation is to get anyone you can into the affected area as quickly as possible, even if they can't offer any real assistance. The town of Lunenburg (where I had once worked in the high school) had gone well over a week without electricity and the citizens were desperate. We had available chainsaw crews, but there just weren't enough civilian power restoration teams to get to the town. Nevertheless, I watched Brig. Gen. Sellars' helicopter touch down in the center of town about a half hour before a squad of National Guardsmen was expected to arrive at the town's shelter. I joined the General and the town's public safety officials in time to see our camouflage cargo trucks roar down main street to the cheers and clapping of citizens. Regrettably our soldiers couldn't help restore anyone's electric power, but their presence was a powerful sign that help was on the way. Lunenburg wasn't forgotten. Sellars just glanced at me and smiled.

Many soldiers and airmen had been on duty for more than a week without a break, so we planned for personnel rotations and allowed troops who lived within thirty miles of their duty area to return to their homes at night. I learned to carry a shaving kit, towel, and change of socks and underwear with me as I traveled through the impacted area. When I finished my business at a fire station or public works building, I'd often ask if they had a shower with hot water. Then, if time permitted, I'd clean myself up a bit. Still, I was beginning to look pretty ragged, so I decided to stand down for a night and go home to check on my family and pick up a clean uniform, new towel, and some fresh underwear.

I arrived home at dusk. My wife and youngest son were gathered in the room with a wood stove. They had closed off the doors to other rooms and stretched a blanket over the opening that didn't have a door to hold in the heat. It was good to be together as we played cards by the dim light of a battery operated lantern and listened to a transistor radio. But I'll never forget how the rest of the house took on a dark, unfriendly—almost sinister aura—that didn't much feel like our family home. I hadn't realized how dismal conditions were for my own family. I tried to find a hotel and make a reservation for them, but it seemed that every room in Massachusetts was occupied. I suggested that she go stay with some of our family in the eastern part of the state, but she said she wasn't going to stay anywhere that she couldn't check on our home daily. There was no arguing with her—my wife is a tough woman when her mind's made up.

Power lines were slowly repaired in many areas as missions continued into the second week after the storm. However chainsaw crews and wellness check teams were busier than ever. Two soldiers on a wellness check sweep discovered an elderly couple who were unconscious from breathing fumes from a kerosene space heater. The soldiers were credited with saving the lives of the two senior citizens. Acts of ingenuity, creativity, and, in some cases, heroism were a daily occurrence.

In the hardest hit areas we began to receive increasing requests for armed anti-looting patrols. At first this seemed like an overreaction. But one night I drove through a densely populated area in Fitchburg. I was struck by the darkness and silence that descended on the neighborhoods of hundreds of homes once the sun set. Here and there you could see the faint glow of a candle or lantern, but the cold and the gloom created a sense of threat and menace throughout the blackened streets and alleys. The need for roving MP patrols was suddenly quite clear.

My wife and son were able to sleep at a friend's house where electricity had been restored and they visited our cold, dark home each day to check on it. But they were at the breaking point. One night a few days before Christmas my wife called me in tears. The reality that we would be unable to celebrate Christmas in our home was too much for her to bear. Although I tried to comfort her with assurances that we'd have a wonderful celebration after December 25, I couldn't find much cheer in that thought.

I decided to head home that night after speaking with my wife to check on the house and pick up some clean clothing. As I drove up the driveway I noticed a light glowing in the top window of our barn. I'm ashamed to admit it, but my first thought was, "Dammit, our son forgot to turn off the barn lights again!" Then it dawned on me and I quickly dialed my wife's cell phone. "We have power again," I shouted into the phone. "Come on home, darling."

Operation Big Ice wrapped up shortly thereafter. I soon turned to the task of clearing away the debris from the storm that was strewn all over our house and yard. I distinctly remember a bright afternoon as I perched with one foot on the top rung of a ladder and one foot on the gutter as I positioned a chainsaw over a tree limb that lay across the roof. I chuckled when I thought about how I'd chew any soldier's ass who I caught trying to do something as dumb and risky as this. Then I fired up the chainsaw.

Our home was battered, but it was once again bright and warm as we prepared to celebrate Christmas.

On the Border

While the military police in our brigade were busy with airport security, the engineers were tasked to assist the Border Patrol with building projects to enhance security along the border with Mexico. Operation Jump Start involved civil engineering projects, like vehicle barriers, access roads, and, yes, building walls, in strategic locations along the Southern border of Arizona.

As a brigade commander I visited our units who were deployed for construction projects and I traveled to Arizona three or four times. I certainly have no civil engineering expertise, so I must admit that my role was primarily to ensure that leaders were properly taking care of troops and to show my appreciation for our soldiers' efforts.

As my flight approached the airport in Tucson on my first trip, I was struck by the way the bright sunshine highlighted the different shades of brown, from the dark shades of the mountain valleys to the reddish rooftops to the light tan of desert sands. I'm sure there were green palm trees and bushes here and there, but everything was brown as far as my Yankee eyes could see.

I rented a white SUV at the airport and joined the stream of other white vehicles on the southbound highway to my destination in Douglas, Arizona.

The Gadsden Hotel in Douglas, where I was staying, is one of the most unique hotels in the United States. The rectangular, 13-story building was built in the late 1800s. In its early days guests watched Pancho Villa's army battle his enemies in nearby Agua Prieta, Mexico, while sipping cocktails on the roof. The colorful lobby is flanked by marble columns and illuminated through Tiffany stained glass. The chip in one of the marble steps of the grand central staircase has never been repaired. Legend has it that Pancho Villa himself rode his horse up the staircase and one of the iron horseshoes left its mark. But the elegance belonged to a bygone era and the hotel had a cavernous, dusty—almost ghostly—feel to it.

I was informed that the officer in command of the company I was visiting had arranged a special room reservation for me. The porter escorted me into the ancient elevator that was operated by a gentleman who was almost as old as the rickety lift. We walked to the end of a long corridor over tattered carpet under light fixtures that must have been as old as the hotel until we arrived at a door in which "666" was scrawled. After opening the door, the porter handed me the key. I thought I detected a wry smile as he said, "Enjoy your stay with us."

The company commander and several sergeants met me for dinner in the hotel and presented me with a black cowboy hat with my rank insignia on it. They also sported similar hats. The atmosphere was lighthearted as they updated me on the progress of the engineering project and joked about some of the unique conditions in the border zone. After a few beers we all agreed we could use a good night's sleep and they headed off to their lodging closer to the border. But before they departed, the company commander couldn't resist telling me, "You know they say this place is haunted. I hope you like your room, Sir."

I'm not a superstitious person, but I have to admit that I had a little trouble sleeping in room 666 that night. Like everything else in the hotel, the furnishings were in need of updating but they were comfortable. However I just couldn't quite fall into a deep sleep. At one point the persistent hooting of an owl awakened me. No sooner had I fallen asleep again then a sporadic pop-pop-pop in the distance woke me up. It sounded just like a military rifle qualification range to me, but it eventually ceased and I drifted off to sleep again.

Before I made contact with our engineer unit in the morning, I decided to check in with the Border Patrol. My assumption had always been that the tension along our Southern border was partially the product of Anglo-Chicano friction, so I was very surprised to find that most of the Border Patrol personnel in the Tucson sector were Latino Americans. After getting an overview of where our engineering project fit into the strategic plan for border security, I had to ask about the strange noises at night.

"I could have sworn that I heard something like a weapons qualification range last night," I said. The agent looked up at me with a slight grin. "Yeah, some bad asses tried to shoot their way across the border last night."

"How often does that happen?" I asked. "More often than we'd like it to," he replied.

Later that morning I joined our engineer unit at the construction site where they were building 20-foot steel wall sections around a Super Wal-Mart. The strategic purpose was obvious: If migrants were able to enter the United States illegally and blend into the crowds of shoppers, it would be impossible to separate them from the many American citizens who passed through the shopping center because the vast majority of citizens in Southern Arizona are Latino.

I donned a yellow construction helmet and joined the company commander on a slight rise to scan the long border wall that our troops were building. It was a warm, sunny spring day and remarkably comfortable for that part of the country. I looked down the slope into a tidy Mexican neighborhood of well-kept one-story houses. In fact, it was almost identical with a suburban setting near New York or Chicago or anywhere else in the USA.

Two middle-aged men were finishing their morning jog as I looked down the slope. When they saw me near the rising border wall, they looked up and shook their fists. Although I don't understand much Spanish, I quickly concluded that the words they were shouting weren't friendly greetings. More than anything I read in the news, this incident brought home the hostility that many Mexican citizens feel when they see our border wall expanding. To many who live south of the border, the ugly steel wall sends a message of superiority, isolation, and xenophobia.

The negative feelings about the border wall and distrust of the government in the border region were evident again when we attempted to eat lunch at a chain restaurant that day. It was quite apparent that the waitress who initially greeted us was uncomfortable with our uniforms. The manager soon arrived to seat us, but he seemed annoyed at our presence and escorted us to a carefully selected table. I hadn't felt this reaction to my uniform since the late 1970s when our nation was recovering from post–Vietnam war anti-militarism.

Later in the day I stopped at the local Wal-Mart for some bottled water and other supplies. As I approached the main entrance, the stream of shoppers parted in a wide swath as people placed as much distance as possible between my uniform and them. I don't think that many of them had legal immigration issues, but I do believe that the culture of the border region is to avoid contact with anyone in a uniform, just to be on the safe side.

I conducted a command visit to another engineer operation during the summer months. This mission involved building an access road along the border through the Tohono O'odham Native American reservation. One of the limitations for Border Patrol operations in the desert was the lack of high-speed road access along remote sections of the boundary between the two nations.

The Tohono O'odham people have occupied the desert for centuries. Their ancestors subsisted on hunting, cactus, and some crop cultivation in the harsh environment. The tribe was mainly peaceful except for one incident in the 1870s when they lashed out at their ancestral enemy, the Apaches. Today 34,000 Tohono O'odham people in the United States live within a largely self-governing reservation about the size of Connecticut. However, other members of the tribe also live in the Sonoran Desert on the other side of the border in Mexico. There is considerable resentment about border barriers and restrictions between members of the tribe.

There were significant limitations placed on this mission. Our troops weren't lodged on the reservation, so they traveled from the Tucson area every day which took over an hour. Once they were on site, they had to be accompanied by a Tribal Council representative and an archaeologist. Both the representative and archaeologist were good-natured, but neither of them worked after 3:00 p.m. and several times operations were halted because one of them had a dentist appointment or a meeting off-site. The mission was further hampered by the greatest factor of all—temperatures regularly reached 110 degrees Fahrenheit, which severely limited activities to 30 minutes out of every hour, particularly for unacclimated New Englanders.

Upon arrival in the area I was amazed that the border is essentially unmarked in the desert. Here and there a strand of rusty barbed wire or a tilted granite marker might be visible, but generally there is nothing to distinguish American sand and scrub brush from the Mexican desert. The area struck me as the deadliest place on the planet. Dented signs warned of the dangers of venomous snakes and lizards, every now and then an emaciated wild horse could be seen slinking along in search of water, and buzzards circled endlessly in the harsh sunlight.

Road construction operations were halted almost daily when a Saguaro cactus blocked the proposed roadway. The Tohono O'odham people believe that the souls of their ancestors reside in cactuses. So each cactus had to be evaluated by several Tribal Council members to determine how close the roadway could pass. Less frequently the archaeologist located evidence of ancient human life and construction was paused or rerouted while he determined if the site was significant.

On at least one occasion, human remains were encountered near the proposed roadway. A call would be made to the Border Patrol who would quickly remove the sun bleached bones without much fanfare. We learned that human remains found in the desert are usually the result of border crossers who die from dehydration or snakebite while trying to enter the U.S. at a remote point to evade arrest. The other cause is more sinister— the desert is a convenient depository for the victims of drug cartel violence because the heat and carnivorous creatures soon remove evidence of foul play. The nonchalant way the remains of these poor folks were collected saddened me when I thought about the urgency we would regard a body or bones found in a park or forest in any other location in the U.S.

One afternoon as I drove along the border path that we would soon improve into a dirt road, I became curious about a low ridge about 300 yards into Mexico. I parked the SUV and looked around. There was nothing in sight for miles, other than sand, scrub, and the distant mountains in Mexico. And so I set out on foot across the border.

I was surprised to find that the far side of the ridge looked like a town dump. There were piles of water bottles, diapers, clothing, and occasional household items like toasters or pots and pans. Some of the water bottles still had liquid in them and the diapers looked like they were recently used. Apparently this barren ridge was the final hiding spot before border crossers made the last dash into the U.S. under the cover of darkness.

As I returned to my vehicle and drove back to the construction site, I drew up alongside a green and white Border Patrol pickup truck. I rolled down my window to greet the agent. "You just had to do it, didn't you," he said with a grin. "What are you talking about?" I asked innocently.

"Everybody who comes down here just has to take a stroll into Mexico," he laughed. "I guess it's something you need to brag about when you get home." I shrugged, rolled up my window, and drove on. But, of course, he was right. Although the border is unmarked in the desert, ground sensors have a greater range than I would have thought likely.

Our last mission in Arizona was perhaps the closest brush we had with the drug cartels who are our greatest enemy south of the border.. A small engineer contingent was tasked with constructing vehicle barriers in the remote rolling woodlands near Patagonia, Arizona. The vehicle barriers were constructed by welding three four-foot sections of steel rail together. Then they were placed along the border at about one-yard intervals in an effort to prevent drug or human smugglers from driving across.

The area around Patagonia consists of cattle ranches, farms, and abandoned mining ghost towns. Although it's hot like most of Southern Arizona, the region has ponds, streams, trees, and green vegetation.

We loaded up our rails and supplies at a large, dusty depot in nearby Naco, Arizona, which is notorious for drug smuggling tunnels. Naco is a small, dusty town that's separated from its Mexican mirror image by a tiny customs station and a large, steel wall. As we loaded up our materials, I looked across the border into the rundown Mexican buildings. I caught a glint of sunshine reflecting off glass lenses, and I prayed they were binoculars and not a rifle scope. As I nonchalantly ducked behind a pile of railroad tiles, I saw the reflection again from the top floor of what looked like an abandoned brick building. Despite the warm afternoon, a chill ran down my spine.

Most of the work took place on wooded hillsides and in sunny valleys, but there was one sector that ran across open high ground. During this phase of the operation we were accompanied by a Border Patrol agent with an M-4 rifle. During all of our activities in Arizona we were unarmed because U.S. statutes restrict the military from the use of armed force within our borders except under rare emergency circumstances. Our well-armed Border Patrol comrade informed us that his station chief thought it best that we have some firepower on site because of recent drug cartel activity in the area. He pointed across the border to a roadway about a mile in the distance and explained that cars would occasionally stop and pop off a few rounds. Smiling at us, he joked that it was highly unlikely that they'd hit anything, but it was the cartel's way of reminding us that they were still bosses on their side of the border. Whenever we saw a car traveling along the distant Mexican roadway we hunkered down a bit closer to frontal cover.

Perhaps the incident that most defines my life as a citizen-soldier occurred during this mission. At this time my civilian occupation was assistant principal of a public high school. When I was called away for military duty, my administrator colleagues picked up the slack. I'm particularly grateful to Dave Uminski, our principal, who never complained or questioned when I needed to pack up and go.

Needless to say the tension was fairly high on the hillside as we placed the vehicle barriers because we realized that our activities were being closely watched by the drug cartels. Late one morning, a middle-aged man suddenly appeared from nowhere and stumbled toward us. He was strangely dressed in a white tee shirt, black polyester pants, shiny loafers and a mesh trucker baseball hat on his head. As he approached, he called out, "Agua, por favor!"

We gave him a bottle of water and motioned for him to sit on the ground in the shade while we called the Border Patrol to come pick him up. For some reason our armed Border Patrol Agent wasn't in the area.

When my Blackberry cell phone buzzed, I assumed it was the Border Patrol making coordination. I answered the call. "Greg, is this you?" the voice asked. "Who is this?" I asked, realizing that the Border Patrol didn't even know my first name.

"It's Dave," the voice continued. "How are you?"

"I'm great, Dave, but I'm kind of busy right now," I said.

"Well, I didn't want to bother you, but we can't find last year's SAT testing results. Are they in your desk?"

"Sure, check the second drawer on the right side. There's an envelope that says, 'College Board,'" I responded.

"Great," he said. "See you soon." I just shook my head and waited for the Border Patrol.

My time on the border taught me an important lesson—immigration and border security are perhaps the most morally fraught, complex issues with which our nation wrestles. Whenever I hear someone pontificate about "open borders" or "shutting down" border access, I quietly ask, "Have you ever been there?"

Taps

The long convoy of camouflage trucks rumbled along the New York Thruway in the summer sun. Looking down the straightaways, drivers could see waves of heat shimmering above the pavement like wispy ghosts. Even with the windows rolled down, temperatures in the truck cabs soared and the dull whine of the engine threatened to lull tired drivers into a trance. One of the lumbering cargo trucks began to weave back and forth. Suddenly it careened into a guardrail, bounced off a rock wall, then flipped onto its side as it screeched to a halt on the asphalt. The driver was dragged along the pavement under the truck. A military ambulance, recovery vehicles, and the commander's HMMWV raced to the site where the battered truck lay on its side like a dead whale.

A hundred miles away I was mowing the lawn in the summer sunshine when my wife appeared in the kitchen door. Over the growl of the lawnmower she called out and motioned that I had a telephone call but there was nothing particularly urgent in her gestures or voice.

In my first year of brigade command I had become accustomed to phone calls about all sorts of matters, usually involving mundane administrative matters. I wiped the sweat off my forehead and pressed the house phone to my ear. I heard the flat voice of Lt. Col. John MacPherson, the tough, seasoned commander of our Military Police Battalion. In an almost detached way, Mac informed me of the fatal highway accident. He described the tragic death of a driver in his battalion who had been crushed under his cargo truck when it overturned on the New York Thruway. The unit was returning home from a successful two-week training exercise at Fort Drum. Mac assured me that the New York State Police were investigating the scene, a serious incident report had been filed at National Guard State Headquarters, and the rest of the unit was now arriving at their armory. I thanked him for his professional actions following the accident and told him that I'd meet him at the unit's armory as soon as I could get there.

After changing into a uniform, I drove to the armory as quickly as possible although it was an hour away. I had never dealt with the death of a soldier on duty in my command before. During the hour's drive to the armory I had a chance to think through all the details of what needed to be done—family notification, recovery of personal items, initiating an accident investigation, and so many other details. I had a brief conversation with Maj. Gen. Mason as I drove. He assured me that the unit would have the full support of State Headquarters for whatever I felt it needed.

I arrived at the unit's armory after most of the soldiers had parked their vehicles but before Lt. Col. MacPherson got there. Troops busied themselves with offloading weapons and equipment, lining up trucks, and all the small tasks that need to be tended to after a long training exercise. But I noticed that they spoke only in hushed tones and slowly shuffled, almost tiptoed, as they went about their work. It was almost like they were fearful of upsetting the quiet that had settled on the armory.

The first soldiers I saw in the company office were the medics. I thanked them for their efforts to save the crushed driver and they began to tell me about the accident scene, becoming more anguished as they talked. Finally one of the medics broke down in tears, saying, "I tried to administer CPR, Sir, but I couldn't find enough of him to do the compressions." I found myself putting my hand on his shoulder and saying, "You did all you could to save him, Specialist. It wasn't your fault that he didn't make it. Thank you for doing all you could."

I remember a similar conversation with the company commander, Captain Rick Cipro, as he recounted what he wished he'd done to prevent this horrible accident. I found myself assuring him that he wasn't to blame for this man's death and I thanked him for all he had done to get the rest of the convoy home safely. The conversation was brief because Capt. Cipro needed to attend to getting the rest of the unit accounted for while he consoled and comforted grieving soldiers. Dealing with his own grief had to wait until after he completed his duties as a commander. Maybe that was a blessing in disguise.

By this time Lt. Col. MacPherson had arrived. We went to a quiet office where he hung his head in exhaustion and talked about all the things he wished he had done that might have prevented the accident. Gently I corrected him. "Mac, there wasn't a damn thing you could have done to stop this from happening. You did all the right things to react to the incident by getting the State Police there quickly and notifying State Headquarters. No amount of blame or regret is going to bring this guy back to life. We need to be concerned about his buddies, his family, and the people who are mourning his death."

After Mac and I alked, I had a brief moment to gather my thoughts. Slowly I realized that my main responsibility as a senior leader was to listen and give absolution. Too many leaders, buddies, and even soldiers who hardly knew the victim would blame themselves to varying degrees for actions that they thought could have prevented the accident. It was my job to dismiss any self-accusation of blame and focus soldiers on their responsibility to one another and what needed to be done going forward.

When I stepped out of the company office, I noticed the furtive glances of soldiers as they passed by me and knew what I had to do next. I called the entire company together in the open assembly area in the middle of the armory. They started to line up in formation, but I motioned for them to gather around me in a semicircle. I don't specifically recall what I said to them, but I know it was permission to grieve, a call to support one another, and sincere assurance that no one was to blame for the death of their comrade. We ended with a moment of silence. Soon the unit was dismissed and soldiers headed home after two long weeks away.

Days later the deceased soldier was laid to rest in a state veterans' cemetery. Maj. Gen. Mason attended along with civilian leaders and hundreds of National Guardsmen all sweating in their dress uniforms. The Army's comprehensive casualty assistance system tended to the family's needs during the time of their intense grief and loss. Under Capt. Cipro's compassionate leadership the company recovered as well as could be expected after the loss of a member of their military family.

Because it involved loss of life on duty, by regulation there was an extensive investigation into the accident which took weeks to complete. Although my colleague, Col. Chuck Maguire, conducted a complete and thorough investigation, regulations call for the brigade commander of the deceased soldier to present the findings of the investigation to the immediate family. I received a copy of Chuck's investigation report to prepare for my briefing to the family. The report found no fault with vehicle equipment, convoy preparations, or leadership responsibilities. It also contained the gruesome details of the driver's death.

On the day of the briefing I arrived for a rehearsal. A conference room was set aside at State Headquarters. Refreshments were laid out on a white tablecloth in the corner. The Department of the Army sent a short, balding, abrasive sergeant major to coach us on the presentation. Without any introductions or recognition of my rank, he pulled me aside and lectured me about exactly what I was and wasn't expected to say during the course of the briefing. Perhaps it was the nature of his specialization that made him so irritating, but his guidance only served to elevate the tension surrounding the briefing. About fifteen officers and sergeants, all attired uncomfortably in dress uniforms, milled about as we nervously awaited the family.

At length a half dozen people stepped awkwardly into the conference room. They glanced at the refreshments after we formally greeted them, but they didn't touch any of the food. As I recall, the soldier's parents, siblings, and a friend—possibly a lover—settled into a row of chairs that was set up in front of a screen. They kept their coats on.

I stepped forward and introduced myself, offering the condolences of all their loved one's commanders, sergeants, and buddies. Then I launched into the antiseptic recitation of the accident investigation report as I had been instructed by the blunt and irksome sergeant major. There was no opportunity to say, "Your son/brother/lover seemed like a really good guy. We're so sorry for your pain and grief at the sudden loss of someone so young and full of life. In a different way we share your loss because he was a member of our military family too. All of us would do anything to have prevented this tragic accident."

The family members sat in stony silence as I rattled off the findings of the report. As I glanced at their faces I could read doubt, mistrust, anger, and deep sadness. There were no tears. When I finished the presentation the soldier's siblings asked one or two quiet questions, but there were no heightened emotions. A cloud of quiet sorrow filled the room.

The family members glanced at one another then rose from their chairs. They nodded to us as they filed out of the conference room, but there were no handshakes and no polite words of parting. The irritating sergeant major caught a late flight back to DC and the rest of us were left to our own unsettled thoughts about the tragic passing of this soldier.

The Army desensitizes soldiers to death right from the beginning. I remember my earliest days in the Army began as we ran in formation while the sun rose through the gloom and someone sang out cheerfully. In particular I remember echoing these lyrics to the tune of "Camptown Races" as we trotted along keeping perfect time with the synchronized crunch of our boots.

> I'm going home in a body bag doo-da, doo-da.
> I'm going home in a body bag, oh da-doo-dah-day.
> Shot between the eyes.
> Shot between the thighs.
> Oh, I'm going home in a body bag, oh da-doo-dah-day.

This shouldn't be attributed to callousness or insensitivity, but rather it's an occupational necessity that those who are entrusted by society to use lethal force can't be too preoccupied with mortality when they're called upon to do their deadly work. When a leader becomes incapacitated, the next in line needs to step up to take command without shedding any tears over the leader's loss. More importantly, when the soldier in front falls wounded the soldiers behind need to step forward to take their place in the ranks without looking down to see the gushing blood or shredded flesh. Needless to say, the elimination of an enemy must never be mourned as the passing of another human being. I was to see the critical importance of this detached view of mortality later in my career.

Although soldiers understand that they might die or they might lose their buddies in the course of performing their dangerous duties, this clinically detached view of death collides with the sentimentality that surrounds the profession of arms. I can't attribute the quote, but some wise person once said that "soldiers are the last romantics," and I wholeheartedly agree.

What this startling phrase means is that soldiers are some of the last people in the world who believe in a black and white narrative to life's stories. Soldiers see themselves as the "good guys" who are locked in an eternal struggle against the forces of evil, the black hats, the "bad guys." A popular tee shirt logo states proudly, "God Bless the Good Guys," over the symbols of the five U.S. armed services. These aren't casual words or a catch phrase—they subtly reflect the belief that U.S. forces are on a divine mission. Beneath the hardened shell every soldier hopes to be the golden knight who triumphs over the sneaky, sinister, low-life evildoer who seeks to burn our homes, kidnap our children, and deflower our sisters. Tobacco-spitting nonchalance barely conceals hearts that thrill to the sounds of the National Anthem, chests that puff out when the Stars and Stripes or regimental flags flutter in the breeze, and eyes that well up when F-16 swoop down out of the sky. While there is something powerful and deadly in the warrior ethos, there is also something innocent and wondrous in the idealistic belief of absolute righteousness.

Perhaps it's this complicated view of death and mortality that contributes to the heightened rate of suicides in the military community. I've presided over enough funerals and known enough buddies who took their own lives to be firmly perplexed by the essential question—Why? But I must leave it to others who are wiser and have a better understanding of human psychology to uncover the roots of military suicide, because I've come to accept that I'll never understand.

Soldiers don't mourn the loss of a comrade at the moment when he or she falls—they can't—but they grieve deeply when the smoke clears and the battle is over. The military never forgets its dead, but it memorializes them in vastly different ways. The pomp and pageantry that accompanies a formal military funeral is rich with symbolism and something wondrous to behold. Anyone who has watched a burial at Arlington National Cemetery knows this.

I was asked to preside over the burial of an elderly brigadier general who was being interred in his western Massachusetts hometown where the borders of Massachusetts, Vermont, and New York meet. The old general had lived a good life that spanned over eighty years and he was fondly remembered by the community. His family requested full military burial honors for a brigadier general, but I don't think they realized what that entailed.

The cannon crew that was tasked with providing the eleven-gun salute traveled west from the seacoast along a route that took them across the width of the Bay State then north through upstate New York until they could find a straight route into the little town in the Berkshire Hills. A platoon of soldiers in dress blue uniforms spent their work day providing a rifle firing squad and a formation of soldiers to surround the burial area. The bugler who sounded Taps and the flag-folding casket detail had traveled hundreds of miles from the Boston area.

After prayers were offered by the grave, the cannons roared, the rifles crackled, and the casket crew executed the crisp, precise movements to fold the U.S. flag that draped the casket. I presented the tri-fold flag to the general's daughter, and repeated the prescribed statement, which must be delivered verbatim. I knew it by heart because I had pronounced it too many times: "On behalf of the President of the United States, the United States Army, and a grateful Nation, please accept this flag as a symbol of appreciation for your loved one's honorable and faithful service."[19]

She was dry-eyed, but overwhelmed by the pageantry. Once the ceremony was over I made it a point to thank all the soldiers who had cheerfully contributed to this elegant send-off for a general whom they never knew. But quietly I roughly calculated the cost of payroll, mileage, even ammunition, and concluded that this sendoff had cost Uncle Sam more than a few thousand tax dollars. Still, it was somehow refreshing and satisfying to realize that the military never forgets its leaders and chieftains, regardless of how much time has passed since their glory days. However I decided to advise my family to forego most of the pageantry when I meet my inevitable end.

I also recall another, quite different, graveside memorial. Howie the Cook was a sergeant in the battalion headquarters and he was a unique character. He constantly muttered incoherently, but he never denied anyone an extra helping, a hot cup of coffee after the kitchen was closed, or a sandwich for drivers who arrived too late for hot chow. Howie lived with his elderly mother and it was rumored that he was secretly wealthy. Perhaps that rumor persisted because he would show up at Christmas parties in a three-piece business suit with a jaunty fedora perched on his head. Then he'd take off his jacket and start cooking.

Poor Howie fell ill one winter and he quickly passed away from the illness. Bad winter weather prevented many unit members from attending his funeral. And so he was buried under a flat marker in the veterans' cemetery without many of his buddies present to remember him.

That summer the battalion happened to be training in an area fairly close to where Howie was buried. At the end of one training day, the headquarters sergeant told me that he had arranged for a bus to take anyone who was interested over to the veterans' cemetery to visit Howie's grave. He wasn't asking for my permission, he was inviting me to come along. About twenty of us piled into the big green Army bus. I think I may have been the only officer on the bus, but rank had no bearing on this trip.

The sun was low in the sky and we could hear birds singing. The sweet scent of freshly mown grass greeted us as we picked our way between the flat grave markers, careful not to step on any of them. Two soldiers set a big red cooler down on the grass when we reached Howie's grave. The headquarters sergeant was the first to speak when we surrounded Howie's marker. "Hardly any of us were able to see Howie off like we wanted to. So I figured we'd have our own little memorial service, the way he would have liked." He motioned toward the cooler. "So grab whatever you want in the cooler and let's remember Howie in our own way."

Everyone reached into the freezing ice water and grabbed the wine cooler, soda, or beer can of their choice. I hoped no one from the cemetery would notice and try to stop us because that wouldn't have ended well. One by one, each of us stepped forward to describe our favorite memory of Howie and offer our best wishes for him wherever he was. One remembrance sounded something like this,

"Hey, Howie, I'm real sorry about what happened to you, man. Just wanted to say that we miss you at the mess tent—except that it's a lot quieter over there and the food tastes better too—just kidding, buddy. I hope that wherever you are the food's good and they don't ever make you scrub the pots and pans… But don't do any more cooking up there 'cause maybe angels can get indigestion too."

After each speaker finished, he or she took a swig and then tipped a splash of their beverage onto the marker saying, "This is for you, Howie." I wanted to just watch and listen, but glances told me that it was my turn. I cleared my throat and said, "Howie, I'll always remember the time we were taking a piss side-by-side and you said, 'Hey I was in OCS once, but I quit. If I stayed in I'd be like a Captain General or something by now.' I just wanted you to know that there's no such thing as a Captain General … or maybe they promoted you to one where you are now. Anyway, thanks for all you gave us and I don't just mean food—thanks for the laughs, thanks for never bitching about the hard jobs, and thanks for always lifting us up. We miss you."

Then I offered my graveside toast. When everyone said his or her peace, the headquarters sergeant said quietly, "I guess we better get back.

They'll be wondering where we went." One-by-one each person stepped in front of Howie's grave for a private, silent moment. Some knelt. Some blessed themselves. Some just stood and poured out the last drops of their drinks.

We were subdued as we climbed onto the bus, but we all smiled, and we all felt a little closer as a team, as a family. I've often thought about Howie's unorthodox memorial service. If we leave our friends with memories that bring smiles and thoughts that bind them closer together, then we will have lived a life of purpose and meaning, indeed—regardless of whether there are cannons or cans of beer to mark our sendoff.

Hubris

I had just assumed command of a brigade, taken charge of a small military facility, and recently had Colonel's eagles pinned to my uniform—life was good. As with most fresh starts in life, I was enjoying a honeymoon with the brigade staff—my orders were followed promptly, every idea I proposed was brilliant, and my jokes were witty. You see, at this stage of the relationship, the people with whom I worked were figuring out my limits, vulnerabilities, and, most important, whether or not I could be trusted if they spoke the truth. But, in my overconfidence and naivety, I had convinced myself that life as a brigade commander was going to be a breeze.

Anyway, it was a cold, raw afternoon as I drove through the post gates and headed home. The dismal weather couldn't dampen my self-satisfaction as I congratulated myself on the auspicious beginning of my new command. Nearing the highway, I spotted a lanky, young soldier, head hunched against the rain, walking down the road. I pulled over and asked him if he needed a ride.

"Oh, thanks," he gasped, wiping the rain off his face as he got into the car. "I'm headed for the train station. Are you going near there?" I told him that I'd drive him to the train and asked where he lived. He was pretty talkative, and told me all about his apartment and his college studies in Boston. Then our conversation turned to military matters. "What do you do in the Army?" I asked.

"I'm a mechanic in the maintenance shop," he replied. "It's dirty work, but I'm kind of glad I picked that job because I'm learning good stuff. When I finally save up enough money to buy my own car, I'll be able to do my own oil changes and brakes and simple repairs like that." Then he paused and looked at me. "What do you do?" he asked innocently.

I chuckled inside as I prepared to answer. "Why, I'm the brigade commander, soldier," I stated in a response that was totally devoid of any shred of humility. He looked puzzled for a moment, then asked, ""Does that mean you work for the First Sergeant?"

Perhaps there was an audible rush of wind as my ego deflated like an old balloon after a birthday party. Slowly I gathered my wits and turned to the soldier. "Yeah, that's right. I work for the First Sergeant, too," I replied, hoping the egg on my face was truly invisible. "So, tell me, will the Patriots make it to the Super Bowl next year?" Perhaps a wise man would have learned his lesson and embraced humility, but I have never claimed to be a wise man.

Several years later, on Christmas Eve day, I found myself awaiting the arrival of a truck company who had spent the last year overseas in support of Operation Iraqi Freedom. My teenage son joined me and I was grateful for his company on the long car ride. At that time I was the Assistant Adjutant General, but I was still a colonel. My promotion to brigadier general was slowly making its way through the gears of the federal government machine, but it had been two years. Frankly I was beginning to doubt if my promotion would ever be approved.

The unit's armory was a whirlwind of activity. The drill hall was festooned with streamers that frequently became entangled in the feet of frolicking kids, many of whom were excited about the arrivals of the two most beloved men in their lives—Santa and Dad—and neither had been seen for nearly a year. Wives, decked out in holiday sweaters, nervously tended to the food tables. They were as anxious as the kids, in a different way, but they did a better job of hiding it. Ear splitting Christmas carols blared from a speaker system that somebody thought was a good idea. The whole place was a loud, spinning, red and green arena of chaos, anticipation, and suppressed joy. Everyone—mothers and fathers, husbands and wives, sons and daughters, lovers, friends, and buddies—anxiously awaited the sound of the buses.

Congressman Jim McGovern joined me as we waited for the troops, who were inevitably delayed coming through Hartford, despite the police escort. I mention the Congressman's presence at this event on Christmas Eve because too often we criticize members of Congress, but we don't recognize their long hours of community support. Jim McGovern was always there when soldiers in his district were heading downrange or coming home.

Finally we heard the sirens of the police escort in the distance and everyone rushed outside as the buses pulled into the parking lot to cheers and squeals of delight. Still accustomed to military discipline, the troops filed off the buses and fell into formation in the armory. I was wise enough to welcome them back in less than ninety seconds and they were dismissed to a stampede of shouts, hugs, and more than a few tears.

I congratulated as many of the troops as I could, and, when the crowd began to leave the armory, my son and I headed for the door. One of our Public Affairs NCOs stopped me. "Can I have a quote for the media release, General?" he asked. "Sure," I responded, "but don't call me 'General' in your article. I'm still just a colonel."

He smiled at me. "Actually, Sir, we were notified that your promotion order came in yesterday. Merry Christmas, General." I thanked him for his good wishes and gave him a very general-sounding quote, but the reality of my promotion didn't really sink in.

*   *   *

Shortly after Governor Deval Patrick was sworn in, he announced that Brigadier General Joseph C. Carter would be appointed as the next Adjutant General. Tall, ramrod straight, with a deep authoritative voice, Brig. Gen. Joe Carter assumed his duties as Adjutant General. He had an impressive record of law enforcement credentials: Chief of Police in the Martha's Vineyard community of Oak's Bluff, Chief of Boston's Transit Police, President of the International Association of Chiefs of Police.

Carter always chose his words carefully and maintained an aloof, almost regal, bearing. Perhaps as the first African American leader in several assignments he was wary of scrutiny. In private I found him to be warm, charismatic, and generous to those he trusted. During the command transition from Mason to Carter I was mainly concerned with the affairs of my own brigade. I welcomed Carter and congratulated him on his promotion, but our relationship was stiff and formal. Because Carter had left his position of Assistant Adjutant General when he was promoted, there was now a vacancy for a brigadier general. I was aware that many of my fellow colonels were actively campaigning for this assignment, but I couldn't be bothered. First, it was never my style to ingratiate myself to anyone and second, I didn't have the political connections I thought were needed to become a general officer in Massachusetts.

Carter chose to leave the Assistant Adjutant General slot vacant for well over a year. Then one day while I was at a training course in Missouri, I received a phone call from Brigadier General Sellars, my direct boss. In an off-handed way he informed me that Carter was accepting applications for Assistant Adjutant General, which required an essay on the candidate's future vision for the Massachusetts National Guard. There was one catch—the application must be submitted within 72 hours. As he signed off the call, I had the distinct impression that Sellars didn't think I had a chance. However I thought, "Nothing ventured, nothing gained," so I emailed my application the following day. I don't think I gave the matter a second thought in the days ahead.

A few days after I returned home from Missouri, our home phone rang. On the other end was the Adjutant General's secretary. "Hello,

Colonel Smith, welcome back. Can you hold for the Adjutant General?" "Sure, standing by," I stammered, bracing myself for the trouble that might prompt a direct call from the Adjutant General.

Moments later, the deep voice of Major General Carter boomed over the line. "Hello, Colonel Smith, did you have a good time in Missouri?"

"Yes, Sir, it was very informative," I replied cautiously.

"Well I'm just calling to see if you'd like to be the next Assistant Adjutant General," he said.

"Yes, Sir," I was stunned.

"What do you mean 'Yes, Sir'? Is that all you have to say about being offered a promotion to general?" he chuckled.

"Thank you, General. This is quite a shock," I said.

"Don't thank me until you see what the job entails. We'll talk more when we meet. Call my secretary to set up an appointment with me. Now go tell your wife the good news, General." I called out to my wife and gushed, "Nora, I'm going to be promoted to General!" She looked at me stoically, then asked, "Does this mean you'll stay in the Guard longer?"

"Yes … probably," I replied. "Oh, shit," she muttered. "My dear, that isn't the way this news is usually greeted," I chuckled. She turned away and silently leafed through the day's mail.

I continued to serve as the commander of the 26th Maneuver Enhancement Brigade while I waited for my promotion packet to crawl through the long bureaucratic process. In the end it took nearly two full years from the time my application was submitted to the final approval of the U.S. Senate.

However in late December 2010 I officially became a brigadier general. The next date on which I reported for duty was the drill weekend in early January. I wore my colonel's eagle on my camouflage uniform because it didn't seem quite right to pin on my own star for the first time. Perhaps I was overthinking the rank transition.

Major General Carter passed me in the hallway and called out, "General Smith, you're out of uniform."

"Well, General, I figured that someone should award the rank before I wore it," I replied expecting that he'd notify me when my promotion ceremony would take place.

"Do you have a general's star with you?" Carter asked. When I replied that I did, he asked me to hand it to him. Then he tore off my velcro colonel's eagle and slapped the star into place on my camouflage shirt. "Now let's get to work, General," he barked as he continued down the hallway. That was my promotion ceremony to brigadier general. However I did host a celebration about a month later at which Major General Carter offered a few more gracious words of congratulations.

Although my wife wasn't exactly delighted about any action that would extend my military career, she gave me a brigadier general's flag for Christmas, which she must have been saving for the day when my promotion came through. Traditionally an Army general's headquarters flies a red flag with the number of stars to which the general is entitled, in my case, one star. Accordingly, a few days after Christmas, I marched out and hauled down Old Glory from the flagpole in our yard. In its place I hoisted up my bright red flag with its one white star. As it flapped in the wind I was filled with pride and self-satisfaction.

Two days later it snowed. As I was shoveling my driveway, our neighbor, a wizened New Englander, strolled over. We exchanged holiday good wishes. "I noticed you put up a new flag in the yard," he observed.

"Yes, I certainly did," I responded, bursting with pride.

"Well, a couple of us were wondering why you wanted to have a Cuban flag on your flagpole," he said with a quizzical look on his face.

Sheepishly I explained the significance of my red flag. My neighbor chuckled and apologized for mistaking my brigadier general flag for the Cuban banner. After we wished each other a Happy New Year, he shuffled over to his house. I waited until my neighbor was out of sight, then hauled down that red flag as quickly as I could. By sunset, the Stars and Stripes were fluttering again over our yard. Later I realized that my neighbor was an Army veteran who would clearly recognize a brigadier general's flag. Had I been bamboozled by a wry Yankee who wanted to serve up a little humility to his neighbor?

An Army general officer's dress uniform is a fairly plain suit that's a shade called, "Midnight Blue," or almost black. Although I wore it proudly, it often created more than its share of awkwardness. When I've been in public places, I've often been approached by friendly civilians who ask, "How long have you been in the Navy?" It has happened so often that I've become quite good at responding without a smirk, "Actually not all that long." But I usually follow up with an explanation.

In warm weather we dispense with the blue/black jacket and wear a white shirt with black shoulder boards and the black/blue pants. Admittedly we bear a close resemblance to airline pilots. I've lost count of how many times I've been confronted in airports by frazzled travelers who approach me to ask questions like, "Can you tell me why Delta 573 to Omaha is delayed?" I usually just smile and point to the nearest service desk. Once I was waved to the head of the line by a TSA screener who winked at me and said, "I've always been a supporter of the Salvation Army."

Perhaps the most embarrassing confusion about my uniform occurred on an Irish warship. They hosted a reception for all naval officers who were in port for a small gathering of allied warships. I was invited as the local land forces commander. Because it was summer, the uniform was Class B—short-sleeve white shirt, blue/black pants, and black shoulder boards. Now I must explain that a U.S. Army brigadier general's shoulder boards are marked by one silver star and one thin gold stripe. In most naval services, all officers have one silver star, but seniority is noted by the number and width of gold stripes on the sleeve or shoulder board. After paying my respects to the ship's captain, I was puzzled when I went to get a cold beer and was jostled at the bar by young officers. Ordinarily young officers prefer to keep their distance from generals or admirals, or at least treat senior officers with some level of courtesy and deference. But here I was dodging elbows and bumps as I tried not to spill my beer. Perhaps even more perplexing, the bartender addressed me as "mate."

After trying to strike up conversations with other naval officers who didn't seem interested in talking to me, two young Irish officers approached me. "Excuse me," they said, "I hope you're not offended, but we were wondering how someone at your age could still be an ensign." (Ensign is the entry-level officer rank in the U.S. Navy.) I looked at them a bit puzzled until they pointed to my shoulder boards. I chuckled and explained that the silver star was the insignia of a U.S. Army brigadier general. The Irishmen were a bit chagrined, but we all had a good laugh and I guess it was a good thing because they offered to get me a jostle-free beer.

All of the confusion about ceremonies and flags and uniforms taught me a valuable lesson in the long run—if you take yourself too seriously, you just end up looking like a fool.

A Mighty Wind

At 4:17 p.m. on June 1, 2011, a tornado tore a 37-mile path of destruction about 300 yards wide that ran through the Berkshire foothills and across the city center of Springfield, Massachusetts. Three people were killed by the flying debris, but it's nothing short of miraculous that many other deaths didn't result from the devastation.[20]

I was scheduled to take command of Joint Task Force Massachusetts, which is responsible for emergency response, on June 2, 2011. However on June 1st I was at a hotel function room chaperoning a high school pre-graduation banquet. My cell phone buzzed and I recognized the voice of my counterpart in the Connecticut National Guard.

"Hey Greg, I just wanted you to know our Blackhawks are ready to assist you if you need them," he said.

"Thanks, but I think we're all set." I replied a bit puzzled.

"I hope so, man, because we hear it's a mess up in the Berkshire Hills," he continued.

"What are you talking about?" I asked. "An EF 3 tornado just ripped through your state within a few miles of our border," he yelled.

I quickly thanked him and called into Massachusetts National Guard headquarters. As I drove to the Massachusetts Emergency Management Agency operations center, I looked up at an early evening sky to the west that was a churning kaleidoscope of purple and orange. I've never seen such a colorful sunset and I hope I never see one like it again.

I met my friend and former boss, Brig. Gen. Sellars, at the operations center. Tom was celebrating the end of his command by taking a long-awaited Florida vacation. In fact he had tickets for an early morning flight the next day. "This is a helluva way to spend my last day on the job," he said. "But tomorrow it's all yours, brother."

After a series of meetings with state officials, we issued orders to deploy military police and engineers with heavy equipment to the devastated area as soon as possible. We also laid on a mission request to fly Governor Deval Patrick and other officials to survey the damage.

In the predawn gloom of June 2nd I waited on the helipad behind Massachusetts National Guard headquarters as the crew went through their operations checks. A Blackhawk holds 13 passengers other than the pilots and crew chief. One by one the passengers arrived. I recall at least four Massachusetts cabinet secretaries, a public affairs staffer, Senator John Kerry (D) and Senator Scott Brown (R), who were uncomfortably seated in adjacent jump seats, cheek to cheek. Last to arrive was Governor Patrick, who insisted on sitting in the gunner's seat. All I could think of was the disastrous photo of Governor Michael Dukakis with his head poking up out of a tank. I believe it cost him the presidency. Any open seats were filled with staffers and security personnel. I remember one secretary who ignored our advice not to sit in the rear seat closest to the open door because of the uncomfortable rush of air. I quietly enjoyed watching his face turn green when we lifted off and he was hit with a blast of propeller wash.

We touched down in Monson, Massachusetts, and were startled by the sight of a neighborhood that had been laid flat. A square half mile area was littered with shattered slivers of wood, household appliances, over-turned cars, and felled trees. On the outskirts of the area, one house was completely inverted—the peak of the roof rested upside down into the foundation.

Dozens of stunned residents picked through the piles of wreckage searching for some of their personal belongings. As I spoke with them, I was impressed by their resilience. No one seemed to be overcome by the enormity of their loss. In fact, most seemed grateful to be unharmed. A few residents had actually begun clearing debris or shoring up sections of structures that could be salvaged.

I recall one woman saying she knew it was serious when she watched as her treadmill was sucked out of her living room picture window. Another woman told me she was thankful that someone had found her checkbook—over one hundred miles away in Vermont! We assured the residents that we would do everything in our power to assist them. Then I coordinated with the fire chief who did an out-standing job as Incident Commander for the relief effort and reassured him that National Guard engineers, firefighters, and military police were on the way to Monson.

As we waited for Governor Patrick to return to the helicopter for our return flight, I chatted with Lt. Col. Dave Underwood, our pilot, a man with a wonderfully dry sense of humor. "So, Dave, were you a little ner-vous flying a chopper with all these VIPs?" I asked. He paused, then said, "Well, General, I don't usually think about such things when I'm flying, but I said to myself, 'If something goes wrong on this flight there's going to be a whole lot of upward mobility in Massachusetts tomorrow.'"

Brig. Gen. Smith listens to reports from Massachusetts National Guard firefighters involved in recovery operations following the tornado that leveled parts of Monson, Massachusetts, in 2011 (Massachusetts National Guard PAO).

On our return flight to headquarters we were able to get a better overview of the tornado area. The powerful winds cut a straight 37-mile path through the hills of western Massachusetts up over peaks and down through valleys, cutting through forests, small towns, and the city of Springfield where it leveled a section of the downtown area. The swath of damage was about a quarter mile wide. Structures within the path were demolished, but houses only a few hundred yards away were untouched. It was almost like a giant had taken a lawnmower and cut a straight path through western Massachusetts.

When we landed at headquarters the real work began. The Joint Operations Center was humming with activity as we responded to requests for brush clearing details, traffic control points, transport, and troops to staff supply distribution points throughout Western Massachusetts.

The Joint Staff is the body of senior officers and NCOs at headquarters who execute all the details of the commander's plan. There are colonels who are in charge of personnel, intelligence, operations, logistics, communications, finances, legal issues, public affairs, aviation, and other areas who make up the staff. All of these professionals report to the chief of staff who orchestrates their actions, coordinates their efforts, and provides a kick in the ass if necessary. Although there's frequent interaction between the commander and the staff, formal communication takes place at Command Update Briefings, usually scheduled for 0800 and 1600 hours daily.

This was my maiden voyage as a Joint Task Force Commander and my first rodeo with Col. Frank Magurn as chief of staff. Frank was a brilliant, experienced full time officer with firm beliefs about how things should run, and so the operation was humming along. However when Major General Carter, the Adjutant General and my boss, arrived for the afternoon Command Update Briefing, something short-circuited. The staff made simple errors in their presentations. As Carter's irritation became more apparent, anxiety increased and they became more hesitant—never a good look for senior officers.

Suddenly Carter stood up, glared at me and bellowed, "General Smith, you clearly have some work to do with your staff." Then he stormed out of the conference room. I was deeply embarrassed, confused, and probably feared that I'd be relieved of command. Without thinking, I called the senior staff to join me in a side office. Then I launched into an angry, expletive-laden explosion about what I thought of their job performance and their fitness for their positions.

When I calmed down and looked at their faces, I realized that I had made one of the greatest leadership mistakes of my career. What I saw in the faces of these colleagues with whom I'd served for years wasn't fear or humiliation for themselves so much as disappointment and shame for my loss of control and unprofessionalism. This wasn't who I was as a leader and it certainly wasn't an effective strategy for achieving improved results. I was ashamed. I hope I had the wisdom to apologize to each of them, but I know I never allowed my temper to interfere with my leadership again. Gradually I regained their trust, but I will always regard that temper tantrum as a stain on my career as a leader.

Because Frank Magurn isn't a man to sulk or hold grudges, staff efficiency, confidence, and performance at briefings with General Carter quickly improved and the tornado response operation continued.

Springfield is a diverse city of about 154,000 people. It's the home of Springfield College, the Basketball Hall of Fame, and the Springfield Armory, where most of the nation's firearms were manufactured throughout history. Dr. Seuss called it home. Like most small cities, it has its share of economic troubles and safety concerns, including a very active gang presence. The Springfield Police identified more than 30 gang organizations and estimated that over 1,000 young people belonged to those groups. The most urgent needs in the city, where nearly 500 buildings were damaged, was to provide emergency shelter and prevent looting. The city called for troop support to operate a shelter in the Civic Center and for military police to patrol damaged neighborhoods.

As darkness fell on the second night of operations I met with the state and city leadership at the city's operations center in a trailer at the Basketball Hall of Fame parking lot. There was considerable concern about safety in the gang infested neighborhoods where electric power was out. The Governor's representative tasked me with providing military police patrols in the area throughout the night. Up to this time, daylight military police patrols were unarmed.

The Massachusetts State Police commander on site, Lt. Col. Tim Alben, whispered, "Let's talk outside." I followed Alben outside the operations center. He said, "Look, General, it's not my call, but I wouldn't send my own guys up into those neighborhoods unarmed in the darkness. Just this afternoon, one of my patrols took random gunfire from some gangbanger up there."

I thanked him and pondered my next move. I reminded myself that the safety of the men and women in the task force was my primary concern. How could I ask them to patrol the gang-infested neighborhoods unarmed after what I had just learned? But I also understood that my next move could cost me my job on my second day of command.

I returned to the operations center trailer and informed the state official that I could send military police patrols into the neighborhoods only if they were armed. He was shocked. "Do you mean to tell me you're refusing the Governor's request?"

"The safety of those military police soldiers is my responsibility," I replied. "I'm not willing to send them up there without the ability to protect themselves."

The official shook his head and stormed away. I quickly called Maj. Gen. Carter on my Blackberry and informed him of what I had done. As a seasoned law enforcement leader, Carter understood the situation and gave me his full support.

Perhaps a half hour later, the state official called me into the operations center trailer. "Distribute your pistols and get those patrols up there as fast as you can," he quietly grumbled. I think I saw Tim Alben smiling out of the corner of my eye.

Over the next few days recovery operations in small towns gradually subsided, but patrols and shelter staffing requests from Springfield continued at a brisk pace. After a full week, leaders in the 211th Military Police Battalion were becoming impatient. Electricity was restored in most of the city and military police patrols seemed to be pointless. Furthermore the unit was facing a combat deployment to Iraq within the next year and needed the training time.

I pushed the state official for permission to withdraw, but my requests were denied. I met with the mayor, Domenic Sarno, several times, but he deftly parried my requests to withdraw with heartfelt thanks for all our troops were doing for the city. I enlisted General Carter's assistance in pleading with the governor and stepped up the persistence of my requests to the state official, all to no avail.

However I knew our requests for withdrawal were taking some effect when I received a phone call from Mayor Sarno. "General, I just called to once again thank you for the good work your soldiers are doing for our city," he began.

"But I heard a terrible rumor that you're planning to leave. I hope it isn't true." "You know that our MP need to train for their Iraq deployment, Mayor, so we have to wrap up our operations in Springfield as soon as possible," I replied.

"Well, I just wanted to call you before I called my good friend the Governor," he continued sweetly. "I wouldn't want to cause any trouble for

you." Needless to say, the Governor's office refused to release us from the Springfield mission.

One day I asked our intelligence section to gather statistics about Springfield's crime rate before and after the tornado. To my surprise the crime rate in Springfield dropped significantly and remained at lower levels once military police began patrolling the streets. It also dawned on me that this added layer of law enforcement came free of charge to the city. Why wouldn't Mayor Sarno fight to keep a National Guard presence in his city?

Mayor Domenic Sarno of Springfield, Massachusetts, and Brig. Gen. Smith share a lighter moment after a press conference about recovery operations following the 2011 tornado (Massachusetts National Guard Museum.)

Eventually the Springfield operations ended after several weeks. Although I sparred with Mayor Sarno over and over, I came to respect his tenacious advocacy for his city and I actually grew to like him.

I learned two important lessons from the tornado relief operation. First, stand your ground when it comes to the safety of the people you lead. Second, it's a hell of a lot easier to get into a disaster recovery operation than it is to get out.

The Global War
on Terror Strikes Home

There was a beautiful spring morning sunrise on Monday, April 15, 2013—Patriots Day in Massachusetts. Staff Sergeant Patrick Smith, my aide, reminded me that, as the commander, I really ought to be visible to the troops providing security at the start of the Boston Marathon before the race kicked off. And so, despite my grumbling, we arrived at the race starting point in Hopkinton as the sun was rising. I shook myself awake, gulped down the last of my lukewarm coffee, and put on a game face to thank the troops standing tall for yet another routine Marathon Monday security mission, or so I thought.

Staff Sgt. Smith accompanied me as I talked with soldiers and airmen along the route near the starting point. I had never met Patrick, a military police NCO, before he was assigned as my driver and aide, but he quickly became my conscience, my wisest advisor, my most honest critic, a brutally funny comic, and my guardian angel. I will always think of him as a friend and a younger brother, although we aren't blood relatives. Standing well over six feet tall with a shaved head and a weightlifter's bulk, Patrick was an imposing presence. A former college football lineman, he enjoyed listening to National Public Radio and humming to the score of *Les Misérables*. When he and I traveled together we talked about everything from football to news to headquarters gossip to the challenges of raising a growing family. He had a wonderfully dry, unpredictable sense of humor that often had me in stitches.

However when we arrived at an official location Patrick liked to don mirror sunglasses, open the door for me, and stiffly act the part of a simple driver. Always lurking a few paces behind, he would scan the area with feigned disinterest in any discussions that transpired. Once we finished a meeting or inspection and we were back in the vehicle, he would then let loose with his unvarnished evaluation of the people with whom we had interacted, often detecting details I had missed. I always found him to be uniquely perceptive, shockingly witty, and brutally honest. Anyone who ignored Patrick's presence or made an improper comment within his earshot committed a grave tactical error.

From my first days in the National Guard as a lieutenant I had taken part in the National Guard security mission along the 26-mile Boston Marathon route. Duty usually consisted of nothing more than asking enthusiastic spectators to stand back on the sidewalk as the runners passed by. The only excitement I ever remember was waving an ambulance onto the route when a runner stumbled and injured himself. Usually we completed the mission and began dismissing troops in the early afternoon.

Patrick and I made our way down the marathon route in advance of the more than 23,000 runners behind us, stopping frequently to talk with the troops on the street. At several points we checked in with law enforcement and military leaders to get a status of the mission and inquire about any emerging problems. Morale was good, troop leaders were coordinated with local police, and it seemed like just another Marathon Monday. The sunshine grew stronger and chased away the morning chill as we arrived in Boston.

The 1st Civil Support Team, or CST, was positioned near the finish line. This full-time organization of 32 personnel is one of the most highly trained, well-equipped units in the Massachusetts National Guard. Its mission is to detect and respond to Chemical, Biological, Radiological, and Nuclear (CBRN) threats and it is often deployed to support large public gatherings. When I reached the CST's van, which housed its state-of-the-art communication and detection equipment, I was greeted by the medical officer. She introduced me to additional CST personnel from Rhode Island and New York who were augmenting our team. I also spoke with several FBI agents who were co-located with the CST. Soldiers of the 387th Explosive Ordnance Disposal Company, who are trained to defuse live bombs, were supporting the CST and I thanked them for standing by in case their skills were needed. Later in the day I believe the CST's resources were augmented by an Air Force military working dog team.

The CST medical officer escorted me to the runners' treatment tent that was located within a few hundred feet of the finish line. I joked with the volunteer doctors and nurses, some of whom were former National Guardsmen, about the many blistered feet they'd treat in the next few hours. As I thanked the CST medical officer for accompanying me on my tour of the treatment tent, I clearly remember saying to her, "Well, I'm sorry you're having such an uneventful day."

Patrick and I walked over to the finish line and briefly chatted with the Adjutant General, Major General L. Scott Rice, and his wife, who were sitting in the bleachers that were set up for VIPs. We stood nearby as the first elite runners finished the race to the cheers of the crowd. Around

1:30 p.m. I told Patrick that we should return to Joint Force Headquarters (JFHQ) at Hanscom Air Force Base. He weakly protested because he was enjoying watching the runners in the sunshine. However I insisted that we leave and confessed that I wanted to get home while there was still enough sunlight to mow the lawn. And I reassured him that even brigadier generals have to mow their own lawns.

We dropped off the SUV at Hanscom and I checked in at the Joint Operations Center. Some units that manned the roads near the start of the marathon route had already arrived at their armories. I asked the staff to keep me posted on my Blackberry, then headed home.

At 2:49 p.m. two improvised pressure cooker bombs detonated, 14 seconds apart, among the crowds on the sidewalk of Boylston Street near the finish line. Three people were killed by the blasts: Martin Richard, an eight-year-old boy, Lu Lingzi, a 23-year-old Boston University student from China, and Krystle Campbell, a 29-year-old restaurant manager. There were 264 runners and spectators injured by the blasts, many of whom lost limbs. Massachusetts National Guardsmen, 1st Lt. Steve Fiola, Master Sgt. Bernie Madore, and Staff Sgt. Mark Welch plunged into the dense smoke to pull away tangled fencing and administer lifesaving first aid.[21]

Left to right: 1st Lt. Steve Fiola, 1st Sgt. Bernie Madore, Staff Sgt. Mark Welch, Massachusetts National Guardsmen who risked their lives to pull victims of the 2013 Boston Marathon bombings to safety and administer first aid. All three soldiers would later be awarded the Soldier's Medal for their heroic lifesaving actions (National Guard PAO).

Moments after the blasts, Lieutenant Colonel Mark Merlino, the Task Force Commander for the mission, called my Blackberry. I was sitting in my car having just pulled over to the side of the road to take the call. "Sir, I need to inform you that there have been two bomb blasts near the finish line," Merlino, a veteran of several Iraq combat deployments, said in an unemotional tone. "There are multiple fatalities and widespread injuries."

"Don't fuck with me, Mark," I blurted out.

"I'm not joking, Sir, you'll hear it on the news soon enough." Then he asked, "What are your orders?" I'm not entirely certain of my response after that, but I recall directing him to coordinate with the Boston Police to secure the blast area, provide any lifesaving assistance we could, and stand by for further orders.

I immediately called Major General Rice and requested permission to activate Joint Task Force Massachusetts, which is our emergency response force. He quickly approved my request and promised to get back to me with the number of troops that Governor Patrick would authorize.

Then I called Colonel Chuck Cody, the Joint Task Force chief of staff, and directed him to assemble the JTF staff in the Joint Operations Center at Hanscom. Shortly after that the cell phone grid was overcome because of all the message traffic in the Boston area. As I sped toward Hanscom I was somehow able to get a message to Patrick to meet me there. Because of the cell phone grid overload we were unable to communicate effectively by voice within the military force, although in hindsight we must have had some residual capacity to send text messages. Our overreliance on cell phones was an important lesson learned and a mistake the Massachusetts National Guard will never repeat.

As I raced down the highway to Hanscom, I was awash in the frantic news on the car radio. I understood that there had been hundreds of serious injuries and multiple deaths, but I was focused on the unknown: What if this was the initial strike in a Mumbai-like coordinated attack? What if there were other follow-on bombs set to detonate? Who were the bombers and what resources did they have? How large was the terrorist network that had attacked our city?

As an Army officer trained in land warfare, my initial plan was to assemble as many armed troops as possible on the Route 128 / Interstate 95 beltway that encircles Boston. My assumption was that any future attacks would be in the metropolitan Boston area because of high-probability targets, like population concentrations and vulnerable infrastructure, such as skyscrapers and the volatile liquid natural gas tanks near Boston Harbor. Rather than having forces committed into the chaos and gridlock of Boston, I wanted to have troops poised on the perimeter ready to deploy to critical locations as needed and I wanted to retain a reserve force in case we needed to surge firepower to a crisis point. I also knew that in any disaster response, any smart leader plans for the worst situation and hopes for the best outcome.

Soon the radio news began to confirm some of my worst assumptions. A fire at the John F. Kennedy Library and Museum in nearby Columbia Point became linked to the bombings. Numerous unattended backpacks and packages were reported as suspicious. (Although in retrospect, it's quite likely that a panicked crowd will leave behind many unattended bags and packages.) Every puff of smoke, petty crime, or speeding vehicle in the city of Boston soon became a suspicious terrorist event.

When I sprinted up the stairs and stepped into the Joint Operations Center at Hanscom the room was full of twenty or so staff officers. There was dead silence. I scanned their grim faces and saw shock, confusion, and uncertainty. Because of the cell phone grid collapse, I had no clear orders from the Governor's office, or the Massachusetts Emergency Management Agency. I had spoken briefly with Maj. Gen. Rice, but not long enough to discuss a plan of action. I had no experience with a domestic terrorism incident and, quite frankly, we had nothing but a vague contingency plan.

But I had enough command experience and common sense to know that what was of greatest importance in a crisis was poise, confidence, and decisiveness—even if I was scared shitless inside. To put it simply, I knew I had to "Fake it 'til I made it."

I don't remember clearly what I said other than that I had confidence in them to lead the force because we had done this before during floods, hurricanes, and a tornado—except this time the impact was deadlier and more urgent. I knew this wasn't the time for speeches, so I began firing off tasks to the staff sections—some of which were routine. But I was gambling that activity would overcome chaos and the paralysis of shock:

> **J-1:** We need a status of how many personnel we have available for duty immediately by location.
>
> **J-2:** Get going on an intelligence assessment. Do we have a bomb damage assessment yet? What do we know about the suspected bombers?
>
> **J-3:** Prepare a FRAGO directing Task Force Patriot to arm up and stand by to support the FBI, Boston PD, and State Police. We need to array armed forces in the armories along Route 128 and we need to get ammo to them ASAP.
>
> **J-4:** Better get going on the logistics plan to feed and house up to 2,000 troops in their armories or mobile locations in the city. Also we need to know where all our operational ground vehicles are located.
>
> **J-6:** We need to get a satellite system into Boston ASAP to restore reliable communications. How quickly can we get an Air National Guard system into operation in Boston?

AVIATION OFFICER: We need to know how many Blackhawks we can get in the air and how soon they'll be ready to fly.
JAG: We need a RUF (Rules for the Use of Force) document ASAP.
PAO: Let's get a brief statement out to the media so people know we're on the way.
CHAPLAIN: …Pray.

And so it went until the Operations Center was buzzing with activity. Just as I had hoped, I could see confidence returning to the staff officers around me. Col. Cody skillfully managed the activity and message flow as chief of staff and soon officers and NCOs were generating questions and delivering results. The staff team was operating like a well-oiled machine despite the anxiety and grief that we all felt.

Major Bryan Pillai, Maj. Gen. Rice's resourceful assistant, was somehow able to relay messages by text. Rice directed the JTF to rush as many troops as possible into Boston after conferring with the quickly emerging Unified Command team. Although I was very concerned about sending unarmed soldiers and airmen into a danger zone, Maj. Gen. Rice suggested that we could deal with the issue of arming troops later on. Consequently the troops who had been guarding the marathon route rushed into an ad hoc assembly area on the Boston Common. Col. George Harrington, dressed in his business suit, left his office near the Common and temporarily took charge of organizing the force. Soon Lt. Col. Merlino, the assigned Task Force Commander, arrived to take charge and began to deploy troops to support law enforcement. I will always remember the image of Col. George "Hatchet" Harrington, in his suit and tie, directing troops on the Boston Common, as the embodiment of the Minuteman tradition in our time.

In emergency operations the Massachusetts National Guard receives mission guidance and authority from the governor through the Massachusetts Emergency Management Agency, or MEMA. We were accustomed to receiving detailed directives from MEMA particularly regarding budgetary limits for numbers of troops authorized. Consequently we had an experienced liaison officer, Lt. Col. Martin Spellacy, stationed at MEMA headquarters to relay information and advise the civilian Director of Emergency Management about military capabilities. When I asked Lt. Col. Spellacy about directives from MEMA, he said, "The only thing they keep saying is. 'Do whatever Boston tells you to do.'" Although our soldiers were in contact with law enforcement agencies in the Boston area, there was little strategic guidance coming from anyone in Boston during the afternoon.

As evening approached, I was confident that the team of staff professionals would direct the force in accordance with our mission to support law enforcement. I decided that I needed to get some clarity on the Unified Command's intent and consult with Maj. Gen. Rice to develop future plans. So Staff Sgt. Smith and I drove into Boston. The downtown Boston streets were nearly empty except for the ring of news trucks parked bumper-to-bumper around the Common. Small groups of reporters were gathered here and there, but they all kept a respectful distance from our troops.

Patrick was skilled at maneuvering through traffic, although when we flew the wrong way down some of Boston's one-way streets I started to question his judgment. However he managed to position our SUV directly in front of the crowded entrance to the Westin Copley Place Hotel, which was serving as a makeshift Unified Command headquarters. As we walked into the first floor lobby of the elegant hotel, I was amazed to see guests laughing and socializing at the hotel bar as if nothing unusual had transpired in the city.

The entire second floor of the hotel, which was a wide open function space, was now occupied by the Unified Command. As we rose up the escalator, we gradually approached a tall policeman guarding the end of the moving stairs. He was decked out in full body armor, a helmet, and eye protection. An M-4 rifle was cradled in his gloved hands. It was almost like a scene from some sci-fi movie and I thought, "Oh no, we're going to have to go through some time-consuming security check to get in here." However, when we reached the second floor, the guard stepped aside and simply said, "Evening, General."

A picture of confusion unfolded as we stepped into the wide open function area. There were well over a hundred police personnel, politicians, and other city officials. There were even a few K-9 teams. Some were talking on cell phones. Some were eating. Some were gathered in small heated discussions. Others were lounging on the couches. I noticed Senator Elizabeth Warren working her cell phone feverishly. Congressman Stephen Lynch conferred with knots of Boston officials. Senator William "Mo" Cowan watched the activity, waiting for his opportunity to help. I spotted Governor Deval Patrick slumped down in a chair, deep in thought, despite the whirlwind of activity around him. I quickly recognized the dozen or so military folks present and asked them to direct me to Maj. Gen. Rice.

My two main concerns were questions I needed answered for future operational planning: How many troops would Governor Patrick be willing to authorize and when would he issue the authority to arm the force? The first question was simple. Rice asked me how many soldiers and airmen I thought I needed to support our security missions. I estimated that we needed authorization for 1500 troops and Rice said that the Governor would be okay with that number. When I asked about arming authority and the timeline to issue weapons, the general motioned for me to follow him to a quieter corner.

Rice carefully explained that Boston Mayor Tom Menino was absolutely opposed to deploying armed National Guard troops within the city. In fact Rice repeated a comment that was made in the meeting he had just attended. According to the general, a city official said, " We're not going to have another Kent State in the City of Boston." I was furious. When I started to protest, arguing that we couldn't put unarmed soldiers and airmen in danger as they pursued terrorists, Rice assured me that he had already made that argument to the Governor, to no avail.

I now had a complicated decision to make. Although Maj. Gen. Rice was my superior officer, in his position as State Adjutant General he held no command authority. In my position as Joint Task Force Commander, I indeed had command authority and also ultimate responsibility for the safety and protection of the people in the force I commanded. If I agreed to continue to deploy unarmed troops onto Boston streets and there was another terrorist act that resulted in military injuries or death, I would be responsible. If, on the other hand, I refused to commit troops without the means to protect themselves (as I had done previously in Springfield), I would add another layer of confusion to an already chaotic situation.

When I considered the urgency of the situation, I agreed to continue to deploy security forces unarmed, but only under the condition that they be accompanied by armed police personnel and have constant radio communication with police. Rice agreed that pairing police with our unarmed troops was prudent and assured me that the Governor and Mayor Menino would support the concept.

Staff Sgt. Smith and I returned to the Boston Common where Lt. Col. Merlino had established a command post by assembling several trailers from which he and his staff directed security forces in Boston. The Task Force Patriot headquarters was also supplemented by the antennae, dish, and trailer of an on-site Joint Incident Site Communications Capability system, or JISCC, which an Air National Guard team had deployed and erected in record time. The JISCC capability enabled the Joint Task Force to establish and maintain steady, reliable communications that weren't disrupted by cell grid overloads.

I conferred briefly with Merlino and informed him that we would continue to provide unarmed security support to the Boston Police, State Police, and the Transit Police departments, provided that our troops were paired up with armed officers and provided with radios. Lt. Col. Merlino and his staff had already established informal, but effective coordination networks with law enforcement. Support to the Transit Police was particularly important because it was believed at the time that terrorists would likely use the subway or bus system to flee the Boston area and we knew that the subway trains and tunnels were highly vulnerable targets.

As Staff Sgt. Smith and I drove back to JFHQ at Hanscom, his usually jovial tone of voice became serious. "Sir, I was thinking that if we had stayed at the finish line like I wanted to, we might have been caught in the blast zone." Here was my moment to be sensitive and compassionate, instead I replied. "Hey Patrick, are you still in one piece? We dodged the bullet, so let's do our job." He chuckled and drove on.

Moments later he spoke up again. "Sir," he said, "I just have one question."

"What is it, Patrick," I prepared myself for another deep reflection.

"What the fuck is a pressure cooker?" he asked. For the first time that day, I enjoyed a good laugh as I realized that few people under forty had ever seen one of the whistling, spitting cast iron pots … and the terrorists had turned into a weapon of death and destruction.

When we returned to JFHQ we learned that conspiracy theorist Alex Jones was flashing images of our Civil Support Team members on his show, "InfoWars," and alleging that they were the bombers. Jones picked out the CST people because they wear black jackets, khaki pants and carry black backpacks, similar to the description of the bombers. He had now created a situation in which we needed to request armed law enforcement security protection for our own people to protect them from vigilantes. This diverted already stretched security resources away from vital missions within the city. I believed then, and still believe, that Jones should have faced consequences for this reckless exploitation of fake news that endangered our troops and wasted valuable security resources.

Throughout my career it has always amazed me how quickly soldiers and airmen adapt to any situation and environment. Within 24 hours of the blasts, the Joint Task Force was smoothly operating on a round-the-clock schedule of briefings, staff working groups, troop shift changes, meal and supply cycles, and all the gears that mesh to maintain an efficient military machine. I have often found that National Guardsmen are at their best when the mission is most critical. I also must emphasize that the high level of organization and staff synchronization was almost entirely due to the professionalism and leadership of Col. Chuck Cody. Chuck had the uncanny ability to insist on top level performance without ever losing his cool or resorting to intimidation. He was consistently able to encourage people to give their best by encouragement, support, and gentle prodding. Col. Cody was the staff leader we needed at this critical time.

My time on Tuesday, April 16, was occupied by the duties of command at JFHQ. I recall a blur of phone calls, meetings, and constant checking on details. As night approached, Patrick stepped into the conference room where I was chairing a routine meeting. "General, your next meeting is coming up in a few minutes," he said, impatiently tapping his watch.

Unaware that I had any evening meetings scheduled, I stepped out into the hallway with him. "What are you talking about, Patrick?"

"I need to get you out of here," he whispered. "You need to be downtown with your troops. They need to see you." Once again, I had been schooled by an Army NCO who was absolutely right.

We checked in with the Task Force headquarters on Boston Common and found the mission running smoothly. As I walked across the Common, I could see clusters of reporters eyeing me hungrily—I knew they were desperate for any tidbit of information, but it wasn't my place to speak to the media, the Unified Command had that responsibility.

I remember walking through Copley Square in the heart of Boston. It had been cordoned off for blocks around the blast area as a crime scene. Usually well-lit and bustling, it was totally dark and deserted behind the steel barriers. Plastic bags and newspapers blew down the street in the moonlight as we came to a checkpoint manned by four young Guardsmen. They were a bit nervous at having a general drop in on them, but they soon loosened up. They reported that they were in communication with Boston Police several times per hour and there were no incidents to report.

We watched Anderson Cooper give his CNN broadcast from a security checkpoint on the opposite street corner, but he kept his distance. While we were there, a server from the Au Bon Pain sandwich shop nearby came over with a bag of sandwiches for the three soldiers staffing the checkpoint. They gratefully, but sheepishly, accepted the gift. After a few minutes a young woman stopped by with a shopping bag containing twenty or so cans of smokeless tobacco.

"I hear you guys love this stuff, so I wanted to show my appreciation for keeping us safe," she said, cheerfully passing the bag around. Patrick and the soldiers eagerly took the cans and thanked her. After she left, Patrick said, "Do you have any idea how much that bag was worth?"

The troops also told me that the manager of the Copley Plaza, a four-star hotel near the checkpoint, had invited them to come in for dinner when they rotated shifts. I asked if they intended to take him up on the offer. "No, Sir, it seems like too much trouble," one of them responded. "It's up to you, but I'd do it because most of us couldn't afford to eat in that restaurant, which is one of the finest in Boston. You might as well enjoy it while you can," I counseled as Patrick, a true connoisseur of fine food, nodded enthusiastically.

My nightly walks with Patrick in downtown Boston all merge together, but certain images linger. I recall watching an energetic young female sergeant bantering with passersby at a particularly busy checkpoint. Her good-natured, but professional presence projected the message, "I'm here to keep you safe, so please do what I ask you to do." Throughout my travels I saw soldiers dealing respectfully and compassionately with the citizens of Boston. Somehow they knew that a strong, reassuring posture was important for this wounded, shaken city at this time. I credit the ability of first responders and soldiers to gain and maintain public trust with critical developments that unfolded later on.

At one point I visited the Explosive Ordnance Disposal teams at the Lenox Hotel that overlooked the blast sites. The EOD teams were unique in that personnel from Massachusetts State Police, FBI, and National Guard immediately came together to work as one unified force. Essentially I had very loose command and control of our EOD soldiers, but I yielded to the reality that these unique specialists shared a common language and craft that transcended agency assignment.

I was most concerned about these soldiers because their tasks were perhaps the most gruesome. Initially EOD personnel were called to detonate many abandoned packages and backpacks, during a time when we believed that the terrorists might have left explosives behind. After several blocks around the blast area had been cordoned off as a crime scene, the EOD mission changed. They were now tasked with detecting, marking the location, and cataloging bomb fragments and human remains. Our Command Chaplain, Col. Rabbi Larry Bazer, was so concerned about the mental health of the EOD soldiers that he requested my permission to marshal behavioral health and chaplain personnel to support these troops as they performed their gut wrenching mission. I believe Col. Bazer's foresight may have prevented future behavioral health issues.

When I entered the Lenox Hotel looking for the EOD teams I was directed to the second floor. I smiled when I saw that the entire floor of the hotel had been converted into a sort of Bomb Disposal Frat House. Off-duty soldiers and bomb techs walked around half-clothed as they munched on snacks. Piles of dirty glasses and plates stood in the hallway, and people sacked out in the bedrooms. I was able to find our soldiers because they were wearing at least parts of their camouflage uniforms. Unlike most soldiers, who are usually somewhat uncomfortable when a general suddenly visits, the EOD team acted like they were expecting me. The young sergeant in charge gave me a thorough, and candid, update on their activities before he invited me to partake in some buffalo wings from the buffet cart provided by the hotel. Then he beckoned me to join him at an open window.

Pointing to the street below he said, "If you lean out this window with me I can show you the blast radius." Then he barked to another soldier to grasp the back of my belt as we stretched out over the pavement. The sergeant then gave me an expert explanation about the blast effects of the pressure cooker bombs by pointing out the blackened shoots and fragments still on the pavement. I left with a better understanding of the EOD mission and the reassurance that our soldiers were well taken care of—and the wings were pretty tasty.

Perhaps my most poignant memory of our nightly walks occurred late one night as Patrick and I crossed the darkened investigation area. We noticed a small group of people gathered in front of one of our barricades. Initially we were concerned that this was some kind of protest or demonstration, but the group was fairly quiet. As we approached the checkpoint, we asked the two soldiers manning it about the gathering. "People have been stopping by tonight, leaving cards and flowers and other stuff," one of the soldiers explained, "but they're pretty peaceful."

We looked down at the base of the barricade and saw a small pile of stuffed animals, bouquets, paper messages, American flags, and other tokens of sorrow and remembrance. This was the beginning of an impromptu memorial that would grow into a mountain of symbols that expressed the grief, compassion, and pride of the citizens of Boston.

On Wednesday, April 17, we learned that President Obama planned to visit the city of Boston on the following day. While many of us harbored some misgivings about the additional security burden of a presidential visit, the ultimate morale benefits for the citizens of Boston were well worth the added layers of protection. We were beginning to see the city return to some degree of normalcy. Moreover intelligence was indicating that the bombings were the work of a small terrorist cell, rather than a larger campaign by a widespread terror network, like Al Qaeda.

My assessment was that the National Guard would play a persistent supporting role in the weeks to come as the FBI completed the investigation and the nationwide manhunt for the killers unfolded. I didn't anticipate the need for National Guard surge forces and capabilities. Future events were to prove me wrong. Lt. Col. Mark Merlino and his staff had commanded the Task Force admirably since the bombings on Monday. Because he only had a limited number of staff officers available and probably because he was a traditional Guardsman like me, with a job that needed him, I decided to relieve his Task Force and conduct a relief in place.

The incoming command was the 26th Maneuver Enhancement Brigade, under the leadership of Col. Frank Magurn. The 26th Brigade had a deep bench of staff officers and many more organic units within its command, including the 211th Military Police Battalion. Almost as important,

Col. Magurn was a wise, intelligent, proven leader. He also happened to be a full-time National Guardsman who would be better positioned to lead a sustained operation without the distractions of a civilian job. Although there were some complaints from soldiers who wanted to remain on the mission, the relief in place was executed seamlessly. The 26th Brigade occupied the forward headquarters on the Boston Common and assumed command of the nearly 1,000 troops securing the city. In the end this was the right decision.

There was a marked change in emotional temperature on Thursday, April 17 as the sun rose on a clear, sunny spring morning. Rather than create a burden, the presidential visit lifted the city's spirits and emphasized themes of strength, resilience, and determination. The National Guard wasn't tasked in the security near the President, but Maj. Gen. Rice and several aides were invited to attend the service at the Cathedral of the Holy Cross in Boston where President Obama addressed the city. I detected that the overall outlook of our force was somehow boosted by the President's visit and the general mood of what we came to know as "Boston Strong."

At some point on Thursday we learned the identity of the bombers as Tamerlan and Dzhokhar Tsarnaev, residents of Cambridge, Massachusetts, who were born in the Soviet Union, but were possibly U.S. citizens. At our afternoon staff briefing, I tasked our J-2, or intelligence section to gather as much information about the Tsarnaev brothers as possible, to include their likes and dislikes, behavior patterns, and social networks. My thinking was that our troops were under a constant threat from an armed and dangerous enemy whose location was unknown. I wanted to have as much information as possible about the enemy.

After the briefing concluded, I was confronted by a young Air Force captain. She identified herself as a member of the J-2 section. "General, I want you to know that I can't comply with the order you just gave," she said. Somewhat surprised, I asked, "Why not?"

"It appears that at least one of the Tsarnaev brothers is a U.S. citizen," she explained. "U.S. law forbids the military from collecting intelligence on U.S. citizens. Your order is illegal."

"Look, captain, these are unique times," I shot back quickly. "You can either get the information we need, or I'll find someone else who will." She turned and walked away without further comment. I was too busy to give this conversation much thought until the operation was over.

In hindsight, she was right. I wish that I could find this officer to offer my apology for treating her so badly. We need more officers who have the courage to stand up to senior leaders when they're wrong—and we need more senior leaders who are humble enough to listen to them than I was in this situation.

As Thursday came to a close, my assessment was that the search for the Tsarnaev brothers was going to be a long, protracted affair. After consulting with Col. Cody, I planned to return to my civilian job duties on Friday. Late Thursday night, Massachusetts Institute of Technology Campus Police Officer Sean Collier, was found dead in his cruiser, shot through the head. The Tsarnaev brothers had taken another innocent life.

Later the Tsarnaev brothers carjacked a black Mercedes Benz SUV at another location in Allston. The car owner escaped and called 911.

Early Friday morning a Watertown police officer spotted the black SUV in his patrol area. He called for backup and tailed the stolen vehicle. Tamerlan Tsarnaev pulled over, hopped out of the vehicle and began firing at the police cruiser. A chaotic firefight escalated as backup police officers arrived on scene. Witnesses report that the Tsarnaevs fired a pistol at police and tossed explosives, including what appeared to be another pressure cooker bomb.

Apparently out of ammunition, Tamerlan threw his pistol at an officer who chased him and tackled him. As two officers attempted to restrain Tamerlan, his brother Dzhokhar jumped into the Mercedes and drove toward his brother. The officers leapt clear of the SUV, but Tamerlan was dragged under the vehicle for some distance before his limp body was tossed aside. Dzhokhar sped off in the damaged vehicle leaving his fatally injured brother behind. After driving a short distance, Dzhokhar abandoned the vehicle and fled on foot into the densely packed neighborhoods of suburban Watertown. By dawn a massive manhunt was underway.

All this took place while I slept. Through some miscommunication at JFHQ, the overnight staff officer failed to notify me. Fortunately Col. Frank Magurn, the Task Force Commander, was informed of the situation and quickly reacted to state police requests for armored HMMWV vehicles to escort police officers on house-to-house searches in Watertown. Magurn correctly used his own initiative to arm the military police soldiers who drove the vehicles, although I believe he quickly received affirmation from Maj. Gen. Rice.

Likewise, the Liaison Officer at the Massachusetts Emergency Management Agency, Lt. Col. Martin Spellacy, used his own initiative to link up with Lt. Col. Dave Underwood, the State Aviation Officer, and coordinate a landing zone for Blackhawk helicopters in Watertown. The aircraft were used to quickly transport ammunition into the assembly area at the Watertown Mall and rapidly move specialized police teams to Dartmouth, Massachusetts, where alleged co-conspirators of the terrorist cell were located.

I woke up at 5:30 a.m. and dressed for my return to school. As I walked into our kitchen I heard snatches of the television news. Quickly grabbing my Blackberry I read my messages, uttering "holy shit!" over and over. I tore off my shirt and tie, pulling on yesterday's camouflage uniform from the laundry basket as I fumbled with the laces of my combat boots. I remember my wife's words as I raced out the door, "You're not going to Watertown, are you?"

"Of course not," I shouted back, but I think we both knew where I was headed.

I don't clearly remember the drive from my home to Hanscom Air Force Base, but I must have spoken with Patrick Smith, Col. Cody, Col. Magurn, and Maj. Gen. Rice as I sped along the highway. By the time I reached Hanscom, plans were underway to deploy an armed military police company from the 211th Military Police Battalion around the search area to act as a net into which the surviving bomber might be flushed.

When I arrived at JFHQ Col. Cody briefed me on the developing events and the Joint Task Force's staff actions up to that point. It was clear that he had the staff effort running like clockwork. I informed him that I intended to go forward to the Watertown Mall assembly area to get better situational awareness. I asked Patrick to get a vehicle and draw pistols, ammunition, and body armor for the two of us.

As we approached the Watertown Mall, I had a strange, surreal feeling. I spent my childhood in Watertown, although I hadn't been there in nearly 50 years. As we drove past familiar landmarks, I was struck by the odd sensation of returning to my old hometown carrying battle rattle and a weapon while hunting an armed terrorist.

Patrick and I were surprised by the large number of vehicles that were already gathered in the Watertown Mall parking lot. We quickly found the command trailer where I coordinated with the Incident Commander, Col. Tim Alben, commander of the Massachusetts State Police. Under Col. Alben's command, the Watertown operation was significantly better coordinated than the Boston operation had been. I give the Watertown Police Chief great credit for yielding incident command to Alben. Having a single commander in place simplified decision-making and facilitated quicker action. Personally I was grateful to be dealing with the experienced, no-nonsense Alben with whom I'd worked on previous operations.

I then sought out the commander of the 211th Military Police Battalion, Lt. Col. Al Aldenberg, who briefed me on the HMMWV police escort and the cordon operation surrounding the search area. Aldenberg (who currently serves as the Police Chief of Manchester, New Hampshire) was an experienced commander who was also a civilian law enforcement professional. He was in total control of the soldiers under his command and was able to clearly communicate with the police officers his force was supporting. Lt. Col. Aldenberg's firm command and control was to prove crucial later that night. Patrick and I then spent the next few hours gaining situational awareness by talking with military police soldiers surrounding the search area. I was particularly concerned that they understood the RUF—Rules for the Use of Force—which dictated that they were only authorized to fire on an identified target in self-defense or to prevent loss of life.

Before we headed back to Hanscom, we checked in at the command trailer for any new developments. At this point it was early afternoon and Patrick and I were astonished at what we saw in the assembly area. SWAT teams and police groups from as far away as New York and Maine were camped out in the overcrowded parking lot. Many of the groups had set up barbecue grills and were offering hot dogs and hamburgers to other police officers. The scent of broiling hamburgers was more like a football game tailgate party than the search operation for an armed and dangerous fugitive. We just shook our heads and departed.

We traveled back to JFHQ at Hanscom to confer with Col. Cody and receive a Joint Task Force staff briefing. As the afternoon wore on with no leads as to the suspect's whereabouts, it was clear that the Joint Task Force needed to prepare for sustained operations. Because the 211th Military Police Battalion had been providing cordon security in the Watertown search area since the early morning hours, I issued orders for the 182nd Infantry Battalion to prepare to relieve the Military Police. Patrick

A Massachusetts National Guard Military Police officer briefs Brig. Gen. Smith near the search area for the Boston Marathon bombers on April 19, 2013 (Massachusetts National Guard PAO).

and I then traveled to the 182nd Infantry's armory in Melrose, not far from Watertown, in the late afternoon.

After the 182nd Infantry Battalion Commander briefed me on the readiness of his command, I asked him to assemble his soldiers so I could address them. I remember the earnest young faces peering at me as they gripped their rifles and took a knee around me. I then launched into a motivational stump speech that was perhaps amplified by my own pent-up emotions. Bill Belichick would have been proud if he could have heard it. As I asked the eager troops if they were with me until Tsarnaev was brought to justice, they roared with bloodlust and fire in their eyes.

Just then Patrick, who must have been holding my Blackberry, interrupted me. He quietly whispered, "We've got Tsarnaev cornered in somebody's boat." Returning to the troops gathered in the circle, I didn't have the time to explain to the young soldiers, now inflamed with zeal to take down the terrorist, that they weren't going to be needed after all. Instead I thanked them for answering the call of duty and beckoned to their commander to explain the change of plan. I'm not quite sure how he reeled his troops back into sanity, because Patrick and I were racing to Watertown by then.

Night had fallen by the time we arrived back at the Command Post in Watertown. I entered the trailer, which was occupied by Governor Patrick, Maj. Gen. Rice, Maj. Pillai, the Director of the Massachusetts Emergency Management Agency, the Watertown Police Chief, Col. Alben and a few staff personnel. We anxiously listened as Col. Alben directed his team to prepare to take custody of Dzhokhar Tsarnaev. For several minutes we were all able to view an infrared image of the search area from a State Police helicopter, but soon the link died and all we could hear was the scratchy radio transmission from the State Police team commander at the boat. I don't believe we were aware of the barrage of gunfire directed at the boat by hundreds of self-deploying law enforcement officers.

We exchanged anxious glances as Col. Alben directed the actions of the apprehending team, but no one spoke. Finally we received confirmation over the radio that Dzhokhar Tsarnaev was in custody and traveling to a nearby hospital for examination. The group in the command trailer breathed a collective sigh of relief, but there was no celebration, only quiet comments of thanks and recognition of a job well done. There had been too much bloodshed, heartache, and anxiety during the past week for any feelings of triumph.

As the civilian leaders prepared to brief the press, I issued orders for our troops to stand down and thanked them for their courage and professionalism. It didn't occur to me until much later that they had been within the sound of the gunfire at the boat, but every military police soldier held his or her fire in accordance with the Rules for the Use of Force. Lt. Col. Aldenberg and every soldier is to be commended for their fire discipline because any MP on that mission would have welcomed the opportunity to take down Dzhokhar Tsarnaev.

Patrick and I drove through the throng of jubilant flag-waving onlookers and headed for Hanscom to wrap up operations. But along the way he reminded me that we hadn't paused to eat for quite a while. We stopped at a crowded Mexican restaurant near the base. The other customers attentively watched the television news and enthusiastically chatted about the capture of the last Boston Marathon Bomber without paying much attention to us. Because the restaurant was close to the base, it wasn't unusual to see customers wearing military uniforms.

Patrick shook his head, "These people have no idea what we've been doing for the past eighteen hours, do they?" I looked around the restaurant.

"Nope, they probably don't, and maybe that's how it should be." We gulped down our food and headed to JFHQ to wrap up the operation.

After Dzhokhar Tsarnaev was in custody we were able to gradually stand down troops from security missions in the downtown Boston area. On Saturday April 20, Red Sox star David "Big Papi" Ortiz shouted out his famous statement that touched the tattered hearts of all Bostonians. "This is our fucking city," became a roar of triumph for a wounded city regaining its confidence. In the days and weeks that followed the Massachusetts National Guard was flooded with calls of congratulations.

A few weeks later I was asked to attend a reception at the Boston Public Library to receive an unnamed public figure from the United Kingdom. On the ride into Boston, Patrick had great fun speculating about the possibilities—Elton John, Kate Middleton, the Spice Girls, Mick Jagger, perhaps the Queen herself!

Arriving at the library, I enjoyed talking with other leaders from the bombing response whom I never had the chance to converse with in a relaxed setting. Suddenly we recognized the tall figure of Prime Minister David Cameron approaching us accompanied by Governor Deval Patrick. Assuming that this was a formal "grip and grin" event, I waited for Mr. Cameron to approach me, expecting a quick handshake and greeting. However I was quite surprised when he said, "General, I have several questions about the relationship between your military and law enforcement."

I was impressed with his insightful questions, but I was more impressed that he actually listened to my responses, some of which were quite involved. He thanked me for the discussion, shook my hand, and moved along. I breathed a sigh of relief. Briefing a visiting head of state had not been on my "to do list" for the morning, but it didn't appear that I had endangered transatlantic relations. However I couldn't help thinking that

UK Prime Minister David Cameron and Brig. Gen. Smith discuss civil-military cooperation while a member of the UK consular staff looks on after the 2013 Boston Marathon bombings (British Consulate in Boston).

my Irish immigrant ancestors would be turning in their graves if they saw their descendant chatting with the Prime Minister of Great Britain.

But the question I was most often asked after the 2013 Marathon response was, "What made this operation so successful?"

I always found it difficult to respond. First, because we had made more than a few mistakes. In fact we spent a great deal of time in After Action Review meetings examining every aspect of the operation to improve our performance in future no-notice disaster response operations.[22]

Second, it was hard to focus on a single element. We had actually benefited from several factors. Past weather emergencies had required close interagency cooperation between the National Guard and first responders. Fortunately the communication links, relationships, and norms established during floods and blizzards had carried over into the Marathon bombings response. Injuries would have been far worse had they not occurred within a few hundred yards of a medical treatment tent staffed by highly skilled doctors and nurses. Casualties were quickly evacuated to Boston hospitals that are the best in the world. At the time of the blasts there were nearly 600 National Guardsmen and the framework of a command structure already on duty for crowd control, which certainly accelerated our response time. Finally we benefited from the mistakes and lack of sophistication of our enemies.

In the end however it wasn't the wisdom and fortitude of commanders that shaped the National Guard response to the Boston Marathon Bombings, although staff officers and troop leaders performed superbly. It was the thousands of independent, smart decisions made by junior officers, NCOs, soldiers and airmen that resulted in operational success. When it counted most, our people rose to the challenge and lived our values of loyalty, duty, respect, service, honor, integrity, and courage. The truth of the matter is that, in the best Minuteman tradition, Guardsmen stood shoulder-to-shoulder with first responders to raise Boston up from the smoke, dust, and carnage to once again become "Boston Strong."

Chinese Intrigue

The Superintendent of Schools sat across from me at my civilian job. A mysterious three-page letter sat between us on my cluttered desk. The letter was hand addressed to the superintendent by name. It had a California return address. I was startled when I read the bold type heading on the first page: "I request National Guards IG Office to conduct a THOROUGH INVESTIGATION ON ACTIONS UNBECOMING AN OFFICER BY MANG BRIGADIER GENERAL PAUL GREGORY SMITH...." I finished reading its contents and looked up at him.

"Level with me, Greg, is there anything in here I need to be aware of?" he asked with a look of concern. "I've never met this woman, and I have no idea why she'd make some of these accusations," I replied. "She must be crazy."

"Well, that's good, because several members of the School Committee have also received letters from her," he responded. "I think they realize that it's something that has nothing to do with our school system, but let's hope she's done with her letter writing campaign." As he left my office I realized that whoever launched this smear attack against me had already been partially successful.

Over the next several days colleagues and school officials sent me more letters that they had received from this woman who attacked my fitness as a leader. It was obvious that they were written by someone who had an incomplete grasp of formal written English, but had some understanding of the military Inspector General complaint system. In addition she had access to details about my military career. What was most surprising was that she had ferreted out addresses of the school district leaders where I worked.

The letters alluded to a romantic relationship that she had with a senior sergeant in my brigade years ago. Now, as a brigadier general, I was no longer a brigade commander. Even more baffling was the fact that her alleged lover had long since retired from the Army and I was due to retire within months.

I recalled that several years ago I had spoken with this sergeant, who was an outstanding soldier, about rumors that he had a relationship with a Chinese national. The concern was that any close ties to a foreign citizen, particularly a citizen of a hostile power, would pose a security concern. He assured me that the matter was largely overblown and that he had been in communication with military intelligence. Although he and I worked closely together, he clearly had no desire to discuss the matter any further with me and I respected his privacy.

Now a woman who alleged that she was this sergeant's lover was sending letter after letter to people in my circle of colleagues and associates outside the military. The allegations she made against me weren't entirely clear, but she attributed all sorts of underhanded chicanery to me in my associations with this sergeant and the Inspector General's office. However, it was curious that she also questioned my fitness for command because I had not served on any combat deployments to the Middle East. Other accusations in the letters were largely false, but contained just enough information about units, operations, and deployments to be intriguing. It was also interesting that she alluded to having resided in Shanghai for the past several years. Most of the information in the letter could have been gleaned from very diligent open source investigation, but the knowledge of my deployment history and unit movements would have required some assistance from someone with access to more advanced sources of information.

I immediately reported the smear campaign to the intelligence section at our headquarters and forwarded as many letters as I could to them. However, I was only aware of letters received by people who informed me, which made me wonder, "How many other letters were out there about which I didn't know?"

I called the former sergeant who had allegedly been involved with this woman and told him what was happening. He was exasperated and said that she had been stalking him, even climbing a tree outside his residence as she waited for him to arrive home. He said that he had notified his local police department. Once again, he denied having a romantic relationship with this woman.

At first I believed that this was simply an effort by an unhinged, jilted woman to lash out at someone whom she perceived was a friend and ally of her actual or imagined lover. Perhaps she reasoned that, after she had harassed me enough, I would contact my former sergeant and ask him to intervene with her. This was a pretty far-fetched explanation, but she appeared to be quite deranged.

Then questions began to nag me:

How did she know that I was a public high school administrator?

How could she understand that letters to the Superintendent of

Schools, School Committee members, and my colleagues would put pressure on my career?

How did she locate the small school district in which I worked?

How much time did she spend tracking down all the mailing addresses to which letters were sent?

How did she develop an understanding of the Army Inspector General complaint process?

How did she obtain detailed information about my assignments and unit movements?

Her detailed knowledge went far beyond any pillow talk that she might have had with anyone.

Although I accused myself of paranoia and building a conspiracy theory in my own mind, the hypothesis I formed was that she must have had assistance from someone with access to extensive research networks and intelligence resources about the U.S. military. If my assumptions were correct, then this woman's letter writing offensive was supported by the Chinese government.

One might accuse me of flattering myself that the Chinese government would waste its resources trying to discredit a brigadier general in the Massachusetts National Guard. But the proof might lie in emerging Chinese military doctrine regarding Information Warfare. Simply put, the People's Liberation Army exploits any form of power or leverage to create chaos or instability that weakens opponents. In particular, "fake news" and disinformation are effective weapons to sow confusion, distrust, and discord. The Chinese employ "wolf warriors," to disseminate falsehoods, lies, and invective against those whom they view as China's opponents. Was it plausible that staff members in a Chinese consulate provided assistance to an angry woman—a willing "wolf warrior"[23]—who wanted to defame a U.S. Army general?

Once I suspected that the Chinese government might be involved, I contacted the Army Criminal Investigation Division office who referred me to Army Intelligence. Days later an unassuming middle-aged gentleman in a business suit met with me at school. He only identified himself and offered his credentials as an Army Intelligence agent once the door was closed in my office. I gave him a brief summary of the letter writing campaign and handed over all the letters in my possession.

After the meeting with Army Intelligence I had no further word of anyone receiving letters from the Chinese woman nor were there any reports of her activities anywhere else. Was the entire affair simply the actions of a highly resourceful "woman scorned" lashing out at an associate of her lover? I think not.

Purple Heart

One of the most moving and rewarding tasks I ever performed as a soldier was to present a Purple Heart to Thomas Copeland, an 89-year-old World War II veteran of the Bougainville Campaign in the Pacific.[24]

It was a cloudy February day. We were returning from a rural part of the state where we were wrapping up emergency operations from a winter storm when I received a message from state headquarters. Apparently the Adjutant General was unexpectedly called to the governor's office and would be unable to present a Purple Heart Medal to an elderly veteran near the area in which we found ourselves. Headquarters asked if I could handle the presentation and meet one of our Family Assistance Coordinators at a designated location.

I was traveling with the city-smart Staff Sergeant Smith who was already unnerved at finding himself among so many trees. He asked sarcastically if we needed passports to enter the veteran's town. I told him he was a smart ass, but he found the rendezvous with the Family Assistance Coordinator anyway. We met up with the coordinator who had the medal in hand and had already made arrangements with the family. He informed me that several other military leaders, veterans representatives, and town officials would be there, as well as the media.

We drove to the veteran's home up a side street of small working class houses in an old factory town. There were half a dozen National Guard leaders waiting for us in front of a tiny weathered shingle ranch house. As we entered the house we were greeted by the scent of fresh baked brownies and the warm smile of the veteran's wife, a spry woman in her seventies. She quickly invited us to eat something from her kitchen table that was overflowing with cold cuts, pies, cookies, and, yes, brownies. We declined her offer of food and she proceeded to introduce us to many friends and family members who had gathered for the ceremony. There were sons and daughters-in-law, cousins, neighbors, fellow veterans, and local selectmen all packed into the small first floor rooms. But the introduction that was perhaps the most memorable was the veteran's granddaughter who was helping with the refreshments. She was a truly beautiful young lady in her early twenties with a radiant smile. I quickly realized that if I noticed her wholesome good looks, my fellow soldiers must be driven to distraction.

Nevertheless we were ushered into the living room. The wood paneled walls were hung with family pictures from better days and most of the furniture had been removed. In the center of the room was a hospital bed in which lay an ashen, but smiling elderly man. He grasped my hand and I could feel the cool, smooth skin that barely covered his bones. "I should stand up when a general comes into the room," he croaked with a grin.

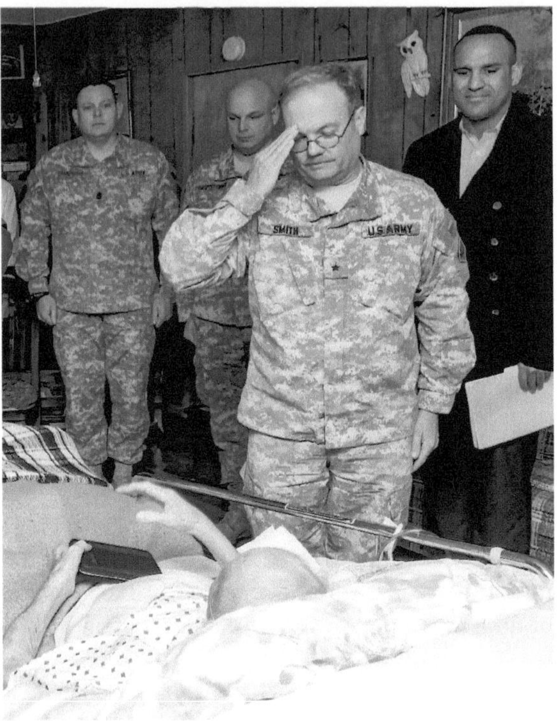

Brig. Gen. Smith salutes World War II veteran, Thomas Copeland, after presenting him with a long overdue Purple Heart medal (Massachusetts National Guard PAO).

"That's okay, Sir," I replied. "We're all here to honor you today." We talked about his combat service in the Pacific as best we could because of his labored breathing. All the while he held my hand. When he had said all he could, I began the ceremony by calling attention and reading the medal citation. When I finished, I pinned the Purple Heart to his hospital johnny, stepped back and saluted him. His eyes were full of tears as he attempted to return the salute. I gently shook his hand and then backed away so his family could come into the tiny living room and congratulate him.

The other soldiers and I lingered for a short time. When we prepared to leave, the veteran's wife took my hand in both of hers. As she wiped away the tears, she said, " Thank you so much for coming today. He doesn't have much longer to live and I so wanted him to have this medal before…." She quickly turned her head away. I simply nodded and patted her hand.

At length the other soldiers made eye contact with me and we made our way to the front door, refusing persistent offers of food. We stepped out quietly into the street, no one wanting to break the silence after this solemn and touching event.

As we reached our vehicles however, I heard a voice say, "Did you see the old man's granddaughter?"

"Holy shit, was she gorgeous," another voice quickly chimed in.

"Who would ever think someone that beautiful would live out here?," asked another soldier. And so it went. The reverence of soldiers has its limits.

Goodbye to All That

At some point in 2014, as we wound down from a minor emergency response, Major General Rice came into the conference room in the Joint Operations Center where I was sitting. He gently closed the door. Rice sat down beside me and quietly asked, "Greg, have you thought about moving on?"

I knew what he was asking. I had been assigned to a general's position for over four years. The traditional agreement was that a general held one of the top jobs for only three years, otherwise it stunted the careers of talented colonels.

Rice continued, "We've got a couple of good candidates for promotion to general, and we owe it to them to make room for them. I'll support you for a second star if you want to pursue an assignment at the Pentagon or somewhere else."

I thanked him for his support, but it only took a few moments to realize that it was time to retire. I couldn't ask my wife to move to Washington for my military career, even if it meant promotion to Major General. I had already asked too much of her over the past 35 years. Also I wasn't willing to give up my career as an educator. Moreover I joined the National Guard to defend the nation and respond to emergencies. Briefings, meetings, visits to politicians and all the drama of Washington wasn't what I signed up for. I came to the stark conclusion that it was time to hang up my spurs. And so, we began the process of transitioning to new leaders.

As my final day in uniform arrived, I packed up all the knickknacks, mementos, and files in my office. A flood of memories passed over me like a tidal wave. There were homely painted rocks and cracked coffee mugs from my days of company command, a handsome sword from the battalion I commanded, framed photos and press clippings from my time as a brigade commander. There was also a growing cluster of newer, more elegant trophies—a plaque with a hatchet, a chromed artillery shell, a powder horn in an oak cradle, nicely framed military prints—recent presentations from the brigades under my command, like tributes to a warlord from the clan chiefs at the end of his reign.

Maybe I could have used a little help loading the boxes into my car, but the staff had left me to my own thoughts on the last day of my military career. They were also occupied by rehearsals and final preparations for the grand Change of Command ceremony later that morning.

I arrived at the parade field that was flooded with sunshine on a clear June morning. The sounds of the band tuning their horns muffled the shouts of the sergeants directing the soldiers to place the chairs and the flags just right. I waved to a few friends and colleagues who were gathering in the bleachers.

If it was up to me I wouldn't have assembled the band, the flag bearers, and the troop formations to witness my final day in uniform. But this day wasn't about me, it was a ceremony to mark the succession of command for a military force that was older than the United States. For 378 years the Massachusetts militia defended the citizens of the Commonwealth and the nation. Throughout the centuries the force always had a commander who relinquished leadership to the next commander. The day's pomp and fanfare was a recognition of that tradition and legacy.

The officer who would narrate the event respectfully briefed me on exactly where I was to stand, sit, and speak throughout the ceremony, then quickly attended to other details. Soon Major General Rice arrived with Colonel Frank Magurn. I made cheerful small talk to mask my nervousness about my part in this grand ceremony.

At last the narrator's voice boomed over the loudspeaker asking everyone to be seated. The band struck up the music to begin the ceremony. We saluted during the National Anthem, bowed our heads for the opening prayer, and Maj. Gen. Rice gave his remarks. The time came for the ceremonial passing of the Massachusetts National Guard flag to Colonel Magurn and I executed the movements of handing over the colors almost mechanically as I had done when leaving my previous commands. To reflect too deeply on all that was passing would have been too much to bear.

Maj. Gen. Rice graciously presented me with an Air Force Commendation Medal and thanked me for my leadership during joint operations with both Army and Air Force elements. Now it was my turn to speak.

I had given many speeches during my time in uniform, but this one was tough. I wasn't concerned about being eloquent or long-winded, rather I was worried that I'd fail to thank all those who had provided me with good advice, had my back, put up with my bullshit without abandoning me, stood by my side in dark days, and trusted me. I'm certain I forgot someone.

As I finished my remarks and turned to sit down, I heard the thump of helicopter rotors approaching like a drumbeat. I looked up to see a

Maj. Gen. L. Scott Rice awards Brig. Gen. Smith the Air Force Commendation Medal at Smith's retirement ceremony in 2014 (Massachusetts National Guard PAO).

diamond formation of four Blackhawks approaching the field. As they swooped overhead in the clear blue sky, the pilots tilted their helicopters from side to side—an aviator's salute. My heart swelled when I understood that the four dark green angels were saluting me on my last day of command—and it was even more precious when I realized that they had carefully scheduled their "training" flights to simultaneously converge on the parade field. Ceremonial flyovers were strictly unauthorized.

I have little recollection of the reception after the ceremony. I know I must have chatted with many of the colleagues and friends who attended the ceremony. My wife and children hadn't come because of the long distance from home. But I guess that was fitting, because this day was all about my farewell to my other family—my military family.

When the crowd thinned out I was pleased to climb into my car alone with my mixed emotions—relief that the ceremony had gone well, gratitude for all the kind remarks, nostalgia for the era that was coming to an end, longing to do it all over again, and perhaps a little bit of fear for what was coming next.

It was going to be a long drive home, but maybe I'd get home in time to mow the lawn before sunset.

Chapter Notes

Preface

1. "The May 4 Shootings at Kent State University: The Search for Historical Accuracy." *Kent State University,* 8 Aug. 2023, https://www.kent.edu/may-4-historical-accuracy.

Son of the Greatest Generation

2. "60,000 War Protesters Rally on Common." *The Harvard Crimson,* 16 Apr. 1970, https://www.thecrimson.com/article/1970/4/16/60000-war-protestors-rally-on-common/.

"ROTC, It Sounds Like Some Bullshit to Me, to Me...."

3. "A Time to Heal: William Sharpe." *The Vietnam War Pennsylvania Archive,* 8 Aug. 2023, https://atimetoheal.wpsu.org/stories/william-sharpe.

4. "USASOC Honors Clandestine Unit From Vietnam War." *Army.mil,* 31 Oct. 2008, https://www.army.mil/article/13809/usasoc_honors_clandestine_sf_unit_from_vietnam_war.

5. "Momma, Momma Can't You See?" *Military Cadence: Largest Source of Online Military Cadences,* 14 June 2018, https://www.army-cadence.com/158/.

6. "Marine Officer's Memory Lives On with New Award." *Worcester Telegram and Gazette,* 9 Nov. 2011, https://www.telegram.com/story/news/local/north/2011/11/10/marine-officer-s-memory-lives/49837929007/.

Birth of a Weekend Warrior

7. "Boston Marks 35 Years Since Pope St. John Paul II's Visit." *The Pilot,* 3 Oct. 2014, http://www.thebostonpilot.com/article.php?ID=172133.

Riot Duty

8. "Massachusetts Guard on Strike Duty." *The New York Times,* 12 July 1981, https://www.nytimes.com/1981/07/12/us/massachusetts-guard-on-strike-duty.html.

Unfinished Race

9. "95 Million Watched the Chase." *The New York Times,* 22 June 1994, https://www.nytimes.com/1994/06/22/us/95-million-watched-the-chase.html.

End of Innocence

10. HMMWV, or "hummvee" is a High Mobility Multipurpose Wheeled Vehicle, which replaced the legendary Jeep as the U.S. Army's small transport vehicle.

Rainbow Soldiers

11. "Inside the War Between Trump and His Generals." *The New Yorker,* 15 Aug. 2022, https://www.newyorker.com/magazine/2022/08/15/inside-the-war-between-trump-and-his-generals.

Public Affairs

12. "Protest at Soldier's Funeral Brings a Massachusetts Town Together." *Los*

Angeles Times, 28 June 2005, https://www. latimes.com/archives/la-xpm-2005-jun-28-na-funeral28-story.html.

Operation Helping Hand

13. "With 235 Served, Helping Hand Wraps Up." The Standard-Times: South Coast Today, 25 Oct. 2005, https://www. southcoasttoday.com/story/news/2005/ 10/25/with-235-served-helping-hand/502 01218007/.

Opportunity Knocks

14. "Ex-State Sgt. Gets 5 Years in Sex Case." *Worcester Telegram and Gazette,* 28 Feb. 2007, https://www.telegram.com/ story/news/local/north/2007/02/28/ex-state-sgt-gets-5/52960242007/.
15. "Rain, Flooding Prompt Governor to Call a State of Emergency." *Seacoastonline,* 15 May 2006, https://www.sea coastonline.com/story/news/2006/05/ 15/rain-flooding-prompt-governor-to/512 13190007/.
16. "Romney Activates National Guard Troops for Logan Airport." *Foster's Daily Democrat,* 11 Aug. 2006, https://www. fosters.com/story/news/local/2006/08/11/ romney-activates-national-guard-for/ 53052123007/.

The Land of "Not Quite Right"

17. "Paraguay." *CIA.gov: The World Factbook,* 8 Aug. 2023, https://www.cia. gov/the-world-factbook/countries/ paraguay/.

Operation Big Ice

18. "Ice Storm Cripples Parts of Northeast." *The New York Times,* 12 Dec. 2008, https://www.nytimes.com/2008/12/12/us/ 12cnd-storm.html.

Taps

19. "What to Expect During Military Funeral Honors." *Military One Source,* 5 Jan. 2023, https://www.militaryonesource. mil/transition-retirement/veterans/ what-to-expect-during-military-funeral-honors/#:~:text=%E2%80%9COn%20 behalf%20of%20the%20president, loved%20one's%20honorable%20and%20 faithful.

A Mighty Wind

20. "Massachusetts Tornado: Recalling the Twister Through Photos on Its 2nd Anniversary." *masslive.com,* 1 June 2013, https://www.masslive.com/ news/2013/06/massachusetts_tornado_ photos_f.html.

The Global War on Terror Strikes Home

21. "National Guard Soldiers Recall Heroic Actions at Boston Marathon." *nationalguard.mil,* 26 Apr. 2013, https:// www.nationalguard.mil/News/Article/ 574411/national-guard-soldiers-recall-her oic-actions-at-boston-marathon/.
22. "Why Was Boston Strong? Lessons from the Boston Marathon Bombing." *Harvard Kennedy School: Program on Crisis Leadership,* April 2014, https:// ash.harvard.edu/files/why_was_boston_ strong.pdf.

Chinese Intrigue

23. "The Disinformation Tactics Used by China." *BBC,* 12 March 2021, https:// www.bbc.com/news/56364952.

Purple Heart

24. "Athol Veteran Finally Gets Purple Heart." *Worcester Telegram and Gazette,* 11 Feb. 2013, https://www.telegram.com/ story/news/local/north/2013/02/12/ athol-veteran-finally-gets-wwii/4910 2222007/.

Index

www.ingramcontent.com/pod-product-compliance
Ingram Content Group UK Ltd.
Pitfield, Milton Keynes, MK11 3LW, UK
UKHW041354190726
13851UKWH00014B/103